Click 'n Connect
Training Your Dog – A Lifelong Jou... ,

Teah Anders
Click 'n Connect
Training Your Dog – A Lifelong Journey

GENTLE TOUCH PET TRAINING

Arroyo Grande, CA

Cover design by Bright Ideas
Front cover photograph by Jerome Ross
Back cover photograph by Jim Flattery and compliments of Samantha Curran and Richard Berg, Evermay Airedales

ISBN 978-0-9796116-0-5

Teah Anders
GENTLE TOUCH PET TRAINING
1886 Deer Canyon Rd.
Arroyo Grande, CA 93420
(805) 481-1490
(805) 481-1497 FAX
teah@clicknconnect.com
www.clicknconnect.com

This book is dedicated to Wags, my dear and wonderful Lhasa Apso, who was my companion for almost 15 years. Wags was my first small dog. When I brought Wags home at eight weeks old, I knew I had to find a gentler way to train. In 1989, my search for a positive training method led me to clicker training.

Table of Contents

Preface

M y dog won't listen to me!" As an animal trainer, this is the comment I hear
most often. Creating a relationship where your dog will listen to you is
built by establishing an understanding that goes both ways. It's based upon having a 'dialogue' with your dog. From my years of study and first-hand experience,
I have found clicker training to be the most effective tool for establishing reliable
and consistent communication with your dog – without having to use force. The
comment I hear most frequently from other dog trainers, who won't teach clicker
training, is that "people just won't be able to grasp the concepts of clicker training" or that "people can't handle a clicker and the dog and a leash and everything
at the same time." While the method does have some particular complexities, it's
important to remember that clicker training is widely and successfully used in
many countries not only with dogs, but also with wild animals at animal parks and
zoos, and with marine mammals at marine parks. My experience has taught me
that given the right information and training most dog owners can master clicker
training. This book was initially written as a simple and helpful handbook to
supplement classroom training. However, the book's content has been expanded
and refined through the years, as I've held classes and addressed questions from
clients. Consequently, the uses for this book have grown as well.*

I have found it helpful to make reference material available so my clients can
refer to it outside of class. Additionally, I believe that this book will be a useful
guide to individuals who, if unable to attend a clicker class, need guidance for
learning clicker training at home. The training explained in this book can be used
in the home to start with puppies as young as six weeks old or be used with puppies (starting at eight weeks old) in a Puppy Preschool class. Additionally, it can
be used with adolescent dogs or adult dogs of any age.

The entire field of clicker training is expanding. In the last four consecutive
years, after I return from a Karen Pryor Clicker Training Expo, I'm inspired by
the emerging developments in the field of clicker training. An example of this
awe-inspiring work was illustrated in a presentation by Alexandra Kurland who
explained how clicker training has been used with a miniature horse, trained to be
a seeing-eye guide for a woman sightless from birth. As studies are being conducted and people all over the world are getting involved in clicker training, more

---

* *This practical guide may be useful for other trainers as a supplement to training sessions.
Trainers may copy and distribute the homework assignments found in this book to their
clients. Other parts of the book may be used with written permission.*

is being learned about this remarkable way of training animals. I have been using clicker training since 1989, and everyday I realize that the more I know the more there is to know. Clicker training is both a science and an art; hence, it is ever-evolving.

As a realist, I know that there's always more to learn, and the fact is that as soon as this book is written, parts of it will be out dated. However, I offer here the cumulative knowledge that I have gained through years of reading, training, and experimenting, hoping that the lives of dogs and dog lovers everywhere can be happier than they already are.

In that regard, I would like to note that I have drawn on the expertise of many other fine trainers and animal behaviorists. One of the trainers that has been most helpful to me in understanding the nuances of clicker training is Kay Laurence from the UK. Other trainers that I have learned from in seminars and books include Mary Ray from the UK, Kathy Sdao, Ian Dunbar, Patricia McConnell, Leslie Nelson, Gail Fisher, Chris Bach, Corally Burmeister, Bob and Marian Bailey, Steve and Jen White, Morgan Spector and Gary Wilkes. Because these sources have been so helpful to me, I've provided a "Resources" section with information about the many books, videos, and web sites on clicker and positive training methods.

Acknowledgments

I'd like to express my sincere gratitude to several people who helped me to publish this book. Thanks to Mary and Greg Lugo for their beautiful photography, and their incredible patience, persistence and responsiveness in helping me gather the photos. Thanks to Jerome Ross for the amazing cover photo of Kiko and me at sunset on the beach. I'd like to express my sincere appreciation to Susan Marsala and Sabine Felsberg for editing and typesetting. Their help has been one of the reasons that I'm finally publishing this book . I know the text is greatly improved because of their assistance. In addition, I am indebted to Dede Watson and Janet Young for their excellent and meticulous editing of the early versions of this text.

Many thanks to Denise Porte, DVM, who offered valuable feedback on several of the puppy-related sections of this book, including helping to structure the Puppy Preschool class. I'd especially like to thank Denise for her constant friendship and willingness to talk about dogs and dog behavior – endlessly. My heartfelt thanks to my husband, Chuck, for his patience and support while I spent hours creating this book. I also wish to express continuing gratitude to my friend, Cinnamon Lofton, who is always there for me in all aspects of my life – including writing this text.

Endless thanks to my friends Katie Hawkins, Ivy Underdahl, and Denny Pontestull. Denny has been with me since the beginning and continues to be a person I admire greatly, as I watch what she can do with her dogs. Katie and Ivy are two of my instructors; their help and what I continue to learn from them is of immeasurable value. Thanks to several of my early assistants, who have moved on, including Alison Christianson and Shirley Keller, for all their help with my classes in the early days. Thanks also to Jayne Bower, one of my new instructors and an assistant, and to Denise Schryver, and Jen Wytmans who have been invaluable class aides. A thousand thanks to Lisa Nichols, who in addition to helping with classes, takes on all my computer data input; I couldn't do it without her. I also wish to acknowledge the help of Georgia Barr and Donna Hedrick who are always willing to substitute for other assistants at the last moment. Huge thanks to my new agility instructors, Diane Baley and Mia Grant, who lead our brand new agility program. Also, my appreciation goes to Juliet Franzen, my Rally-O instructor, who was willing to learn all the rules and keep them straight. And thanks to Elaine Cordero, who makes a conformation handling class possible and fun at our facility, and to Patty Wiedeman for introducing me to the wonderful sport of Musical Canine Freestyle which is perfect for any clicker trainer! And also thanks to Gary Wilkes who, back in 1989, introduced me to this amazing method of training.

I'd like to particularly thank Kay Laurence who has shared so many training ideas with me and continues to be an inspiration for me.

Additionally, I'd like to acknowledge my Gentle Touch Pet Training staff members who made themselves and their dog's available for photos. While this book is certainly written with the pet or companion dog owner in mind, I wanted to include the array of titles and awards these dogs and their owners have worked so hard to achieve. I can still remember, not that long ago, when many people did not believe that positive training methods, such as clicker training, could be used to train a dog to the level of reliability required for competition. Many members of our staff not only compete, they compete in multiple venues and activities, achieve high levels of reliability and have clicker trained their dogs since kindergarten! Denny currently has the only Bull Terrier in the country that has achieved a Rally Excellent Title and certainly is among one of the few who have been awarded the Versatility Award Excellent – the highest level a dog can achieve, from the National Bull Terrier Club of America, recognizing all her, and Fright's, accomplishments.

For the photo opportunities, thanks to:

Denny Pontestull with her Bull Terrier, Frighty, *CH Ardry's Frightfully Fun! VAX, CD, RE, OA, NAJ, CGC, TDIOA;* her Chihuahua, Cucuy, RE AXJ, OA; and her adopted field pointer Twitchy, CGC, CD, RE.

Ivy Underdahl and her Swedish Vallhunds, Blaze, ARBA Master CH *Osafin Blaze To Glory* AXP, OJP, CGC, HRD1s, HCT, STDs, N-Vers, O-NAC, OAC, OJC, NGC, TN-O, TG-O, WV-N, RS-E, JS-E, GS-O; and Skye, ARBA CH *Vastgota Stormy Skye* HCT, CGC.

Katie Hawkins and her Rough Collie, Quinn, *Evermore's Mighty Quinn,* OJC, OAJ, OA, RA, HIC, CGC, W-FD, VC; and her Sheltie, Echo, *Breezeway's Echo of Scamper* OJC, OAJ, OA, CGC.

Mary and Greg Lugo and their Great Danes Maud, BISS Ch CHROMA Maid to Order CGC (TDI) and Simon, *D and T's Von Shoaf American Idol.*

Diane Baley and her Labrador Retriever puppy, Quiz, *Deep Run's Right Answer.*

Jayne Bower and her Golden Retrievers, Dustin, *Emberain Ticket to the Show* and Meryl.

Donna Hedrick and her Toy Poodle, Shasta, *Marweg Silver von Shasta, CD, RE, OA, OAJ, CGC, ThD.*

Teah, the author, has included the following dogs from her family (current and past) in the book: Lhasa Apso, Wags; Pug, Hally, *Winsome's Halcyon Days*, RN, CGC, W-FD; Corgi/Australian Shepherd Mix, Chili, rescued from the streets of Mexico; Chinese Crested Powderpuff, Cambria, *China Road Cambria;* Anatolian Shepherd, Sahara, *Woody Acre's Sahara*; Lhasa Apso, Crystal Moon and Keeshond/Collie mix, Kiko from a local shelter.

Finally, a big thanks to all of my clients (human and dog – and the occasional llama, pig, cat or bird) for all I have learned from them over the years.

And last, but never least, my loving thanks to each of our dogs: Sahara, Chili, Kiko, Hally and Cambria, and my past dog companions, especially Wags, Crystal Moon, Bear, Andrew, Skye and Shanti, and to our clicker-trained llama, Epiphany, as they have all been my greatest teachers.

And one more, thanks to Tina Williams for her last-minute, midnight editing of this book!

About the Author

Teah Anders is owner and trainer for Gentle Touch Pet Training, which was founded in 1999. She is a Certified Pet Dog Trainer and professional member of the Association of Pet Dog Trainers. She currently teaches puppy, beginning, and intermediate clicker training classes at her facility. In addition, Teah teaches Rally-O and Musical Canine Freestyle and is President of the West Coast Musical Freestyle Club. She also works with clients and their dogs in private, in-home training and behavior sessions. In addition, Teah donates her time regularly in helping local dog shelters learn more about positive training methods and

Pictured here with Teah and Chuck (from left) are Chili, a Corgi/Australian Shepherd (and who knows what else) mix from the streets of Mexico; Hally the Pug, Sahara, an Anatolian Shepherd; Cambria, a Chinese Crested Powderpuff; and Kiko, a Keeshond-Collie mix adopted from the Humane Society.

helping 4-H students learn clicker training. She has successfully taught thousands of people the clicker training method. She is an AKC evaluator for Canine Good Citizenship tests and administers CGC tests quarterly at her facility and at community events. Teah also hosts seminars each year bringing world class trainers such as Kay Laurence, Steve White, and Kathy Sdao to California's Central Coast.

Teah holds a B.S. degree in business and an M.A. degree in Natural Resource Policy, Communications, and Management. Although Teah learned clicker training in 1989, it was not until her move to the Central Coast of California that she found the opportunity to move from the corporate arena, where she worked with environmental issues, to help people to live happier lives with their dogs.

Teah lives with her husband, Chuck, five dogs, a cat, two birds, seven llamas, and two goats in Arroyo Grande, CA.

Getting Started

Introduction

I'm sitting here on a sunny California morning watching our dogs – Hally, our little Pug, is sitting in the sun, tummy exposed to the warmth, eyes half-closed with a dazed look of half-sleep on her face. Pugs love to warm themselves in the sun. My heart feels warm just watching her.

Across the yard, Cambria, our Chinese Crested Powderpuff, is romping and jumping like a deer. She's still a pup – well, an adolescent now, about 7 months old. She's busying herself, as usual, and vacillates between running and jumping, exploring gopher holes, and seeing if she can entice Sahara or Chili to play with her. Just watching her makes me laugh. A Chinese Crested is not quite all dog – they are part creature.

Sahara, our adult Anatolian Shepherd, is laying quietly on the highest point in the yard. From her favorite vantage point, she can see over our wooden fence and to the street in front of our property, all the while keeping a careful eye on the llamas and goats that she likes to watch over. She is calm and intent, yet at any moment she could jump to her feet, move at a speed unimaginable in a large, 135-pound dog, with her hackles up and tail raised to confront any incoming intruder or predator. When I look at her, I just marvel at what a wonderful creature she is.

In the corner of the yard is Chili. He's like a piece of my heart. Some of us "dog people" talk about our "heart" dog. He is definitely one of mine. He was rescued from the streets of Mexico at about 8 months old by my friends Robin and Ben. Robin, a veterinarian, brought him to her clinic and doctored him up for about 2 months. He had lost all his hair and was malnourished. I volunteered to simply help her train him and fell in love at first sight. He is about 6 years old and is a Corgi, Aussie and who-knows-what-else cross. As an adolescent, I found him easy to train and work with. As he approached adulthood, he developed a number of serious aggression issues. He has been both a challenge and one of the best dogs I've ever lived with. He has been a great teacher, and he has helped me to be compassionate and understanding with my clients that live with "difficult" dogs. He reminds me of the duality of life – like having a child whom you hope will be a doctor and instead that child decides to be an artist. Not a bad thing all-in-all, just different than what you had imagined. That's how Chili has been for me, and, yet, I love him all the same.

Kiko is in the corner of the yard and has found a small hole though which he can catch a glimpse of the new neighbor's dogs. He is entranced. Suddenly he breaks into barking and jumping around. He stops and sniffs the air. He's a Kees-hund/Collie cross that we adopted from the local Humane Society about 8 years ago. He's now approximately 10 years old. He's had both knees operated on and can run like the wind again. I like to watch him. Even though he came to us with major behavioral issues, including aggression towards strangers, children, and serious resource guarding, he is a total love bug. He will melt into your arms and cuddle the way herding dogs often do.

Lying close to me is Crystal Moon. My little Princess. She's a Lhasa Apso and for so many years ruled the pack as dominant female. Now at 16-1/2 years old, she has begrudgingly surrendered that job to Sahara. She has only 25 % of her sight left, and her hearing is not good. Some days she's stiff from arthritis, and some days she acts like a puppy again. She still eats well and appears to enjoy life. I tear-up at times knowing that her time with me on earth is nearing an end. I comfort myself knowing that she'll join her partner, Wags, who was my male Lhasa Apso and her playmate for 12 years. Wags passed four years ago. I still miss him.

The journey through life with each of our dogs, especially for those of us who consider ourselves "dog people," is amazing and wonderful. The connection we establish with our dogs through positive training is the icing on the cake. More than just having a dog that will come when called, stay when asked, or spin or weave through my legs in a musical freestyle routine, I have developed a deep connection with each dog. That is the beauty of training your dog. The benefits far outweigh the time invested. This book is about how to get started training your dog with an amazing and effective method of training called "Clicker Training." More than that, this book is about a journey you will take that can teach you how to connect with your dog and establish a relationship based on trust and mutual respect. When training is successful, it's a wonderful feeling, but it is life-journey you must travel together, and all traveling companions must learn and do their part. As with all adventures, there are things to learn, tasks to perform, and obstacles along the way; however, as you go remember that you don't want to miss the fun.

Mapping the Course

Before you step foot on this new trail, it's important that you consider what is unique about this journey. Knowing what to expect and developing an appropriate set of expectations is key to managing your end of the dialogue. In the *Handbook to Higher Consciousness*, written by Ken Keyes, Jr., in 1975, Keyes outlines 12 pathways that will help one to cope with and improve their lives. Having studied and used his 12 pathways for many years, I've come up with my own 12 pathways in regard to dog training. Described below are several essential concepts to keep in mind as you begin:

Pathways for Training Pups

- Give up the need to "control" your pet. Clicker training is based on giving your dog a choice. You will not need to force your dog to respond with the correct behavior because the dog will choose the behavior you want because that's the behavior that's been reinforced.
- Be aware that your perception of how your pet should behave often conflicts with a dog's natural instinctive behavior. Remember, these are dogs. Not humans. Be patient and train your dog by utilizing that instinct, and then make a place in your thoughts for your dog to act the way you would like them to. "My dog is calm and sits to greet strangers."
- Every training challenge provides you with an opportunity to appraise whether or not you are calm, focused, and capitalizing on your training techniques. If you get frustrated, breathe and take a break. You will learn a lot about yourself from your dog!
- Stay in the moment with your pet – focus on how your pet is doing today, and don't be preoccupied with past problems or future expectations. Rather than saying "my dog never comes when called," do the training, and then say, "it's typical for my dog to come when called."
- Take full responsibility for how you are training and be aware that your attitude can influence your pet's reactions.
- Accept your pet completely at all times. Remember, these are dogs, not humans, and it's up to us to train them so that they can be successful in a human environment. Be aware of your reactions to your dog's behavior. Be aware of your consistency and commitment to train your dog.
- Maintain a positive communication with your pet. If challenges arise in the training process, examine your attitude and your expectations. Then examine your training methods.
- Be compassionate with your pet and be aware that your dog may not always understand what you want.
- Keep a positive state of mind when training your dog. If you are angry, work on your attitude first, before continuing your training session.
- Strive to feel as one with your pet and all living things.
- Continuously monitor your emotions – your dog does. Create a place in your thinking for your dog to do well in training or competitive situations – visualize!
- Perceive your pet as a unique entity deserving of the best you have to offer.

Blazing the Trail

When I started training 30 years ago with my German Shepherd mix, Shanti, the common method of training was using negative reinforcement with choke or pinch collars and lots of punishment. This "force base" training method was developed in a military setting with German-bred, German Shepherds.

Clicker training has actually been around for longer than most people realize. The clicker method we use today is an outgrowth of work that began in 1945 by two Harvard University graduate students, Keller and Marian Breland. They had just finished four years of work with well-known theoretical behaviorist, B.F. Skinner. The Brelands were clicker training dogs 15 years before Keller Breland introduced the work to U.S. Navy dolphin trainers and marine mammal trainers in 1960. This method was originally popularized primarily by marine mammal trainers and really caught on with dog trainers in the 1990s. Other animals, such as horses, cats, birds, llamas and many wild animals are now trained using this method. I recently met several trainers who work with giraffes and fruit bats with clicker training! The Brelands created a method of training that was the foundation of the modern clicker-based training method. Marian went on to marry Bob Bailey, and although Marian has passed on, Bob Bailey continues to teach clicker training today.

In 1984, Karen Pryor, previously a dolphin trainer, published the book, "Don't Shoot the Dog." This excellent book helped add to the knowledge and understanding of this method of training. This book brought the idea of clicker training to the forefront for dog trainers and is still a must-read today. Today, Karen Pryor Clicker Training continues to educate the public about this amazing training method through the Clicker Expos held annually.

Many other trainers have contributed ideas to this method since that time. Trainers such as Bill Campbell, Ian Dunbar, and Suzanne Clothier, among others, helped to raise awareness that harsh methods were not necessary. Clicker training methods have been fine-tuned and popularized through dog training seminars around the world. Gary Wilkes certainly deserves mention as one of the pioneers in this field. In more recent years, other trainers have come forth to help catapult clicker training to a new level including Kay Laurence from the UK, Kathy Sdao, Steve White, Corally Burmaster, Bob Bailey, Leslie Nelson, Alexander Kurland and others.

Basic Clicker Training Tools

*C*ollar – Nylon or leather buckle collar, Martingale collar or head collar.

Clicker – Box or Button Style

Leash – A six-foot nylon or leather leash. Please do not use an extendable or chain leash for basic training. They both have their uses – they just don't make good basic training leashes.

Treats – Prepare lots of treats, cut up into small pieces. Whatever goodies you prepare for the first session with dogs, double it! (Most people don't prepare enough treats for the first training session.)

Bait bag – Having a bait bag or goodie bag is most convenient. You can also use a fanny pack. Otherwise, wear an article of clothing (such as a sweat shirt or apron) with a large pocket. You'll need somewhere to stash the treats because you can't hold them all in your hand. At home, you can put them in a bowl and place them on the counter. In class, this doesn't work as well.

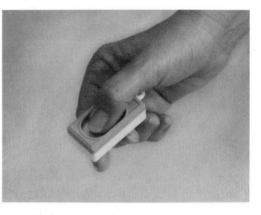

A clicker is most commonly held between the thumb and forefinger and is the tool used to mark the behavior you like and to act as a bridge between that behavior and the reinforcement.

Training is easier with the basic tools and the food easily accessible. Pictured here is a good bait bag to hold the food; a box clicker, a button-style clicker and an extendable target stick.

Target stick – We will teach the dogs to first touch and then target (or follow) our hands. The next step is to teach our dogs to follow a target stick. You can either make one out of a wooden dowel and put a plastic tip on it or many target sticks are available commercially.

Management Tools
That Can Be Helpful During Training

Head Collars – Head halters (also called head collars) are a wonderful invention. They make it possible to gently and safely prevent your dog from pulling while you're teaching your dog to walk with good manners on a loose leash. They do not choke your dog, and the design sends instinctual messages that you're the boss. Dogs have a natural opposition reflex that causes them to pull away from you when you pull on their collar. Head halters also remove your dog's natural opposition reflex. With the head halter, a gentle pull puts pressure behind the dog's ears. While you're training loose leash walking, it's important that you no longer let your dog pull. If you do allow the pulling, you'll be undermining any training that you're doing. For this reason, I find that many people find it helpful to use a head collar while training their dog.

There are a number of manufacturers of head collars. The two I have used most frequently are the Gentle Leader® made by Premier Pet Products and the Snoot Loop® available from by Dr. Peter Borchelt of Animal Behavior Consultants, Inc. I find the Gentle Leader easiest to adjust, and it works quite well on most dogs. For some dogs, depending on the shape of their face and muzzle, I may instead recommend a Snoot Loop. The Snoot Loops work well on brachycephalic (short-nosed) breeds. Both head halters are effective. A newer head halter more recently available is the Comfort Trainer® designed by Mariam Fields-Babineau and Alice DeGroot, DVM. I have limited experience with this collar, although on first review it seems effective. The Halti® is also widely available. I personally prefer the head halters that allow for easy adjustment to specifically fit a particular dog.

I consider a head halter to be a training aid, and once the dog is trained, you will no longer need the head halter to walk your dog. For most of my clients, I recommend that the ultimate goal is to work up to walking your dog on a regular buckle collar. The head collar can be used as a management tool during the training process. I also recommend head halters in situations of great distractions (until your dog is trained in these situations), such as dog training classes, or a veterinarian's office. When I do consultations on seriously aggressive or fearful dogs, I may recommend the head halter be left on most of the time. However, with most of the dogs in my classes, the head halter is only used for working on loose-leash walking or walking your dog at other times to prevent pulling (until he's trained). The collar does not need to be left on the dog for the rest of your clicker training exercises and should not be left on an unsupervised dog.

The fit of the head collar is important for it to be effective. It's helpful to get guidance from a professional trainer or someone trained in fitting head collars. If you don't have the benefit of working with a trainer, be sure to review any written or video instructions available with the collar. If the collar does not fit correctly, it will not be as effective in training. It is also advisable to check the fit of the head halter regularly. (It is nylon and may stretch, or your dog may get heavier or slimmer.) For both the Gentle Leader and Snoot Loop head halters, the collar needs to fit snugly. I suggest two fingers (side-by-side) between the collar and your dog's neck. (The Gentle Leader instructions specify one finger, although I still use two.) The nose loop should be snug enough not to pull beyond the fleshy part of your dog's nose. Remember the piece behind the ears fits high on the dog's neck, unlike a regular buckle collar. You can leave your dog's normal buckle collar and tags on while using the head halter. The leash attaches underneath the dog's chin.

You will get one of three reactions from dogs when first exposed to a head halter. Some will walk happily off into the sunset as if they are now well leash trained! Bear, our 90 pound Labrador/Rottweiler adopted at 7 years old, was one of these dogs. The day he came home, I took him to the beach, and he practically pulled me off my feet! I returned to the car and got him a Gentle Leader, and he walked as if he had been trained for years! Some dogs will sulk. If your dog sulks, make sure not to reinforce this behavior by comforting ("Oh, poor baby…") or you'll get more sulking next time you put it on. Instead, get your dog busy and out for a walk. Reinforce lots for brave behavior and walking with good manners. Other dogs will have a tantrum. (I've seen everything from a level 1 to 10 tantrum!) These dogs are having a fit because they no longer feel like they're running the show, and besides this new thing feels weird on their face! The key with head halters is that you need to take time to get your dog accustomed to his new training equipment, much like you would teach a horse to accept a bridle and saddle. Work up slowly a little at a time, make wearing the head halter very reinforcing (a walk and lots of treats!) and keep redirecting your dog and catching good leash manners so that you can reward. Although I will admit that some dogs cannot seem to get comfortable with a head halter, most often in my experience, it has been that their person does not like the head halter and has not taken the time to get the dog used to it or to reinforce the dog's good behavior for wearing it.

When you have taught your dog to walk on a loose leash, you can wean your dog from the head halter. Do not do this all in one step. First, move the leash from the head halter to your dog's regular collar and leave the head halter on. After several more practice sessions, you can remove the nose loop on the Gentle Leader and leave the rest of the collar on. (You can't remove just the nose loop on the

Snoot Loop or Halti.) Eventually, completely remove the head collar. If at any time your dog's behavior deteriorates, "go back to kindergarten," including putting the head collar back on until the behavior is strong enough to slowly remove it again. You may always choose to use the head collar in situations of very strong distractions or for aggressive dogs when you want to feel you have more control.

I've talked to several very fine trainers who do not recommend head halters. They do not recommend them primarily because folks don't take the time to introduce their dogs to a head halter, or because the head halter inhibits the dog in some situations (including shaping exercises), or because people become dependent on them and never take the time to teach a good loose leash walk or heel with a regular collar. Although all of these situations can be true, I've got to say that for many of my clients, who do not spend a ton of time training their dogs, this is an easy, quick and, for the most part, gentle option in managing some dogs. I honestly don't know how some of my clients could make it through their first couple of group sessions and control their dog without one!

No-Pull Harness – A no-pull harness is designed to help manage a dog that is pulling. There are several different brands and several different styles of no-pull harnesses available. I like the no-pull harnesses that have a connection for the leash on the front of the dog's chest. One brand is the EasyWalk Harness® available from Premier Pet Products. The harness helps to alleviate the natural opposition reflex which contributes to the dog pulling against a leash. The no-pull harness is a good management tool that can be used during the time when you're teaching your dog to walk on a loose leash or to heel. I recommend to my clients that they work towards the goal of training a loose leash walk or a heel with just a buckle collar; however, the no-pull harness can be helpful in the interim.

The advantage of the no-pull harness over the head halters as a training aid to help alleviate pulling is that most dogs do not require much time to get used to the no-pull harness. In my experience, the majority of dogs can wear them immediately with no need to get them used to it. The no-pull harnesses can also be very helpful for small dogs that pull and cannot pull you as hard as a big dog. The no-pull harnesses are a nice management option for people working with a brachycephalic (short-nosed) breed such as a Pug or Shih-Tzu that don't wear head halters easily because of the shape of their faces.

I don't believe that the no-pull harness gives you the same psychological effect in calming the dog that the head halters do. Nor do they give you the same level of control of a dog's head (as would be a concern in the case of aggression). However, some dogs fight a head halter so much that just wearing the halter becomes a distraction to training. For some small percentage of dogs, this may just be their temperament, and they do not accept the head halter. In many cases, it's more likely that the handler did not take the time to properly desensitize the dog to wearing the head halter. Either way, I've seen cases where the no-pull harness is a nice alternative to the head halter and still gives the client a management tool to use during the training process.

I've heard some trainers express concern that the no-pull harness may be unnecessarily restrictive to the dog's natural movement. Like everything in life, training tools are a trade-off; ultimately, you have to decide if a tool such as a no-pull harness is right for you and your dog.

Long Lines – Long lines are used as an interim step before you let your dog off leash out in the real world around distractions. The idea is the dog is supposed to think he's not on a leash. So don't use your long line as a leash and don't keep it tight. There are some dogs that know for sure they are not free and yet it's still a step closer to off leash than a normal six-foot leash. It's a safety device in case your dog makes a run for it, in which case you can step on the end of it to catch your dog. You can also hold on to the end, leaving the leash loose. (Watch out that you don't hurt your hand if your dog makes a sudden dash!) You can also tie it to a fence, piece of furniture or tree while you're training.

A long line can be a simple 20-25 foot length of cord attached to your dog's collar. You can also purchase commercial long lines from catalogues up to 40 feet in length. I like the 30-foot "Tracking Line" available from J&J Dog Supplies (see "Resources" section) the best. Some of the other long lines are too thick and heavy for our purposes.

You can use a long line with a Gentle Leader or other head collar as long as you don't think your dog will run all the way out to the end of the line, going as fast as he can. We don't want him to flip himself or to hurt his neck in any way. If you like, you can attach the long line to your dog's regular buckle collar and leave the head collar on. Be extremely cautious in using a long line with a Greyhound, as they can reach great speeds very quickly. With Greyhounds or other very fast breeds, you may be better off going right to working off leash in a safe, fenced area.

Examples of exercises you can work on with a long line include "stay," "come," "sit" and "down" from a distance. Now, you can move 25 feet or 40 feet away from your dog, depending on the length of your long line. I usually take a long line to the beach with me and work some stays and recalls around distractions. The long line can also be used to tie to a piece of furniture, i.e., if you're working with a dog that rushes the door. Basically, the long line can be used for any exercises you want to work outside a fenced area to ensure your dog doesn't dash away.

Caution: Long lines can be dangerous, so be careful! Watch out if you're hanging on to it, and your dog makes a wild dash; it can give you a rope burn, so hang on to several layers wrapped around your hand. Also, be careful not to stand on it inadvertently or to get it wrapped around your ankles! This can result in more rope burn and even being flipped up in the air and landing on your back! (That happened to me once with a very enthusiastic 80-pound German Shepherd.)

Once your dog is responding well with a long line, the next step is to find a safe, fenced area unfamiliar to your dog, and work him off leash. (Perhaps a baseball diamond, friend's yard or fenced pasture, tennis court or school, etc.) Work your dog off leash in several safe, fenced locations before ever working off leash without a fence.

The Journey of 1,000 Miles – Taking Your First Steps

3

Teaching Your Dog Self-Control

Teaching your dog self-control and establishing a relationship with your dog will contribute immensely to your training success. Just as children can and should be taught to use self-control and restraint, so can a young dog. If taught early in the dog's developmental stages, chances are you will have an adult dog who maintains self-control. Note that I say *'self-control'* here. This is not about you "making" the dog do something or tack-

Frighty, a Bull-Terrier, demonstrates exceptional self-control as she lays quietly next to a real, roasted chicken.*

ling him to the ground to show him who's boss. This is about the dog learning to actually calm himself down and chill out a bit. Nope, you don't get to chase the cat, bird, horse, child, skateboard, bicycle, or other dog. Nope, you need to just sit here for awhile (yes, and be bored) while we do nothing. The idea of self-control can translate to many things including walking on leash and paying attention to you. In addition, over arousal is the root cause of many dog-related issues such as barking and aggression.

There was a study known as the "marshmallow" study which began in the 1960s, conducted by researcher Walter Mischel pertaining to self-control in young children. As a quick summary, four-year-old children were left alone in a room with one marshmallow and told that if they could wait for the time when the adult returned they would get two marshmallows. Interestingly, some children could resist, others busied themselves trying to hide behind their hands and what not, some simply licked the marshmallow, while others took some bites, and some just gave in and ate the whole thing. In our society today, the idea of delayed gratification isn't all that popular – hence all of us are running around with our credit cards! These same children were re-visited by the research team in high school,

---

* *Caution: Never allow your dog to eat an entire chicken since they may choke on the bones.*

and it was discovered that the ones that had good "impulse control" early on were doing very well in school and in their lives – as in not involved with drugs and alcohol. They took another look at these students in college and again noted that those with an ability to use self-control had better SAT scores, and, again, their lives were pretty much together versus those who "ate the marshmallow" and were having more problems. So what does this mean for us as dog trainers? Simply put, there is a lesson here when it comes to working with dogs. Teaching the dogs self-control helps them to mature and live better lives.

Since this finally dawned on me, thanks to several great trainers like Kay Laurence and Suzanne Clothier, I've started to teach self-control exercises in all my classes and especially in puppy and adolescent dog classes.

So here are some specific things you can do to teach your dog to strive for self-control:

Calming Ovals

Kay Laurence, a great trainer from the UK, recently introduced us to a simple and effective exercise to help calm and focus your dog. The result is not just a dog that calms down; this simple exercise also seems to calm the handler – which in turn calms the dog down! In addition, a natural outgrowth of this self-control exercise is that your dog will begin watching your body language more closely (such as moving with your shoulders), focus more on you instead of the outside environment, and understand that they cannot control your actions. As a result, calming ovals will help with your loose leash walk or heel and be an overall help in calming your dog – especially in quieting down an aroused dog.

First, it's really important that you hold the leash as specified so that the dog does not get inadvertent body signals that they may interpret as "I should pull!". Also, this method protects you from getting thrown off balance, pulling a muscle or injuring yourself if the dog makes a sudden move. When you hold the leash as instructed below, you'll find that you will have a much better center of balance from which to operate – and your dog knows it!

Use a 6-foot long nylon or leather leash and a regular buckle collar (tight enough that it won't slip over the dog's head), or if necessary you can use a martingale (limited slip) collar. Put both arms out straight in front of you and face your palms up towards the sky (yep, pretend you're going to do the Macarena!). Now, slip the loop of the leash over one hand and around the wrist, take up some of the excess leash by wrapping it a few times around your hand. Place that hand against the center of your body – between your sternum and belly-button. Place your other hand over the top of that hand. This gives you a secure hold with both hands.

To begin doing the "calming ovals," it's also important that you do not click, do not treat, do not talk to the dog or give the dog any attention. Your dog is about to find out that nothing it can do will change the handler's behavior. You are completely neutral in this exercise. With the dog to your left, begin walking clockwise at a SLOW pace, (a dawdling gait is appropriate for this exercise) in an oval pattern. It's very important that your dog does not trot, pace, or run during this exercise. You need to go slow enough so the dog will walk. The oval can be about 6 feet long. Your dog will probably stop to sniff or be distracted by various things. Fine, just keep walking. Do not jerk or pull on your dog, just keep your hands as instructed and keep walking. When you get to the turn in the oval, if your dog crosses in front of you, use what we call "big feet." This is a very deliberate large step either in front of or under your dog. The result is they will generally scurry back to your left side. If they go to your right side, stop and bring them back around to your left. You can walk the oval anywhere from 10 to 20 times. When the dog is walking calmly, and focusing more on you than the outside environment, you can start figure eights. Do this often with your dog to teach the dog how to calm down. You can also use the "calming ovals" in situations where your dog is getting aroused, such as before you go into the agility field for practice or before you enter a ring for a public freestyle demonstration. You'll be surprised at how much this will help to calm the dog. As I said earlier, an important outcome from this exercise is that you will have an improved loose-leash walk or heel because your dog is learning to focus on you instead of everything else in the environment.

Eventually, you can add some distractions. Start by arranging a distraction on one end of the oval pattern, so that the dog can retain calmness on the rest of the oval, and then approach the distraction again. Once this is going well, you could add another distraction. At some point multiple distractions can be used. Remember to keep your pace SLOW!

We consistently use this exercise to help calm the dogs before a group class. Many dogs find going in and out of the door of our training center quite exciting. You can do the "calming oval" pattern as you move slowly towards, then half-way through the door, and eventually all the way through the door – either coming or going. Do a few ovals, walk a little ways, and do a few more. Perhaps, do the oval walking all the way to your car from the training center or all the way into the building the next time you come to class.

After Kay was here and gave a presentation on walking ovals, I added this technique to my classes. I immediately saw a significant improvement with many dogs using this simple, yet effective, protocol.

Getting From Point A to Point B

Sometimes, you get stranded with your dog! We call it being caught between a rock and a hard place! You may need to move physically from point A to point B, but you find that trying to move forward is difficult. Maybe your dog was previously calm and cooperative, but now you need to get somewhere, and you suspect that the dog may get aroused again. However, you still need to move. For instance, you may be coming into or going out of a class, or going from the waiting room to an examination room at the veterinarian. Here's a simple technique you can use which will help you to avoid letting your dog practice pulling. Just wrap the leash tightly around your hand until it is quite short (the dog shouldn't have enough leash to pull too far ahead) and walk very quickly to where you're going. If the dog's on your left, wrap the leash around your left hand taking up excess slack. Be sure the leash is not so tight that it lifts your dog off the ground or in any way makes the dog uncomfortable. You just want it tight enough that the dog doesn't have much room to pull. This is just a very controlled walk that does not give your dog a chance to pull.

Parking Your Dog

Another real gem that comes from Kay Laurence is a method that she calls "parking." This is an extremely simple but very effective exercise that can be done once the dog is used to a leash. Teaching your dog to "park" is, also, another great exercise for learning self-control. Your dog should be at least 4-months old when you start teaching parking. For several years, I've taught "settle" and "stay" in various ways. However, I often found it to be a "catch 22." If a dog settled appropriately, then I clicked and treated, and the dog was, ironically, all excited again! So the click and treat would cause the dog to naturally contradict the behavior I was hoping to achieve – "settle" or "stay." With Kay Laurence's method, you don't use the clicker, treats, or any praise or attention. You are generally withdrawing your attention altogether during this exercise. This will help your dog understand that sometimes he just needs to hang-out, relax and be content because sometimes life is boring for a dog! In other words, "the grownups are talking!"

You will need a 6-foot long nylon or leather leash attached to a regular buckle collar that fits well and will not slip over the dog's head. Take hold of the collar and rotate the collar so that the ring where the leash attaches is pointing towards the ground. (This will be the signal to the dog that they are being "parked.") You will not use a verbal cue. Let your end of the leash fall on the ground, and step on it in the middle

with both feet, then gather up the extra leash in your hand. (I usually "park" my dog on my left and stand on the leash and hold the excess leash in my right hand.) Make sure that the leash is loose enough that your dog is not pinned to the ground and make sure they are comfortable. They should be able to stand up, sit or lie down, although not jump up on your upper body. Now, pay no attention to them whatsoever. Remember do not click, treat, talk to them or look at them. While I am teaching this behavior, I often engage in conversation with someone who is nearby. Your dog may initially jump or squirm around a little bit. However, you'll be surprised how quickly your dog gets the message that it's time to quiet down and hang-out for a while. Start with short sessions (about one to two minutes) and build up to longer sessions slowly.

When "Parking" your dog (we also call it "The Grownups are Talking"), be sure to leave enough leash for the dog to stand up or lie down comfortably, yet not jump up on the upper body of the handler. The handler then withdraws all attention. This is a quick way to communicate to the dog that they are not always the center of attention and sometimes life is boring. This helps them to gain self-control.

The "Tug-and-Calm" Game

Get a great toy – preferably something your dog would like to tug on. Attach it to the end of a horse dressage whip, fishing pole, long stick or the like. Start by dragging the toy on the ground in a big circle and getting your dog to chase the toy – like you would use a fake mouse on a string to play with a kitten. Once the dog gets the toy, let the dog hold it. Now, play a little game of tug. To get the dog to release the toy (this is not about teaching "give"), take hold of the collar under your dog's chin and pull up with a steady pressure (be careful not to choke the dog) and simply wait until your dog releases the toy. It could take awhile at first, so be patient and calm. Immediately "hug" the toy with both hands against your chest and wait until the dog calms down. The dog must quit jumping, barking and, perhaps, the dog will even sit or lay down. If your dog jumps up on you, hold the toy at your chest and go to a corner where you turn your back on the dog and face the corner for about 20 seconds (giving the dog a "time out"). Now, get the dog playing again and go through the same steps. If you get your dog too aroused, and the dog is not willing to give up the toy, bring the arousal level down a bit the next time you play. If your dog's not getting aroused enough to grab the toy, pull it along the ground, talk silly and get them aroused. Once you've played the game awhile, your dog should release the toy easily to your hands when you stop. Your dog should also begin to calm down more quickly. When you're at this point, add a cue to the behavior of "calm down." Something like "chill out," "relax," or "easy." Whatever works. Once your dog has learned this cue, you can use it other times when your dog is becoming aroused, and you need to bring the arousal level down a notch. (Refer to the "Resources" section and take a look at the DVD *Whippets* and the book, *Learning Games,* available from Kay Laurence.)

Other Self-Control Exercises

In addition to these techniques, you will find a number of other behaviors that we teach in class that also help the dog to learn "impulse control." You can find details on these in other sections of this book:

Under "Let's Walk" see *Goal Method*

Under "Tricks" see *Hold Bone*

Under "Door Rushing" see *Wait at Door*

Under "Training Exercises" see *Settle, Stay,* and *Leave-It*

Once your dog has learned *stay,* you can do all kinds of distraction training that help to teach your dog restraint. OK, now you need to stay while I roll a ball past you!

Voyagers Working Together: Building a Relationship

Like all shared journeys, this one involves some work, and your first task is understanding the importance of the relationship between fellow travelers. I've called this book *Click 'n Connect* for a reason. The reason is that your relationship with your dog is the entire foundation upon which your training is built. If you create a relationship based on mutual trust, respect, and communication, your training will be much easier. I recently attended a Suzanne Clothier seminar, and one of the things she said struck me as a form of "necessary wisdom" which all dog owners should embrace: "If you join your dogs in their world, they are much more interested in joining you in yours."

I've recently changed my approach with Chili, my little rescue from Mexico. He has times when he becomes very "needy," for lack of a better word, and just wants to be as close to me as he can (on my lap if possible). Often, I've thought ,"uh oh … problem – pushy behavior," and sent him away to "go to bed" (a redirect). However, lately, I've just reached over and touched him. I don't say anything; I don't do any more than that; I have simply allowed my hand to rest on his head or neck in a simple act of acknowledgement. Voilà! He calms right down!

The author, Teah, is pictured here with her little Pug, Hally. The relationship between each of us and our dogs will enhance training and simultaneously training will naturally enhance our relationship with our dogs.

I often get clients in my class that have busy lives and yet have taken on the responsibility of a dog. They work or keep very busy with activities during the week. Sometimes, these unfortunate dogs are left in the backyard all day (and some even all night). Some are simply left to wander around the house. (Hey, I had to work away from home for 25 years in an eight-to-five job, so I'm not knocking it.) My point is, however, whether you're home a lot, a little, or only in the evenings and weekends, take some time to connect with your dog. Training, of course, is a wonderful way to build a strong connection.

I can't tell you how many of my clients have told me a similar story of woe about their dog. It goes pretty much like this: My husband (or wife) doesn't believe that dogs should come into the house. Our dog has a nice backyard. We're busy with the kids, so there's no time to take him to a class and no time for walks. This basically means he's alone 24/7, except for feeding and vet visits and an occasional bit of attention from a family member. However, they do like to take him to the beach sometimes or walk him downtown to the local coffee house. These clients all would like a dog that behaves well on a leash and will sit quietly while the family does whatever. They are honestly surprised when they take their dog out and the dog reacts in a very aroused state. The point is just this simple. If you want a well-mannered, balanced dog, you are going to have to spend some time with that dog in training and creating a relationship.

Once the relationship is established, further training and behavioral issues get easier to deal with. How do you create a relationship? The same way you do with a person. Spend some time with them. Sometimes, you can even do what they want to do instead of what you want to do. Above all, do some training. Clicker training is amazing for this because the relationship, the connection, is just simply a side benefit of doing the training! After you've got the basics, consider some kind of dog sport like agility, tracking or musical canine freestyle. When you do, you'll see your relationship blossom!

Following the Signs –
Essential Steps in the Training Process

4

You are about to embark on a wonderful journey with your dog. It's a journey that can result in much greater communication between you and your dog and a much more satisfying relationship. As you learn to train your dog and your dog begins to understand and learn, you will see many changes take place. A bond and a strong connection will develop between you and your dog. Once your dog has been trained, it will be more fun to live with your dog and to take your dog places. You will also find that your dog seems to enjoy being with you more.

This training course is primarily for you. Over the next six weeks, you are going to learn tools and techniques for training your dog. If you are in a group class, your dog will have the opportunity to work around the greatest distractions – a whole room full of dogs – an experience which is good for your dog. However, the training that will take place in this six-week class is mostly for you. The learning that will take place for your dog will happen in the training sessions that you do each day.

Remember, you are learning a new process here, so be patient with both your dog and yourself. If you are feeling frustrated or angry, end the training session on a good note (with something positive) and take it up again later or even the next day if necessary. With this method of training, you'll find that both you and your dog look forward to training because it's fun!

Once the six-week session is over, your dog will perform quite a few basic behaviors on cue. Also, you'll understand more about how to work with undesirable behaviors. Hopefully, this six-week session will not be the end of your training. Training and working with your dog is really a life-long endeavor. There are always more behaviors and tricks that you can train, and your dog will enjoy learning. Some dogs have a "vocabulary" of over 200 words! There are lots of great books, web sites and informative videos available to continue your training efforts (refer to "Resources" in Appendix 4).

After you and your dog have mastered the basics, you may want to progress to more advanced training. Our intermediate training generally consists of working around a higher level of distractions and teaching your dog more complex behaviors. With clicker training the sky really is the limit. I've seen clients and friends progress to very high levels of accomplishments in dog sports – with dogs that have been clicker trained from eight weeks old. There are a multitude of activities available for either competition or to simply have fun with your dog. Some examples include: agility, musical canine freestyle, tracking, therapy visits, obedience, herding, search and rescue, flyball, and Frisbee (see "Other Activities to do with Your Dog" in Appendix 3).

Amazing Fright

Fright, my Bull Terrier, was definitely the dog I needed to push me. There is so much I wouldn't know if not for her. My other dogs were pretty much amenable to whatever I might ask them to do and made me look good as a trainer, but not Fright! But that being said, Bull Terriers are powerful, impetuous dogs, often with a very high prey drive. They are not for the inexperienced or fainthearted. They need a confident leader to help them safely traverse our human world. They also happen to be perpetual clowns; they adore being your best buddy, sharing a pizza, hanging out, going on car rides, but they have just about zero interest in doing things to please you. Bull Terriers tend to have a very self-important world view and, in fact, consider themselves to be your equal. They tend to think their ideas, such as "let's de-stuff the couch!", are simply brilliant and much more interesting than yours, "let's heel!"

Fright is exactly this type of dog, and clicker training helped us bridge this huge gap in ideas and discover a common language with which we could communicate. Fright may be thinking "Boy, mom, I'd kill to have that ball," while I am thinking, "I'd kill to have you heel ten feet with me." Because of Fright's impetuous, autonomous nature, the click was an immediate, crystal clear statement to her from me that "THIS is what I want!" And I believe clicker training was paramount in her grasping and becoming skilled at behaviors far above the level that most Bull Terriers can achieve. Along our journey, Fright has earned many awards and titles, including the Bull Terrier Club's "Versatility Award Excellent" and is the only Bull Terrier in the nation to have earned the Rally Excellent Title.

Denny Pontestull

Think of your relationship with your dog as a cooperative partnership. Your end of the deal is to strengthen behaviors you like, so catch your dog doing something right. Your dog's end of the deal is to realize that certain behaviors result in rewards and to be happy to repeat those behaviors. Above all, have fun with training, and enjoy your companionship with your dog!

Training Concepts and Tips

Practice, practice, practice. For best results, practice daily. For many dogs, and definitely for puppies younger than six months old, shorter, more frequent sessions are most effective. When you are just beginning training with your dog, keep the sessions short, perhaps just 2-3 minutes. You can quickly progress to 5-minute sessions three or four times per day. Once you and your dog are getting comfortable with the concepts, you may prefer to work in two 10-minute sessions per day prior to feeding. You get the idea – fit training into your life in the way that works best for you and your dog.

Consistency. Be consistent in your training. For instance, if you do not want your dog to jump up and greet people, do your best to ensure that you and other members of the family never reinforce this behavior. At the same time, make sure you do reinforce the behavior you would like, such as sitting to greet people. Practice greeting the dog and perhaps even tethering him so you can avoid the jumping up altogether (see Chapter 9 – "Exercises for Dealing with Problem Behaviors").

Feeding. Take control of your dog's food by establishing a regular feeding schedule. If you are "free feeding," that is feeding by putting a dish down and letting the dog eat when it wants, or feeding at irregular times, STOP! Adult dogs can be fed twice per day. If you have a young puppy or small toy breed, check with your veterinarian, as your dog probably needs to eat at least three times per day. Do your primary training sessions *before* you feed your dog. Your dog will pay more attention when he's hungry. If your dog has the potential of a weight problem, consider cutting portion size with regular meals. Depending on how many treats you're giving and how often, if you are worried about weight gain, simply take the food out of the bowl and into the training session! Mix a little ground-up dried liver treat with kibble to make the kibble more desirable. You can also provide a low-calorie food (available from your vet) and low calorie treats such as broiled chicken.

Release. Use a release word to let your dog know the training session is over. Examples are: "Go play," "freedom," "release," "done," "finished," "that'll do," or "break." ("Okay" isn't the best release word because it's used so often in everyday conversation.) When your training session is over, simply say your release word so that your dog understands the training is over for the time being. We will also use the release word later in training to release your dogs from duration behaviors such as "stay" or "let's walk."

Distraction. Begin training sessions in a familiar area, such as your living room or kitchen, with *minimal* distractions. In the beginning, you want your dog to pay attention to the training, not to the sights, sounds and smells in its environment. As training progresses, you will slowly and systematically expose your dog to increasing levels of distractions.

Attitude. Monitor yours during training. If you are feeling stressed out, take a few deep breaths and relax for a moment. Your dog will react to your attitude, so a relaxed, positive attitude during training will aid your efforts. If you become angry or frustrated, end the training session on a positive note. Have your dog do something he knows, click, treat and release your dog. Go back and do the training later when you are feeling better.

Expectations. Your dog can have a bad day, just like you. Sometimes your dog doesn't feel well, is unable to focus, or is very distracted. Also, your dog may be experiencing a learning plateau where he temporarily "forgets" everything. Be patient. This will pass. If your dog is not responding well to training, again, make sure that you end the training on a positive note. Have him do something easy; then click, treat and release him. Return to training later.

Assimilation. Blend training into your daily life. In addition to the "official" training session each day where you teach specific behaviors, start teaching your dog throughout the day. Place some treats and clickers around your house in strategic locations, and praise and click now and then for behaviors you like.

Observation. Catch your dog doing something right! Always look for a win. Look for ways you can catch your dog doing something right. Do not deliberately test your dog to see if you can get him to do it wrong. Instead look for opportunities to help him succeed. In the beginning, as you shape the behavior, it doesn't have to be perfect. As your dog progresses, require more exact behavior before giving the click and reward.

Guidelines for Beginning Clicker Training

Charging the Clicker. Before your dog can begin to associate self-control and correct behavior with the clicker, you must "charge the clicker." The purpose of "charging the clicker" is to get your dog familiar with the sound of the clicker and for him to start to associate the clicker with a treat. The first time (and only the first time) you introduce your dog to the clicker, click and treat (without asking your dog to do anything) ten to twenty times. You do not need to repeat this with subsequent training sessions. Again, only "charge the clicker" the very first time you introduce it. If your dog seems fearful of the noise, see instructions below under *Noise Sensitivity.*

Verbal Marker. In addition to teaching your dog that the click marks the right behavior, a verbal marker can also be taught. The verbal marker can be used in situations where you don't have the clicker or in teaching a few behaviors where it's difficult to use the clicker and handle the food, toys, etc. An example is in teaching "give-it" or in working on handling exercises. To teach a verbal marker (I use the word "yes"); say the world "yes" and give your dog a treat ten to twenty times.

Always click first and then treat. The sequence of click then treat is very important. As an example, if your dog knows the cue: 1) say "sit"; 2) your dog sits; 3) click and treat. If your dog does not yet know the verbal cue, "sit": 1) prompt your dog to sit or wait to capture a sit; 2) click and treat.

Only click once. Resist the temptation to click additional times.

Click and treat every time your dog performs a behavior. In the beginning, while your dog is learning a behavior, it's most effective to click and treat for each behavior being trained. This is called *continuous reinforcement*. We're teaching our dogs that when they hear the click, it means, "that's what I wanted and a reward will be given for that behavior." Even if you click in error, go ahead and treat for right now.

Click while your dog is performing the behavior you want. The click marks the behavior you will be rewarding. For instance, if you're working on sit and your dog's hind end hits the floor that is when you click.

Give Lots of Rewards. Be prepared with about 10 small treats in your hand so that you can quickly reward after the click. A high rate of reinforcement in the beginning will speed up your dog's learning! In other words, don't be stingy! When training a behavior, or anytime you're shaping a new behavior, be sure to click and treat often. This will help encourage your dog and give him needed feedback.

For now, the click marks the end of the behavior. Once your dog has done the behavior correctly and you've clicked, it's okay for him to get up. (For several behaviors that require longer duration, such as "stay" and "heel," we will also teach a verbal release word. More on that later.)

Eliminate food lure. If using a food lure, eliminate the food lure as soon as possible and begin using an empty hand to lead your dog. We don't want to make the mistake of turning the lure into a bribe. A bribe is something you have to show your dog in advance of getting the dog to perform the behavior. A reward is given after the behavior has been offered as payment for a job well done. The luring movements will eventually turn into your hand signals.

Noise sensitivity. Some noise-sensitive dogs might need a slower introduction to the clicker. If your dog seems fearful of the noise of the clicker, you'll need to introduce him more slowly to the sound. You can muffle the sound by placing two fingers on the metal part of the clicker, wrapping some tape around the clicker, wrapping a cloth around the clicker, or placing the clicker in your pocket. If your dog still seems fearful, you'll need a training partner for a few minutes. Go into another room where you and your partner can see each other, and have your partner stay with the dog with treats ready. Keep the clicker muffled for now. You click, and your partner will treat. (If your partner can't hear the click, then you'll need to signal your partner with a hand signal so he knows when you've clicked.) Systematically and slowly, move closer to your dog until you can stand right in front of your dog with a muffled clicker. Then slowly allow the noise to be louder (take one layer of tape off or take the clicker out of your pocket and place it behind your back, etc.). If your dog cannot adjust to the sound of the clicker (I've only encountered four such dogs in 18 years of clicker training), you can choose another marking device (such as a whistle) or a spoken word such as "yes." Karen Pryor Clicker Training also has available some "electronic" clickers that have other noises to mark behavior (see "Resources" section of this book).

The "Training Game" – Time for Fun!

The "Training Game" is a great way to help people understand clicker training. It's very simple and fun to play. I always demonstrate the game at class orientation and suggest that my students play it at least twice the first week. Once they are the "trainer," and the other time they are the "dog." When you play the dog, you'll learn something about what your dog feels like! When you play the trainer, you'll get some important lessons in timing.

The game is simple. It works as follows: The person who is going to be the "dog" leaves the room. The trainer thinks of something they want the person to do when they re-enter the room. In a classroom or group setting, the group can come to an agreement about what they want the "dog" to do. It can involve getting the person playing the dog to do something like turn on a light, pick up a book, or sit in a particular chair. You can also see if you can get the "dog" to do something physical with their bodies, such as wave, stamp a foot or turn in a circle.

The trainer uses no words, just the clicker to indicate when the "dog" is getting closer or heading in the right direction. If the "dog" is not getting close to what the trainer wants, the trainer must ignore the person playing the dog. The game is similar to the child's game "Hot & Cold" – "You're getting warmer." The audience also has to restrain themselves from offering verbal hints if you're in a classroom or group situation. I like to use little pieces of candy for the treats after each click. I usually offer either several pieces of candy or something special as the jackpot when the "dog" finally accomplishes the task.

Motivation

A basic law of learning is that behavior that is reinforced tends to be repeated. A *primary reinforcer* is an object, event, or activity that your dog will work to obtain. The main purpose of using a reinforcer is to motivate your dog and increase the behavior immediately preceding the reinforcer or reward. I usually talk to my classes about what I call the "Lassie Syndrome." That's the belief that dogs just want to please us. What is probably more accurate is that dogs do what works for them. In short, if the behavior is reinforced it will continue. If the behavior receives no reinforcement, it will eventually extinguish. While it's true that dogs can read our energy and they are happy if we're happy, I would not say that dogs just want to please. It doesn't matter how much you love your dog and how much your dog loves you, if you go to a field to train and a squirrel runs by, any dog will break concentration and consider running after the squirrel. We have to make ourselves interesting and be sure to be reinforcing to be effective trainers.

Reinforcers

Food is the best reinforcer for training. Food is a powerful reinforcer, and it's easy to carry and distribute. (For instance, freedom is another strong reinforcer for a dog, but it's not easy or timely to let your dog go run in the middle of a training session!)

Food: The treats you use need to be small (about the size of a pea); soft (not crumby) and your dog must love it! For most dogs, some high value food reinforcers include small pieces of: hot dog, chicken, steak, fish, dried liver, or cheese. Some dogs even like vegetables, fruit and cereal. Our dogs love tri-tip! (Tri-tip is a local version of beef similar to London broil.) There are also lots of healthy, small commercial dog treats available. In general, dry dog biscuits and kibble are not great rewards. Biscuits are big and hard and take too long for your dog to eat (interrupting the flow of training) and may result in crumbs all over the ground and a lot of sniffing by the dog. Many dogs don't get all that excited about their kibble (unless they are chowhounds in which case kibble may work for you). It's a good idea to vary the treats so your dog doesn't get "burnt out" on the same reward day after day. In general, it's best to feed your dog after the training session, not before. A hungry dog pays more attention. On the other hand, if your dog goes into frenzy at the mere sight of food, you may want to feed a partial meal before training. Do what works best for your dog.

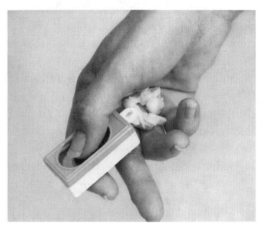

For most dogs, food is the best reinforcer to begin your training. The majority of dogs like food more than just about anything else. Also, it's easy to cut up into small pieces and use without interrupting the flow of the training. And, yes, you can learn to hold treats and a clicker in the same hand!

If your dog's weight is a concern, you may need to cut back on your dog's regular food rations or feed reduced calorie food and/or find low-fat treats your dog likes. Around low distractions, you can simply take the food out of the food bowl and into the training session. Since kibble may not be very exciting, you can use some regular kibble with a little ground-up dried liver mixed in to make it more enticing. Save the better treats for training new behaviors, group classes, and distraction training.

Affection: Some dogs get so aroused in classroom situations that they do not eat. If this is the case, you may need to use praise/petting as a reward until the dog becomes more comfortable in the setting.

Play: While some dogs are not that driven by food, they will do just about anything for a favorite toy such as a squeaky toy or a tennis ball. If your dog loves toys, keep one set aside especially for training sessions. Also some dogs love the activity of playing. A big payoff can be a game of hide & seek, retrieve, or tug of war (as long as you control the game, and your dog plays by the rules).

Freedom: Getting to run free in the field, getting out of the kennel, taking a walk, or running on the beach can be very powerful reinforcers for your dog. Usually, freedom as a reinforcer is used once you have accomplished some basic training such as having a reliable recall. Otherwise, your whole training session might be about getting your dog to come back to you! (*Note:* Do not let a barking dog out of the crate, because freedom is a powerful reinforcer. You will reinforce the barking. Wait until he's quiet for at least a few seconds, and then release him.)

Toys can be very strong motivators for some dogs. When the author, Teah, trained Chili to control himself around her goats, a ball was his favorite reward. For Chili, when surroundings are distracting, chasing a ball is even better than food!

Instinctive Behaviors: Dogs are hard-wired for a number of behaviors: They like to chase squirrels, play with other dogs, and sniff the ground. Different breeds can have other very strong instinctual behaviors. (For instance, my collie mix loves to chase and heard our llamas!)

Praise: Affection, attention, petting and praise can also motivate many dogs, but will not be a strong motivator for some dogs. Give them their favorite stroking or scratch behind the ears or give them a tummy rub. (Our, lab, Bear, loved to be vacuumed!). Using a praise word, such as "good boy!" is also effective.

The Premack Principle: Simply stated the Premack Principle says that the opportunity to engage in a desirable activity reinforces the behavior required to earn the opportunity. For instance, coming to you in the park is reinforced by releasing your dog to go dig gopher holes when he comes! Trainers have discovered that if a behavior is shaped in the beginning and the dog has a purely positive association with doing that behavior, that behavior itself can be so rewarding that it can be used to reward another behavior. This reinforcement is often used in agility. For instance, when the dog does the A-frame correctly, getting to run through the tunnel can be a reward.

You need to find out what your dog likes best. A dog will choose the payoff that has the most appeal at that moment. This is why you have to manage the training situations and minimize distractions at first. If you start up a training session with a handful of kibble (mild motivator for many dogs) in the backyard, and the neighbor's cat is running across the yard (major motivator for most dogs), guess which motivator most dogs will go for? A general rule is, the higher the level of distraction, the better the treat must be. A more in-depth discussion of distractions can be found in the section on "Distraction Training" in this book. For now, make sure your rewards equal a high payoff and that you keep outside distractions to a minimum.

Getting the Behavior

There's a number of different ways to get behaviors from your dog. You may have to use some methods to evoke one behavior and other methods to encourage others. Often, these methods can be combined. Each has advantages and disadvantages. In clicker training, we use primarily four methods: Shaping, capturing, targeting, and luring. I have also included a very brief description of the rarely used practice of physical manipulation. A brief description of each method follows.

Shaping

To shape behavior, you reward small, incremental movements leading to the final result. An example is the children's game "Hot & Cold." – "You're getting warmer." Shaping is a very effective way to train a behavior. The fun of shaping is that once your dog has been shaped a few times, she will begin to recognize when you are in training mode, and will actively attempt to get you to click. She may offer different behaviors to see which one you're clicking. When shaping, you can actually ascertain when "the light goes on," and she figures out what behavior will earn her a reward. It's critical to break the behavior down into very small incremental steps so that you can reinforce a little each time she gets closer to doing the final behavior. If she loses interest, you may have progressed too quickly. It's also important to keep shaping sessions short and positive with few distractions. You are probably wondering how your dog will know what behavior you are clicking. She won't. She'll figure it out when she finally offers the intended behavior and then you click and treat. A basic law of learning is that behavior that is reinforced tends to be repeated. Now the hard part: Be patient, and avoid the temptation to prompt your dog by luring or using physical manipulation (see "Shaping Guidelines").

Let's Boogie, Man

My Chihuahua, Cucuy, (means "the boogieman" in Spanish) is four and a half pounds of pure machismo and talent. As canny and intelligent a dog as I've ever seen, trained only with a clicker, his first behaviors, tricks and many of his agility and obedience skills were taught by pure shaping, and I think this contributes to his confidence, razor-like focus and dedication on the agility field. Ten screaming Border Collies can be milling all around him at the in gate, and he absolutely dismisses them, concentrating on his own warm-up routine. He is the fiercest little competitor I've ever run next to. He's only 7 inches tall, but in his world he is a Wolfhound and owns the whole field and everything on it.

Denny Pontestull

Cucuy was trained only by clicker training, and most of his behaviors have been shaped. He inevitably draws cheers from the crowd at any Agility event.

Shaping Guidelines

Shaping is a wonderful tool. When shaping a behavior we are teaching a behavior by getting tiny little baby steps towards the final behavior. Shaping is fabulous because it teaches your dog to think and to be creative. We're shaping movement and shaping choices that the dog makes. Once your dog understands how to be shaped and you understand how to shape, training becomes even more fun! You can shape your dog to do just about anything they can physically do.

For example, suppose you wanted to shape a behavior such as "go to bed." That's one we do in class regularly and it's an easy one for people and dogs to get started with. Place a mat on the floor, have treats ready and watch your dog for any attention or movement towards the mat. Suppose your dog just looks towards the mat. Great! Click and treat that. Perhaps your dog will move a step towards the mat, click and treat. Toss the treat so that the mat is between you and where you toss the treats. That way your dog is more likely to move back towards you and perhaps move towards the mat. Suppose they sniff the mat. Good! Click and treat. Keep building the behavior a little at a time. Other steps that might be involved are: put a foot on the mat, then two feet, walk over the mat, stop and stand on the mat, sit on the mat, lay down on the mat. Wow, once they lay down, that's exactly the behavior you're looking for! Click and treat that repeatedly. After that, we help to generalize the behavior and add the cue (see "Go to Bed" in the training section of this book).

Shaping Tips:

- Prepare for your shaping session
  - Have an idea what you want to work on ahead of time.
  - Have your treats cut up and ready to go
  - They need to be treats your dog loves
  - Ideally, prepare treats that are a different color than the floor surface so the dog can easily see them, and time is not wasted looking and sniffing for the treats.
- It's helpful to sit in a chair when free shaping. This way the dog will understand when you pull up a chair and place a new object on the ground that you'll be free shaping. This helps to alleviate the common problem of a dog that offers tons of behaviors as soon as you pick up the clicker.
- Keep the session short (perhaps 2-3 minutes), take a short 30-second to 1-minute break, then continuing shaping session for 2-3 minutes.
- Start with easy shaping exercises while you and your dog learn how to shape.
- It's easier to shape movement.

- Raise the criteria in small steps so that the dog can be successful and get reinforced plenty.
- Shape for one criterion at a time. (For instance "go to bed" – work on getting the dog on the mat first, and, then, work on duration on the mat – not both at once.)
- If what you're doing isn't working, do something else!
- If behavior deteriorates, make it easier and rebuild behavior.
- Work in an environment with low distractions.
- Use your treats to re-position your dog for success.
- End on a positive note.
- When you start over the next session, you may need to lower your criteria a little bit (make it easier again) and then rebuild to where you were before moving on.

Advantages: Shaping is so much fun, and you'll find dogs trained through shaping are often creative, self-confident, and very good at what they do! The wonderful thing is there is nothing to fade (as there is in luring or targeting). Once you've shaped a behavior consistently, the dog understands the whole behavior on its own.

Disadvantages: Because shaping uses baby steps towards a final behavior and requires that you are patient and wait for the dog to think of and offer behaviors, this method may seem to take longer in the beginning. However, once your dog becomes "clickerwise," and you become a good shaper, you can train very quickly!

Capturing

Just watch your dog and patiently wait until the behavior is offered. For instance, wait and watch until your dog lies down. Then click and treat. This can be done while sitting on your couch watching TV! Once your dog learns the clicker process, she will actually begin offering behaviors on her own. Waiting and catching a new behavior can become lots of fun with a "clickerwise" dog.

Advantages: This is easy and works well on simple behaviors your dog would naturally and regularly offer.

Disadvantages: This option has limitations because it's doubtful your dog will offer more complex behaviors on her own (such as spinning three times to the left).

Targeting

Teach your dog to touch your hand with his nose on the cue "touch." Then you can teach him to target a stick. You can then use the stick to get him into different positions (such as bow) or to accomplish different behaviors (such as heel). Targeting is actually another form of luring (see below), only now you don't have to use food. We can also teach a dog to target a mat with his paws.

Advantages: Targeting is an incredible training tool. It's easy and fun for most dogs to learn behaviors using targeting. Examples of behaviors that can be taught with targeting are endless and include: heel, finish, turn the lights on/off, spin, bow, etc. When using paw-targeting to a mat, we can easily teach back-up, front, or lateral moves.

Disadvantages: You must fade the target (slowly and systematically eliminate the target stick) until you can get the behavior without the target object present.

Luring

With luring, you basically turn your dog's nose into a magnet. Where the nose goes the body will follow. Luring is usually done with food although a toy can also be used in some cases. You can also think of luring as imagining that you have string attached to your dog's nose and that you're pulling her into the position. Luring with a tasty treat is a shortcut to getting behaviors easily. For instance, to get your dog to sit, simply place a treat in your hand and move it slowly over her head until her hips hit the ground. Then click and give her the treat.

It's important to fade the lure (eliminate the food in your hand) as soon as your dog begins to understand the behavior. My rule of thumb is to lure three times with food and then see if I can lure with an empty hand (pretending I have food). You still click and reward for the sit. The empty hand is soon turned into a hand signal. After three lures with food and three lures with an empty hand, I'll often offer a "*nose-tease*" (wave the treat in front of the dog's nose, then put it behind your back or in your pocket) to see if my dog will now voluntarily offer the behavior. If necessary, I may lure a few more times with food, then without, etc.

There's often confusion as to what makes food a lure, what makes it a bribe, and how a reward is different from a bribe. A lure is used only in the beginning if necessary to get your dog's attention and to help her to understand what behavior you're after. (Lures may also be used when you begin training your dog around distractions to hold her attention when you need to "go back to kindergarten.") You need to fade the lure as soon as possible. However, if you've been working with your dog for a while, and you find it necessary to still show her food to get her to do anything, your lure has become a bribe. A bribe is offered *before* the behavior in order to get the behavior. A reward, on the other hand, is given *after* a behavior and is payment for a job well done. For instance, you ask your dog to "down," and your dog lies down, you click and treat. The treat is a reward.

Advantages: This is a great way to warm up your dog and give him an idea of what you're after. Luring can be a fast and easy way to help your dog understand some basic behaviors such as sit, down, stand, rollover, etc.

Disadvantages: Luring tends to focus the dog on the food instead of the behavior. Whenever you use food as a lure, you need to fade the lure (eliminate the treat) as soon as you can so that your dog doesn't become dependent on the food as a bribe. The biggest problem with luring is not the fact that you've used a lure and need to fade it. The bigger problem I've noticed with my clients is that some people find the lure such as easy way to get a behavior that they have a hard time fading the lure. If you're going to lure, follow the rule of luring a few times, then quickly move to an empty hand to lead your dog into the behavior.

Physical Manipulation

By physically positioning the dog, you can place the dog in a position. An example is pushing down on your dog's hindquarters to get her to sit. This is the method used least in clicker training. If you feel you need to use physical assistance for some behavior, make sure it's very gentle. Use the minimal physical assistance necessary and don't forget to fade this physical help as soon as possible.

Advantages: Physical manipulation makes the human feel like you're getting something really quickly!

Disadvantages: Clicker training is about giving the animal a choice. We want our dogs to learn to take responsibility for their own actions and think for themselves. Physical manipulation does not foster either creativity or help dogs think for themselves. And, of course, physical manipulation has to be faded (eliminated) as soon as possible or your dog may become dependent on your "help" to perform the behavior.

Adding the Cue

Teach the behavior first, and then add the cue. The cue is simply your request for your dog to do a behavior. It can be a verbal cue or a hand signal. Actually, a cue can be a lot of things; however, let's just discuss verbal or hand signals here. In clicker training, we generally use the word cue instead of command. This is only because the word "command" is often associated with punishment if not followed. Think of a cue as your request for your dog to do something. They can comply and get a click and treat, or not and get nothing.

This is different from methods of dog training where the command is taught first and then behavior is lured, physically manipulated or corrected. In general, you won't begin using the cue until the behavior is being performed consistently, reliably, and the way you want it. Keep in mind, it's not saying the word that teaches your dog a behavior, it is instead associating her behavior with a reward that helps her to learn. Also, waiting to add the cue will help avoid the "sit, sit, sit" syndrome. It will also avoid the situation where your dog totally ignores your cues because she doesn't know (or perhaps care) what you are asking for.

When do you add the cue? This is something you will need to decide for yourself. The question to ask yourself is whether or not you are satisfied with your dog's response. Once you add the cue, you are naming the behavior that exists at that time. That means if you add the cue "down" to a behavior of lying down very slowly, that's exactly what it will mean to your dog – lie down slowly. So if you like the behavior as it is, add the cue. If you'd like a better response, i.e., quicker, more precise, etc., then do not add the cue yet.

Once your dog is performing the behavior consistently and the way you want it, then you can add the cue. As trainer and behaviorist Gary Wilkes puts it, when you'd be willing to bet $20 that your dog will do that behavior within the next few seconds, you're ready to attach a cue. You can also consider the 80/20 rule. This rule states that if your dog gets it right 80 % of the time (8 out of 10 times), it's time to add the cue.

To teach the verbal cue, say the word immediately before your dog performs the behavior (not during or after). Then click and reward. Give the cue only once (again avoid the "sit, sit, sit" syndrome). It could take a minimum of 20 to 50 repetitions of the word before your dog will understand a particular word is linked to a specific behavior.

Sometimes, we think we've taught a cue as a verbal cue or a hand signal. Instead, sometimes we're surprised to find out what the cue actually is for the dog – a head movement, how we hold our body, something else happening in the environment.

Twitchy and the Truck

My super-high-RPM rescue Pointer, aptly named Twitchy, had learned to heel beside me out the front door, down the front walk, and while we turn the corner to my white truck; then, on a verbal "OK" she would rocket into the front seat. Since heeling with Twitch is a little like having a vibrating scud missile hovering at your hip, I usually went out prior to this and opened my truck door. One Sunday, we were practicing obedience heeling in a local K-mart parking lot, and to my chagrin, I found out that what she had actually patterned was when any door opened on any white vehicle she read that as a release cue to go for a ride! I had a light line draped over my shoulder and attached to her buckle collar, and she was heeling beautifully, 110% attention; then, blip! She shot like lightning into the back seat of a white Camaro, as their door opened. Thankfully, the couple in the back seat thought it was hilarious that she was sitting sedately in their laps, waiting to go for her ride. I realized at home, as we turned the corner, I had been consistently releasing her at the same time as her eyes fell on my open truck door, and unbeknownst to me the "white vehicle, open door" was actually her release cue, not my "OK." Since she had picked up this information in a super-high state of excitement, (attention heeling) with the ultimate reinforcer "go for a ride with Mom," it was practically Holy Scripture to her. As I got a much better hold of the light line, and control of our heeling practice, I noticed she would, in a micro second, fixate on any white vehicle with an open door, and prepare to launch into it. I got a few of the drivers of white vehicles to help me explain this situation to her, with lots of roast beef and paying for attention every time they opened their doors. But since I "trained" this behavior so well, seven days a week for over a year, I expect to be working on this one for a while!

Denny Pontestull

Varying the Reinforcement Schedule and Varying Rewards

A variable reinforcement schedule refers to reinforcing behaviors on a changing schedule as opposed to continuous reinforcement, which means you give a treat for each behavior. Variable reinforcement schedules can mean that you actually set a new schedule, every third behavior for instance, every two behaviors (twofers); or on a random schedule.

Variable reinforcement schedules are often compared with people playing the slots. Once you sit down, you think you just might win the next round! One of my trainers, Ivy, talks about how for years after winning at a slot machine in Nevada, she would always go back to the same place and same slot to see if she might win. Once you've won, you're even more likely to sit there for a while thinking maybe next time!

Some research done with animals actually points to the fact that the anticipation of the reward may be more reinforcing for the subject than the actual reward itself. It's the fact that you've done the thing right and are going to get something good that makes you feel good. The good reward is the icing on the cake! That may be why variable reinforcement can be used to speed up behaviors or to get them to a more precise degree (see "Building Speed and Accuracy" section of this book).

Variable rewards refers to changing the reward for various behaviors from different foods, different amounts of food (jackpot – lots of treats); to toys, to games; to praise and stroking; to life rewards (letting them run in the field, jump up on the bed, etc.).

An example of variable rewards would be:
click and give one treat (hot dog)
click and give two treats (hot dog)
click and praise and stroke your dog
click and give a favorite toy
click and play
click and a jackpot (5 pieces of cheese)
click and go for a walk

I should mention here that there is a debate in the animal training world. Some very, very fine trainers, don't use variable reinforcement schedules much at all, saying that the continuous reinforcement will keep behaviors stronger. Some good trainers, (scientifically speaking especially), claim that variable reinforcement is the best way to go. I always suggest to my clients that they experiment with their own dogs and see what seems to get them the results they are wanting.

As for me, I'm somewhere in the middle. I use continuous reinforcement for some time until behaviors are quite strong. I do, however, vary the rewards. Later when my dog is doing very well, I may move to a more unpredictable schedule of reinforcement – but then again, I move toward being more unpredictable period (I'm turning quickly here on a heel!) just to keep them interested and on their toes anyway.

On the Road Again: Generalization

I went to the hardware store last week and was looking around for something, when a very nice blond gal came up to me. She said "Hi! Haven't seen you in a while; how's everything going?" Quickly I accessed my memory bank. Oh boy … who is she? I recognize her. Let's see, a client … hmmm can't associate her with a dog. I usually can remember the dog's name if not the person's. OK, we live in a small town, do I know her from one of the restaurants, shops, bank? Then, she said, "How's Julie? I haven't seen her since she had her baby." Ahhh relief, I've got it! She used to attend my self-help class, we call "Living Love." OK, it's Kathy. Now, I know who she is and where I know her from! I bet something similar has happened to you. In this situation, are you "stupid"? What about "stubborn"? I would say it's not either of those; you have just gotten some information out of context and can't quite put it together yet.

So often clients come to class and say, "I let my dog run on the beach today, and he wouldn't come back to me! He's so stubborn!" Usually the client claims that the dog is very well trained at home. I call these dogs "kitchen wonders." They can do anything they are asked to do in the kitchen (where they were trained) and pretty much nothing outside the house (where they've received no training!).

Generalization means the ability to transfer knowledge from one situation to another. Generalized learning is natural for people. For example, I learned to drive in an old '61 VW bug. When it came to the exciting moment to buy a new (used) car 10 years later, I purchased a '70-something Mercury Cougar, an automatic. I jumped right in my new car, checked out the great stereo and heard that engine roar, and I was off. I knew how to drive the car, even though it was quite different from my old VW bug. That's generalized learning. People do it pretty well, dogs don't do it as well.

In order to get generalization, your dog will need to practice the behaviors you've been teaching in different settings with many different distractions. Have you ever taught your dog a cute trick, then you decide to go to the neighbor's house and show them how cute it is? You probably ended up saying, "Yeah, but he does it at home!" If you want your dog to apply what she has learned in any situation, you need to teach each behavior in a variety of new situations. This sounds like a lot of work, although it really isn't. You'll need to relax your expectations a bit, and backtrack when necessary, but your dog will pick it up quicker this time.

Below are listed some different exercises to help your dog generalize learning. Teach each change individually – in other words, don't teach new posture, new orientation and new location all at the same time. Again, be ready to "go back to kindergarten" if necessary until you rebuild a strong behavior in the new situation.

Change your body posture: If you've been standing, sit down. If you've been bending over, stand up straight. Get creative: kneel or lie down, jump up and down, stand on one foot, etc.!

Change your orientation to the dog: Change where you are standing in relation to your dog. If you've been standing directly in front of him, position him on your left side and give him the cue. Next, get him to sit on your right side. (If necessary, go back to luring to get this change.) You can even take this as far as turning your back to your dog and giving him the cue! Don't skip this step, or you will condition your dog to only sit in front of you, and when you progress to walking on leash, you'll have a hard time getting a sit at your side.

Change the room you're working in: Move to different rooms within your house. Once you get to a new room, go back and change your posture first, then your orientation, etc. in the new room. Be willing to backtrack if necessary. Notice that your dog is starting to get this "generalization" stuff as he's learning quicker and quicker now.

Move the training outside the home: In the beginning, you need to keep distractions low, so you'll stay in your house to train. Eventually, you will want to train outside and in different outside locations. You might start with your backyard first and work until your dog's behavior is strong. Then, move to the front yard, perhaps next to the street outside your house, then to a local park, and finally to the beach. Remember to be prepared to lower your expectations each time, and then you'll be able to progress through the changes quickly to the end. (You'll need a leash or long line until your have trained a reliable recall.)

Once your dog has learned to generalize his skills, he will get better at it. When he is well trained, you may find that you go to a brand new place where he's never been, and "voilà!" He does what you ask!

Distraction Training

The more tempting the distractions, the more difficult it is to keep your dog's attention focused on you. Imagine you're standing in the park with some kibble working with your dog. A squirrel runs by. Guess what? You've just lost your dog's attention. In fact, she may have taken off after the squirrel! Even though you might have captured your dog's attention in the living room rewarding with kibble, chances are in this situation it's not working. Distractions go hand-in-hand with generalization. When you have a dog that performs perfectly in the house (our "kitchen wonder" again), and then you go to the park, and she acts like she's had no training whatsoever, you are experiencing a breakdown in behavior due to distractions and lack of generalized learning in that environment.

You must balance distractions with reinforcers. A general rule of thumb is the highest motivator for the greatest distractions. You need to keep your dog's interest and allow her to realize that you are the most interesting thing in her world at that moment. If you're going to the beach or park for the first few times or working on a new behavior in one of these locations, then bring a yummy treat she really *loves*. I've found my clients often want to use fewer treats in this situation or use treats of lower value to the dog, thinking that their dog is doing so well in the house or their yard, they must be ready for the distracting outside world. It's just the opposite; you'll need the better reinforcement now until the dog can handle the distractions.

Do not put your dog in a position to fail. Just like working with generalizing a behavior, start training in an area of very low distractions (such as your living room.) As you strengthen the behavior, and it becomes reliable, start moving around the house, and then out to the backyard, to the front yard, to the park, to the beach, etc. If, for instance, you move to the backyard and the neighbor's dog is going bonkers on the other side of the fence, this may be too great a distraction in the beginning to retain your dog's attention. If you can't get your dog's attention at all, your distraction is too great. There's no point in continuing the training in this situation. Put some distance between you and the distraction and work at that distance. When you've got your dog's attention again, you can move a little closer. Progress a little at a time closer to the distraction, until your dog can concentrate. This may need to be done over a series of training sessions.

Distractions during training should include all of the senses:

Auditory different noises for example a phone, doorbell, a car driving up
Scent   smells of different treats, areas where other dogs may have marked
Visual   movement such rolling balls, tossing toys, bicycles, skateboards, children running
Tactile touching the dog

You need to move up the hierarchy of distractions slowly as if progressing towards the peak of a pyramid (see illustration, p. 56). You would not skip levels (such as going from a squeaky toy to a cat) and expect your dog's behavior not to break down. As distractions become greater, you must be willing to lower your criteria and backtrack if necessary. You must work with each distraction, getting reliable behavior, before progressing to a greater distraction as you work your way up the pyramid.

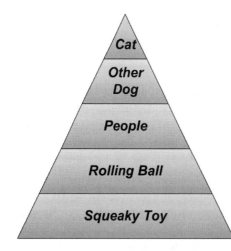

Cat

Other Dog

People

Rolling Ball

Squeaky Toy

Start with low-level distractions and slowly increase the intensity of the distraction, as if progressing towards the peak of a pyramid.

Above all, set-up for success when working with distractions. For instance, if you're working on long-distance recall, and you know your dog likes to chase sheep, do not start working recall where your dog can see sheep. Begin working in an area of low distractions; slowly work up with the distraction in the distance. Move closer and closer to the distraction until your dog can maintain focus on you despite the distraction.

Establishing a Reliable Response

Getting your dog to respond reliably to your cue is a critical part of clicker training. As you've progressed through training, you've gone through a number of steps. First you shaped, captured or otherwise established a behavior. Once the behavior was offered readily, a word or signal was associated with the behavior. As your dog learned the cue, it became a trigger for that behavior.

Once you've starting using a cue, you want a reliable response. In dog training lingo, this is called establishing *stimulus control*. Stimulus control means:

The dog recognizes the cue: You either give a hand signal or verbal cue (or both) and your dog performs the behavior. (Example: You say "sit," your dog sits.)

The dog responds with the behavior requested: The dog can now differentiate between signals. You ask for one behavior and your dog does not offer a different behavior. (Example: If you say "sit," your dog actually sits; he does not lie down instead.)

The behavior is not offered in the absence of the cue: This means if you don't ask for the behavior (during training) the dog will not offer that behavior. (Example: You're sitting there thinking of what you want your dog to do; you're silent.

Meanwhile, he comes over and offers a roll over.) Well, great. Except … you didn't ask for it.

No other behavior is offered in response to the cue: That means if you say "sit," your dog doesn't stand and stare at you or walk away. No other behavior is offered!

It's important to make sure the dog offers the correct behavior when he's asked for it. Suppose you say, "sit" and your dog looks straight at you and lies down. Oops! He doesn't really have the cue ingrained yet. This is all a part of fine-tuning training and getting a reliable response.

During the initial phase of training, you wanted your dog to spontaneously offer a behavior. At that point, it meant they were starting to catch on. Now it's necessary to raise your criteria since your dog has learned the cue. Now what we want is for the dog to wait and listen to us and respond when we ask for the behavior. In other words, we don't want them to offer it (during our training session) unless they've been asked. (Obviously, your dog will do whatever behavior he pleases, like sit or down, etc., outside of the training session, and that's to be expected.) The bottom line is this: *Once a behavior is on cue, you no longer click and treat for spontaneous offerings of that behavior during training.* Instead, say the cue, then when she does the correct behavior, click and treat.

At a certain stage in training, clients will often complain that their dog "knows" the cue but often does something else. I suspect that the dog may not really "know" the cue yet. There are a couple little training exercises you can play to firm up reliable responses.

The Cue/No Cue Game

- Ask your dog to "down" and click and treat. Do this a few more times.
- Now, just stand silently with no hand signals. If your dog lies down, just ignore him. Move to reset the behavior and ask your dog to "down" and click and treat.
- Move again to reset the behavior and stand silently. If he lies down again, do nothing (no response). Go back and forth between asking for the behavior and not asking. What you're looking for is: eventually on the turn when you don't ask, your dog stops, hesitates, and looks straight at you. If he could talk, he'd say "What do you want?" Great! Now go ahead and ask for a down, click and treat. It's in that moment of hesitation that the dog has stopped to listen and wait for your cue!

The Two Different Cues Game

If your dog is having trouble differentiating two behaviors such as "sit" and "down," you can use this game back and forth with both behaviors. Ask for a sit, a down, several downs, nothing, several sits, back and forth until he has to listen because he can't guess what's next!

The You Think You Know What I'm Going to Ask For Game

Another way to play this game is if there are times you always ask for a sit, like to put the leash on for a walk or when giving your dog dinner or a bone, surprise your dog and start asking for different behaviors, even tricks such as roll over or up pretty. Mix it up so that he doesn't know what's coming and has to listen. Otherwise, sometimes these behaviors such as sit become automatic, and the dog isn't really listening or paying attention. I ask for different behaviors each day before feeding – not always "sit."

Whisper, Jumping Jacks and Turning your Back

In my intermediate level clicker class we play some games that are fun and help you figure out where your dog is at on responding to the cue. I start with simple behaviors such as "sit" and "down." We work with these variations when giving the dog the cue:

- *A verbal cue* – no hand signal
- *A hand signal* – no verbal cue
- *Whisper the cue*
- *Sing the cue*
- *Face sideway to the dog and give the verbal cue*
- *Turn your back on the dog and give the verbal cue*
- *Sit down and give the verbal cue*
- *Sit down and give the hand signal*
- *Kneel down on the floor and give the cue*
- *Lie down on the floor and give the cue*
- *Do some jumping jacks and give the cue*
- *Jump on one leg and give the cue*

You get the idea. Vary the way you look and the way you sound, and help your dog to know the cue no matter what!

One last note, be careful of becoming a bit impatient as a trainer. Have you ever been in a hurry to leave and asked your dog for a "sit" to put the leash on and he lies down instead? Ah, but you're in a hurry, so you attach the leash and out the door you go. Just remember, you just reinforced your dog for a different behavior than you asked for. We are always training – either the response we want or something else.

Making Good Time: Building Speed and Accuracy

Building speed and accuracy to improve your dog's performance is called "fluency" in dog training jargon. Fluency is what gets you an immediate response, any time, any place. Fluency is what takes the behavior to another level and makes it possible for the dog to perform the behavior around distractions. Three characteristics make up fluency:

Latency: The amount of time between when you say the cue and you see your dog begin to respond to it. (The ideal latency is zero.)

Speed of Performance: How fast the dog actually performs the behavior. For instance, how long it takes him to lie down.

Accuracy: How straight is the sit? Is the down nice and straight with legs tucked under your dog?

To get fluency in the behaviors, you can work with three behaviors: sit, down, and stand. These three behaviors are actually six position changes for your dog and, therefore, seem like six exercises to her. These are also referred to as "puppy push-ups":

- sit from stand
- down from sit
- stand from sit
- sit from down
- down from stand
- stand from down

At this point, choose to reward for the quicker responses, speedier behaviors, or more accurate performance. Do not click and treat for slow responses or inaccurate behaviors.

To improve latency, establish a "limited hold" or amount of time you will accept between your cue and the response. In the beginning, you may set a limited hold of say 4 seconds, and as time progresses, you will systematically raise your criteria for a quicker response (i.e., 3 seconds, 2 seconds, 1 second and zero). Simply choose to reward the quickest responses to your cue. If you've established a limited hold of 2 seconds and your dog takes 3 seconds to respond, that does not merit a click and reward.

Work on only one characteristic at a time. I recommend working on a quicker response time first. Next, work on speed of performance. Unless you are showing your dog in formal obedience, I'd leave fine tuning accuracy until last. For most companion dogs, your time will be better spent on getting a good quick response and a speedy behavior. Use the following exercise to build speed and track your progress:

– Time how many position changes of puppy push-ups you can get in one minute. Only treat for the quickest performance of behavior. Use this exercise to determine where you need to improve. If you notice that the problem is in response time, stop and work on improving latency over a few sessions by working on quickening your limited hold. If you notice the problem is in speed of performing a behavior, stop and build speed in that behavior. For instance, work just on a faster "down" for a little while. When you feel you've improved, time puppy push-ups again for one minute and see how you've progressed.

Fortunately, working on puppy push-ups can help encourage fluency in other behaviors. As you work through the above exercise and get faster puppy push-ups, you will notice that you are also getting a quicker recall.

Fading the Clicker and Treats

The clicker that you have been using throughout this six-week session has been a way to mark the desired behavior. The official training term for the clicker is a *conditioned reinforcer* or *secondary reinforcer*. It's also called a "bridge," because the sound of the click bridges the time delay between the behavior and delivery of the reinforcer. A bridge (the clicker) conditions your dog to perform a specific behavior and lets him know a reward may be available for that behavior.

The clicker is a training tool. When your dog knows the behavior, you can eliminate the clicker and the treats. However, keep in mind that whenever you teach something new, you're in an unfamiliar area with a high level of distractions, or the dog's responses deteriorate, you'll need to use the clicker again. This is because using the clicker is the most effective way to train.

You can also replace the clicker with a verbal marker, such as "yes." The "yes" then becomes the bridge instead of the clicker. The "yes" is taught the same way that you "charge" the clicker; by saying "yes" and treating ten to twenty times. Then reinforce with a treat, praise, a game, or whatever, the same as you do with the clicker. As you eliminate the clicker and treats, you'll still use praise as reinforcement.

The "yes" marker can also be used in the rare case of a noise-phobic dog, where the dog is afraid of the sound of the clicker. In eight years of running my training school, I have encountered only four dogs that were afraid of the clicker and could not be desensitized to it. All four of them were noise-phobic dogs that were afraid of other noises as well.

Reading the Map: Developmental Stages

All dogs go through a number of developmental stages in their lives. It's important to understand at least a little bit about what your dog is going through. There are many fine books and articles available on this subject. I specifically suggest items by Dr. Ian Dunbar and Suzanne Clothier. I will very briefly highlight the developmental stages below:

Birth to 8 weeks: Learn to be a Dog

In this stage, ideally a puppy stays with its mother and siblings and basically learns to be a dog. They learn about inter-dog communication at this time, including vocalization and body language, to play and inhibit bite, substrate preferences and not to soil the den, and sometimes, they learn whether to be fearful of or aggressive towards people and other dogs.

3 Weeks to 13 Weeks: Early Socialization

This starts when the puppy's eyes and ears open. This generally occurs in the two- to three-week timeframe (eyes first, then ears) and allows the puppy to have their first impressions of the world. During this period, we would hope that puppies meet new people, see new things (hats, umbrellas, bicycles) and hear new noises. Reputable breeders will begin socialization at an early age.

8 to 9 Weeks: Ideal Time to Bring Home Puppy

At about eight to nine weeks is generally considered the best time to bring home a new puppy. They usually adapt very easily at this time – up until about 12 weeks – bonding with the family, learning housetraining and bite inhibition, having an opportunity for socialization, and learning boundaries and rules of your home. This is not a good time to send your puppy off to a board and train facility – you will miss out on important bonding!

14 to 20 Weeks: Late Socialization

At about 14 weeks, puppies can go through a fearful period of time when change can be scary. This is not a good time to adopt or bring home your new puppy.

Somewhere in the 18-20 weeks time period, the critical socialization period ends depending on the breed of your puppy.

20 Weeks to 1-1/2 to 3 years: Adolescent Period

The adolescent period lasts until the puppy reaches full maturity. Depending on the breed, most dogs mature somewhere between 1-1/2 to 3 years of age. In general, herding breeds and smaller breeds mature more quickly, average size breeds mature at about 2 years of age and giant breeds mature more slowly at about 3 years old. At this age, dogs are still socially immature although sexual maturity begins. This can be the most difficult stage in raising a young dog. First they are getting big, yet they are still pretty clumsy! They do not have long attention spans yet. In addition, fear periods can occur between 8-12 months and are often related to movement and noises (skateboards, fireworks) or things we wear and carry (hats, umbrellas, brooms). Episodes of increased aggressive behaviors can occur during this period.

1 1/2 to 3 years: Social Maturity

At this age most dogs will mature and for some it's a period when they begin to calm down a little bit. Status and hierarchy are important relative to people and other dogs in the family. This is usually the age when inter-dog and other aggression can begin to show up. This is one reason it's important to socialize a puppy early.

8 to 10 years: Senior Years
(small dogs and herding breeds later, giant breeds earlier)

During senior years, your dog will slow down a bit; although many can still have a wonderful quality of life during this time. Just like for people, with better diets available and medical advances, dogs are living longer and having more quality of life into later years.

10 to 14 years: Geriatric

Most dogs have reached old age by this time. Much depends on the general health, breed and genetics of your dog. During this phase in life, your dog will slow down quite a bit. Often eye sight and hearing diminish. For many dogs some arthritis can set in. It's a time when you need to go a bit easier on your dog.

Bite Inhibition

Bite inhibition means if and when your dog bites someone (you or someone else), he will not chomp down hard and, therefore, will not seriously hurt someone. Remember, it's not that bad dogs bite, and good dogs don't. Any dog can bite. It's a natural canine behavior. For instance, suppose your dog is quietly snoozing and your visiting grandchild happens to dive off the couch and jump on top of him and startle him. Many dogs would automatically turn around and snap at whatever has scared them!

I first learned about bite inhabitation from Dr. Ian Dunbar who was instrumental in popularizing the idea of puppy kindergarten classes in this country. In one of his seminars he mentioned that bite inhibition is perhaps the most important thing you teach your puppy! It's very important to begin teaching bite inhibition as soon as possible. You want to work with young puppies before they have their adult teeth and fully developed jaws. The truth is, puppy teeth might hurt, and yet it's doubtful the dog will do any serious harm at this age. Don't make the mistake of never letting your dog mouth because you'll miss the critical chance to teach bite inhibition safely.

It's natural for puppies to mouth you with their teeth. If they were still with their littermates, they would all be playing and chewing on each other. With littermates, the other puppy tells them when the pressure is too great. Puppies usually give out a high-pitched loud yip, and if that doesn't stop the mouthing puppy, he may growl or walk away and refuse to play for a while. Now that our puppy lives with us, it's up to us to teach the puppy that it must never chomp down hard on humans. We want them to think, "Wow, those humans are sure delicate. You can't bite hard at all!" When you bring home your little ball of joy, and all of a sudden he turns into a "land shark," here's what to do.

When your puppy is young, you can let them chew on your hand a bit. This is a natural mouthing behavior on the part of the puppy and is not aggression. You rarely have to encourage it because most puppies will grab whatever they can get in their mouths. As they begin chewing and you feel any pressure that hurts, let out a high-pitched, loud "yip!" That's just what another puppy would do. Keep your hand still. Your puppy should interrupt his behavior, and if he returns to chomping down on your hand it should be a bit lighter now. Some puppies (oh those Terriers!) take the "yip!" to mean "let's play harder!" For these little tikes you might want to let out a loud growl like a mommy dog would do. It sounds more like a loud "Buuuff!" than the typical "Grrrrr" sound. The "yip" or the growl is meant to act as an interrupt. We would like to see the puppy momentarily pause and lighten up the pressure on the mouthing.

If you yip or growl loudly to interrupt the behavior, and the puppy chomps down harder, get up and walk away. If necessary, you can tether your puppy to a piece of furniture so that he doesn't run after you to continue mouthing. Give the puppy a short time-out (a minute or two).

Once you've gotten the puppy to the point where the mouthing doesn't hurt (he's eased off on the pressure), you begin teaching him that any amount of pressure on human skin is too much. Now, begin yipping or growling (or walking away if necessary) at any pressure at all. Once you've interrupted the behavior, let him take your hand again and see if he's lightened up. If so, he's getting the message.

Finally, once your puppy understands to mouth gently, you want to reduce the frequency of mouthing. First teach your puppy the "leave-it" cue. Then you can use "leave-it" to let the puppy know you don't want any mouthing. When your puppy grabs your hand, say "leave-it." At about five to six months of age, you want to make sure they are responding to the "leave-it" cue. When the puppy backs off, click and treat for this behavior. Now give them something else to chew on (like a Nylabone® or Kong®.)

I don't recommend allowing any mouthing from an adult dog. Sorry for those of you that like to get down on the floor and rough house with your dog!

You'll need to continue bite inhibition exercises throughout the life of your dog. You can regularly hand feed your dog and, also, do some handling exercises, such as gum massage, lip massage, and brushing teeth to check and help ensure good bite inhibition.

Handling

Handling refers to being able to touch your dog on different parts of her body and have her cooperate with you. Working with your dog on a regular basis to be able to handle her is quite important. You need to be able to examine your dog, including looking in her ears or mouth, handling her tail and hindquarters, touching her tummy, picking up her paws, clipping nails, and giving her a bath. A dog that can be easily and safely handled will make your life easier. I can also guarantee you that your veterinarian and groomer will really appreciate working with a dog that can be easily handled.

An effective way to get your dog comfortable with handling is to shape the behavior, just as you would shape any other behavior. You can click and treat when she allows you to handle her. Some dogs have no problem with this. Other dogs have a lot of sensitivities and can become protective and aggressive. Ideally, this kind of training takes place when the puppy is less than four months old. If you have an adult dog that is not used to being handled, be cautious and use common sense. Remember, biting is normal canine behavior. In reality, all dogs have the potential to bite. The adults in the family should work with handling. Chil-

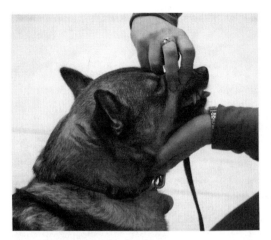

Dogs that experience positive-handling exercises and desensitization to sensitive areas, especially when young, will be much more comfortable when faced with common situations in life: an examination from a veterinarian, a trip to the groomers, baths and nail clipping at home, eye drops, brushing teeth, oral or topical medications or the occasional removal of a sticker.

dren, if allowed to do these exercises at all, should be very closely supervised. Remember, your dog is probably frightened and is not reacting out of spite. Throwing a screaming baby into the water is not the best way to teach her to swim, and using the same principles, wrestling your dog to the ground to clip nails is neither the best nor the safest approach.

Tips for working with handling

• Work with handling frequently. This is something you need to continue working with throughout the life of your dog. You don't do it once or twice and then never again.

• Look inside your dog's ears, then take a few moments to rub her ears. Most dogs like this. Be sure that you are able to differentiate between a growl and a pleasurable moan. Some dogs moan when you rub their ears.

• Rub over your dog's eyes. Don't worry; they'll probably shut their eyes. This will help prepare for having eye drops put in their eyes.

• Massaging your dog's gums is an excellent way to relax her and get her used to having her mouth handled for future tooth brushing or oral medication. Use common sense with this exercise.

• When you work on her tummy, give her some tummy rubs while you're at it.

• If your dog seems very frightened, or snaps at you, you will need to desensitize her first before continuing. To desensitize, take small incremental steps towards your final goal, and shape your dog's behavior for success at each step. Set up for success and click and treat frequently for cooperation.

• Pick up each paw and feel each nail. Work up slowly to clipping nails if your dog is not used to it. You can first let her smell and get used to the clippers. You may want to "pretend" you're clipping nails a few times first and let her adjust to the sound of the clippers. When you do clip, take just a little bit at a time until your dog becomes accustomed to this procedure.

• Use the T-Touch technique as demonstrated in class to massage your dog. Linda Tellington Jones developed T-Touch, and she has both a book and "how-to" video available (see "Resources").

After we adopted Kiko, as an adult dog, I discovered that he was aggressive when handled in some areas. Initially, it was a bit of surprise because he was fine with a bath and brushing. However, when I got out the scissors to snip some clumps of hair on the inside of his rear legs, he quickly snapped at me. Realizing he was frightened, I decided to desensitize this area. For two days in a row, I simply gently rubbed the inside of his legs and clicked and treated for his cooperation. By the third day, I brought out the scissors. I let him smell them, and then I simply rubbed them over his legs, clicking and treating when he relaxed into it. By the fourth day, I made little snipping noises with the scissors and did not actually cut any hair. On the fifth day, I snipped out some of the clumps with no problem. I still clicked and treated. By the sixth day, I could snip out the more severe mats, and he was fine with it. I kept the sessions short. Certainly, my husband and I could have restrained him and taken care of the problem in about five minutes. However, that would not have taught him anything, nor would it have helped him to trust me and to get over his fear of my working with this area of his body. Working with him patiently and shaping the behavior I wanted, I was able to accomplish the task.

However, let me be very honest to say that I continue working with him. When a dog has a severe handling issue, I'm not sure it's ever really "fixed." You can minimize their fear and, therefore, improve their reaction to the handling. When Kiko got severe allergies and the area became inflamed and painful, I did not even attempt to do handling exercises at that time. One time, his allergies were so bad, I just had the veterinarian sedate him so that we could shave his tummy. I figured it was not worth the stress to all of us. Through persistent and positive desensitizing, I've improved his ability to tolerate handling. I still wouldn't say he loves it, depending on what I'm doing; however, he does not get as stressed out and aggressive.

Having lived with a dog that can get quite aggressive with handling when he's in pain, it makes me redouble my efforts to communicate to others not to evade this kind of handling work. Be proactive. Work with your puppy when she's young, and, hopefully, you'll help to eliminate any serious problems later on.

Body Blocking

I was sitting in a Puppyworks seminar listening intently to Patricia McConnell, who has her Ph.D. in Zoology and also owns her own dog training consulting business. She was talking about the effectiveness of using "body blocks" while working with dogs. The funny thing is, I've been body blocking dogs my whole life. It always seemed second nature to me. The more she spoke, the more I realized I take this skill for granted and needed to begin specifically teaching this skill in my classes. Body blocks are a great tool to use when you need your dog to understand space issues. Effectively using space can be helpful in teaching dogs not to jump, to wait at doorways, to "leave-it" on the ground, etc.

Dogs have different ways of maintaining dominance over each other. One way they achieve dominance is through the use of space. In other words, they control space rather than controlling the other dog. Living with six dogs in the house, I see this often. You might be surprised by how my female Lhasa Apso, Crystal Moon, has controlled the space around her for almost 17 years. You can utilize this use of space to your advantage. For instance, suppose you're working on getting your dog to wait at the door rather than run out. Each time your dog attempts to make a run for it, simply move forward into your dog. Lean towards them slightly and take up the space they want to move into. (Also see the "Door Rushing" section of this book.) I also use space when teaching a dog to respect boundaries, like staying behind "the line." In addition, space can be used subtly in teaching behaviors such as "stay" (lean a little towards the dog) and "come" (lean a little away from the dog).

Ethologists (people who study animal psychology) even have a name for one of these body-blocking movements, a "shoulder slam." This is the act of wrapping your arms around your torso and thrusting your shoulder or elbow towards the dog. Doing a "shoulder slam" appears to be understood by dogs as a status-related gesture. It's more effective than using your hands and legs to block him because he seems to understand it more readily. Note that it's important to lean your body in towards the dog, so that you're taking the space away from him. I've also used this move when a dog jumps on me. Generally, they'll get off. Be mindful of which way you're leaning (into him or away from him). Take a look in the "Resources" section of this book and read one of Patricia McConnell's books to learn more about this topic.

Socializing Pups
and Introducing Dogs to New Situations

Socialization generally refers to exposing your dog to other dogs and people. We are introducing them at a young age – when they are malleable – to others that we would like them to be "sociable" with as they grow up. In some households – such as mine – I also want my puppies to get comfortable with other animals such as cats and birds.

We need to familiarize our puppies with lots of different objects they will encounter throughout their lives and places and different environments where we would like them to be comfortable.

Puppies are in their developmental stage where they are most easily socialized and introduced to new things between the ages of 8- and 18-weeks old. At this stage, they tend to more easily accept new things (people, dogs, places). Some of us who have rescued dogs or have older dogs that were not socialized, unfortunately, can't go back; so you need to begin where you are today. The reality is that your older dog may never be the dog she could have been had you had the opportunity to socialize her at an early age.

Puppies

Young puppies should meet as many new people as possible. You need to introduce your puppy to tons of people (all ages, sexes, nationalities, sizes, bearded, bald – you get the idea!). Ian Dunbar, veterinarian and trainer, who popularized the idea of puppy kindergarten, has said that your puppy should meet at least 100 new people by the time he is three months old! So don't make the mistake of thinking that introducing your dog to a few family members or friends will be enough. You need to expose them to a significant number of strangers. I like to carry my puppy (because of Parvo it's not safe to let them walk around on the streets yet) into my hairdresser's where all the gals go crazy for the puppy. I've gone into my accountant's office, the bank, local stores, etc. There are lots of folks willing and ready to meet your puppy!

Your puppy needs to be socialized with other dogs before 4-$\frac{1}{2}$ months old. The problem, of course, is that your dog does not have full immunity at this age against diseases that he can get from the urine or feces of infected dogs. For this reason, you need to be careful about how you socialize a young puppy. You can have people over to your house, you can take your puppy to other people's houses (carry them from the car into the house), and you can find a safe puppy kindergarten class (ideally taught indoors). Puppy kindergarten classes are a wonderful opportunity to let your puppy socialize with other young puppies and lots of different people. Ideally, it's also a good idea to let your puppy meet some adult dogs that are willing to put up with a puppy. This means you may want to introduce your puppy to friends' or family members' dogs – ones you know have all their shots and easy-going temperaments. If you have several dogs, don't make the mistake of thinking you're socializing your puppy. They need to meet dogs outside their own pack.

Quiz, a 14-week old Yellow Lab, falls fast asleep after a fun puppy play period at her Puppy Preschool Class.

Your puppy needs to be introduced to lots of new things at this age as well. Let your puppy be introduced to rolling things (bicycles, skateboards, rollerblades, wheelchairs, etc.) and noisy things (vacuum cleaners, garbage disposals, weed eaters, lawn mowers) and things that people wear or carry (hats, bicycle helmets, scarves, umbrellas, canes, sun glasses). The more they are introduced to now, the better they can handle these things in the future.

Cruising with Your Pup: 12 Puppy-Confidence Builders

All experiences need to be positive for your puppy. Your puppy should approach these new experiences with curiosity and interest. If your puppy seems anxious, uncomfortable or fearful, do not continue the exercise. Your puppy will let you know when he is comfortable and when he is not. Follow the puppy's lead. Every time your puppy is exposed to something new, be sure to include lots of clicks, treats and praise for a calm reaction. In addition to being exposed safely to lots of people and dogs, there are many other objects and situations that a puppy should be exposed to. Ideally, by about 5 months old, your puppy has:

- Experienced 12 different surfaces: wood, wood chips, carpet, tile, cement, linoleum, grass, wet grass, dirt, mud, puddles, gravel, asphalt, grates, uneven surfaces, on a table, on a chair, etc.
- Played with 12 different objects: fuzzy toys, squeaky toys, large and small balls, hard toys, funny sounding toys, wooden items, paper or cardboard items, milk jugs, metal items, car keys, etc.
- Experienced 12 different locations: Start with your yard, then a friend's or family member's home or yard. Prior to vaccination or lead walking, you can carry them in your arms, put them in a car or doggie buggy. Then you

can take your dog to locations such as: schools, parking lots at shopping centers, sports grounds, open country areas, heavy traffic areas, airport, dog classes, your veterinarian's office, etc.

- Experienced 12 different noises: Start with low-level noise, by keeping the source of the sound at a distance; we don't want to frighten the puppy. Work closer to the noise if your puppy can handle it. Include things like: garbage disposals, garage door opening, doorbell, children playing, babies screaming, big trucks, motorcycles, skateboards, washing machine, shopping carts rolling, power boat, clapping, loud singing, pan dropping, horses neighing, vacuums, lawnmowers, leaf blowers, a party, etc.

- Learned "I want" does get it when I work for it. Learning should be established at least 12 times a day on as many different interactions as possible. If the pup wants attention or something else (dinner or a toy for instance), ask for self-control by asking for a behavior such as sit or down (once the puppy has learned these behaviors) before giving the reward.

- Learned the "Grown-ups are talking" 12 times a week, where the pup is ignored for a few minutes when demanding attention.

- Exposed to 12 fast moving objects (don't allow to chase): skateboards, roller-skates, bicycles, motorcycles, cars, people running, cats running, scooters, vacuums, children running, children playing soccer, squirrels, cats, horses running, cows running, etc.

- Experienced 12 different challenges: climb on, in, off and around a box; go through a cardboard tunnel; climb up and down steps; climb over obstacles; play hide-and-seek; go in and out a doorway with a step up or down; expose to an electric sliding door, elevators, umbrella, balloons; walk on a wobbly table (plank of wood with a small rock underneath); jump over a broom; climb over a log, bathtub, etc.

- Handled by the family 12 times a week: hold under arm (like a football), hold to chest, hold on floor near owner, hold in-between owner's legs, hold like a baby, hold in lap, stoke head including muzzle and around eyes, look in ears, mouth, in-between toes, trim toe nails, bathe, brush, etc.

- Eaten from 12 different shaped containers: hands, wobbly bowl, metal bowl, cardboard box, paper, coffee cup, china, pie plate, plastic, frying pan, Kong, other interactive food toy, Bustercube, spoon fed, paper bag, etc.

- Played with people and dogs as much as possible. Don't do anything extreme and maintain a regime of interruption for treats; include: tug games, retrieve, chase and catch. End game for any "error" bites on skin.

- Experienced some alone time: Puppy must learn separation and being comfortable being alone. Pup should be left safely alone, away from family and other animals (5-45 minutes) 12 times a week. Vary the times of day, sometimes in the dark, in the car, in the crate, etc. Sometimes, the surrounding is quiet, sometimes noisy. Being alone should not be so traumatic as to induce screaming. The pup should begin in a crate in a room where people are present and become settled before the people leave. At first, stay close so you can hear and supervise the puppy.

Juvenile and Adult Dogs

Unfortunately, the "socialization" stage of puppies is a narrow window. It slams shut once your puppy has reached about 4-1/2 to 5 months old. You can still work on introducing your adolescent or adult dog to new things. Even if your dog is no longer in the "socialization" stage, it's still possible to help them become more comfortable with their surroundings. As your dog becomes better trained, you will want to take her more places with you. You also have more communication with her, and, hopefully, she will be more confident if you've done some training with her before exposing her to new situations. When working with an older dog that has not been exposed to other dogs, new people or new situations, use caution when introducing her to new things and be prepared to show lots of patience. Do not attempt to proceed too quickly. Give your dog time to get used to new situations. You can expose them to new situations a little at a time. Bring out the food treats and the clicker, and click and reward for any acceptable behavior. Ignore (when it's safe to do so) any behavior that you don't like. Below are some examples of some things you can do:

- If your dog hides under a chair when a visitor arrives, just ignore her. Ask your visitor to sit quietly and ignore your dog. The minute she shows her little face, click and reward. Don't "force" her to greet your visitor, allow her to approach the person when she's comfortable. You can comfort her to some extent if she's frightened, but don't overdo it. Instead, act happy, laugh, and lighten up. Let your dog know this is not that scary.
- If your dog has not been around children, you should have her on a leash (and perhaps a head collar) and proceed gradually. Ask the children to do something quiet. Do not allow them to scream and yell and move quickly. Work with this a little at a time and use common sense. Monitor your dog's reactions closely. Click and treat often for acceptable behavior. You can even have the children give her treats, if appropriate.
- If your dog has not been around other dogs, proceed slowly and with caution. You might start with short walks and get her used to seeing other dogs. If you have a friend who can take another dog on a walk with you and your dog that would be ideal. Another option is to find a friend with a good-natured dog and see if you can introduce them slowly on "neutral" ground. (Your dog may protect her own territory). Use common sense. You can

also set up "puppy play dates" with friends where you can closely monitor the doggie introductions. Dog parks are not the place for introducing dogs that have not been socialized. You have little control of the dog's entering the park. Save the dog park until you know your dog is comfortable with other dogs.

- Be very careful with introduction to other species, such as horses, birds, cats, etc. You can always create a training experience around other animals. Work with these situations gradually. Set up for success. Click and treat often for calm or acceptable behavior.

- If you're taking your dog to do something new, such as her first boat ride, bring along lots of goodies and the clicker. Click and treat often for calm and acceptable behavior. If your dog hides and acts afraid, you can comfort her a little. Then, just make sure she is safe and ignore her for a while. As soon as she peeks her head out or wags her tail, begin clicking and treating for any brave behavior.

- Allow your dog to investigate or observe new situations at her own speed, and click and treat often for acceptable behavior. If your dog starts to get very frightened, consider removing her from the situation. Attempt to introduce her more gradually, and click and treat for calm reactions (see discussion on systematic desensitization below.) Do not force your dog to do something that is frightening her. If your dog is really frightened of certain kinds of situations, you may want to contact a professional trainer or animal behaviorist to work on a specific issue.

The good news is, even with an older dog, you can still get her used to different kinds of circumstances. She will never learn about new circumstances unless you take the time to teach her. Proceed gradually, use common sense, and use lots of clicks and rewards.

Systematic Desensitization

Systematic desensitization is the process of desensitizing a dog to something she is afraid of. It's best to put distance between your dog and the object that triggered the fear. For instance, let's say you're introducing your dog to the first cow she's ever seen. If she walks nicely by the corral, click and treat. If she seems okay and so does the cow, they can even smell each other through the fence. However, if she lunges and barks or hides behind you, immediately put distance between your dog and the cow. Back off as far as necessary until she seems calmer, let's say 30 feet away. Now, see if you can get her attention focused back to you ("watch," "sit," etc.). Once things are going well, move five feet closer. Work on some basic behaviors and see if you can keep her attention on you. Now, move five feet closer, and so on. If you reach a point (say 10 feet away) where she gets upset again, back off to 15 feet again, get her calm and focused on you, and end the session. Go back another day and start at 15 feet, and then move gradually closer. Although this may take some time, systematic desensitization can be very effective for helping a dog to overcome fears and begin accepting new things.

Blaze's Bumpy Ride

Several months ago, my family, my two Swedish Vallhunds, and I were all piled in a van for a trip to Monterey and back. We live in California, about three hours south of Carmel and Monterey. We had decided to take a "scenic route" home which ended up being very curvy, and very long. Our driver, a family member whom we all love, was driving in a way that began to upset everyone in the car. He was not being safe, in our minds, and the cloud of fear and anger in the car was palpable.

On that road, we went over two "cattle guards" at very fast speeds. These were the metal open-slatted guards that completely cross the road to keep cattle in their proper places. The loud bangs even startled me, but I thought nothing of them until I looked down and saw my two-year-old-dog, Blaze, trembling with fear. He jumped up in my sister's lap, and she hugged and cuddled him. I held him and realized immediately that we needed to change the situation. I thought he was going to have a stroke! By now, he was shaking so hard his ears were trembling; he was drooling and panting as well. So I asked if we could please stop the car to take a little rest. We finally did that, and after a while Blaze seemed fine. I was relieved, to say the least.

A month later, we were on our annual fishing trip to the High Sierra. Crossing a cattle guard, even in a large quiet truck, caused Blaze some stress. Later in our little car, we crossed another one. Soon after that we left for home, and Blaze shook for almost 5 hours during the car ride, but was seemingly fine whenever we got out of the car.

As soon as I got home, I went to my lists, my breeder, and my clicker trainer for help. We decided to use something called "counter conditioning." I learned as much as I could about it, and then grabbed Blaze and some of his favorite treats, and we went out to my car. We sat in the car, chatted, and ate hot dogs. That's it. That was the first day. We did that again the next day with his favorite treat, Great Bait. And so it went. Gradually, we added the "negative elements" while shoveling treats, praise, toys; and all of the "positive elements."

Eventually, we started the car and later drove around the barn; the next day we drove down the driveway, and after about two weeks we drove the two mile stretch of road that it takes to get to the highway. At about 2 ¹/₂ weeks, we made our firsts trip, it was to agility class which he loves, then to another class and the beach, then to a dog park, and so on. Every trip meant great things would happen. I was training him almost exactly the way I had trained him when he was a tiny puppy. This was how I had taught him to love car rides.

While we drove on the highway, and hit a few bumps, Blaze began to show concern. I held my clicker in my left hand (don't tell the highway patrol!), and the instant I saw him relax I would click and treat him. In the fourth week, he actually decided to lie down!! I gave him a jackpot! He may not have understood why, but I was so happy I wanted to give him a handful of treats and a bushel of hugs.

The finale is that by the time we were due to take an airplane trip across the country for our National Specialty, (which we were prepared to cancel), Blaze was confident, not noticing scary noises in or out of the car, and ready to go. He showed no signs of stress when we picked him up at the baggage claim. He barked. He wagged his tail. No drooling, panting or shaking. To say I was thrilled is such an understatement. As soon as we got in the car, he fell asleep. Then I cried tears of joy.

I believe in the training methods of positive reinforcement. I believe in counter conditioning, and desensitizing, and I am grateful to those of you who have had these problems before, tested the training, and passed it along. Thank you for giving me back a happy, calm, car-riding dog!

Ivy Underdahl

Simon Struggles with a Road Hazard

I let my Great Dane, Simon, out for his bedtime "potty" break one night last summer, and when he came running back into the house I knew I had a problem. He had been skunked. He had been "hit" directly in the face, and he was completely traumatized. I needed to get the skunk spray out of his eyes right away, so I took him to the shower and started rinsing his mouth and eyes. He was very good, and we took care of his face and got him "de-skunked" right away. But now I had a new problem.

Simon, who had always been very good about being bathed in the shower, would not go anywhere near the bathroom. I tried coaxing him in, and he balked like a little mule. I knew better than to try forcing him ... after all he weighs 125 lbs. It was time to get the treats. I began with the clicker and treats standing next to the bath-  *room door. Simon would walk past the door. I would click and treat. He started walking past more often; then, he started stopping next to the door; then he started hanging out with me in the bathroom. I started making sure I had my clicker and treats with me when I was brushing my teeth in the morning. I would leave the door to the bathroom open, and Simon would come in and get clicked and treated. Once Simon started hanging out in the bathroom with me, I tried closing the door for short periods of time. Remember, this was done very gradually over a period of days ... just a little bit every day.*

Simon started looking for me in the bathroom. He was beginning to think this was a really special place again. Now, it was time to try the shower. I left the shower door open and threw treats into the shower. NO WAY. Simon wasn't ready for that yet. So we spent another week just getting clicks and treats for being in the bathroom with me with the door closed. Then, I tried tossing a treat into the shower again ... this time he very cautiously went into the shower to retrieve the treat. I had to be careful not to push too fast with Simon. I spent another three days just tossing treats into the shower and letting Simon go in and get them. Then, I tried closing the shower door ... oops! Simon didn't like that at all. Three more days of just tossing treats. Next, I tried getting in the shower and calling Simon in ... it worked!

We progressed from there to where Simon is easy to bathe in the shower again. He likes to go into the bathroom and do a little "spin" in the shower to show me what a "good boy" he is ... so good that some mornings my husband will let Simon into the bathroom, and I find myself suddenly sharing the shower with a Great Dane!

Mary Lugo

In this section of the book, I will describe how to teach each of the basic behaviors that we use in our basic classes. I will give you some options for training, through shaping, targeting or luring. For every behavior you train, once you establish the behavior, you'll need to: 1) add duration, 2) add the cue, 3) generalize the behavior and 4) test the behavior around distractions. Tips on each of these four items are listed below.

Duration: After he has offered the behavior a number of times on his own, you can begin to slowly increase the length of time the behavior is performed. The next time your dog does the behavior, don't click immediately. Wait a few seconds, then click and treat. By delaying the click a little while, you're teaching him to hold the behavior until he hears the click.

Add the Cue: Once the behavior is happening reliably, and you like the way it looks, add the cue. The cue can be either a verbal or a physical hand signal. For the verbal cue, say the word (such as "sit") right before he begins to perform the behavior. Verbal cues may take 20 – 50 repetitions. For the hand signal, if a luring movement was used, it can easily be transitioned into the hand signal. Any hand signal can be taught for a behavior by simply giving that hand signal prior to the behavior. Again, this will take repetition (see the "Hand Signal" section of this book).

Generalize: To further strengthen the behavior, change your body posture (if you've been standing, sit down and give the cue), change your orientation to the dog (for instance have him sit on your left side), and move to different locations (another room, backyard, front yard).

Distractions: Slowly add distractions to the training.

Name

You can easily teach your dog his name by simply saying his name and when he turns to look at you, click and treat. You can do this exercise throughout the day. If he does not look at you, do nothing (do not click and reward). Wait a few moments and repeat the exercise. Extend your eye contact slowly by delaying your click.

Attention

The dog looks you straight in the eyes when you say "watch." This is a very important exercise, as it is vital to everything else you do. If there's an emergency, you need to be able to get your dog's attention immediately. The purpose of this exercise is to have your dog check in with you. You can use a word such as "watch" or "look at me" as your cue for the attention behavior or simply teach the behavior as a default without a verbal cue.

When teaching the "Attention" behavior, we want the dog to look straight into our eyes and focus his attention on us, rather than the external environment.

Shaping: It's great fun to shape this behavior and a good experience in starting to learn to shape effectively. You do not need to say anything; shape this behavior a little at a time.

- Click and treat any time your dog orients towards you.
- Click and treat whenever your dog looks towards the center of your body.
- Click and treat any time your dog looks towards the upper part of your body.
- Click and treat for any looks towards your head.

- Click and treat for even momentary eye contact.
- Click and treat for longer eye contact a little at a time, a half second, one second, two seconds, etc.
- Once your dog is looking at you readily and you've prolonged the behavior, begin adding distractions.
- Put a treat in your hand and extend your arm out to your side. Your dog will probably look at the treat. Wait and click as soon as your dog looks back at you (away from the treat) and gives you eye contact. Watch your timing and make sure you click at the second your dog looks back at you.
- Hold treats in one hand and then the other as a distraction.
- Eventually, move your hand and click and treat at the second your dog re-commits eye contact to you.
- Continue this until you can wave your hand around and your dog keeps looking at you instead. Now take your dog out in the world (on leash) and continue working on this behavior around distractions.

Sit

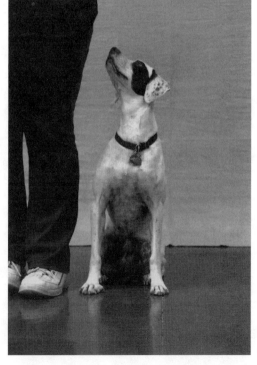

"Sit" means that your dog should place his hindquarters on the ground. This is an important behavior that you will use often.

Capturing: Sit is a behavior that any dog offers frequently. This can be easily taught by capturing.

Just wait until your dog sits, then click and treat. Do this a number of times and before you know it your dog will be running up to you offering sits! Just add the cue "sit" right before your dog sits, and he will learn the word quickly. It's also helpful to teach the hand signal for this behavior.

Twitchy, a field-bred Pointer adopted from a local shelter, sits at Denny Pontestull's left side during a training session.

Shaping: Yes, you can shape a dog to sit.

You can click for each movement closer to sitting. For instance the dog raises his head up and looks up at the ceiling, click and treat. When a dog raises his head to a certain point, the hindquarters have to hit the ground. You could click for any squatting movement beginning in the hindquarters, etc.

Luring: Luring is another way to teach "sit."

While the dog is standing, hold a treat in your closed hand right over the dog's forehead. (For a small dog, you may want to sit on the floor for comfort.) If the dog sits, click and treat. If the dog doesn't sit, then move your hand backward towards the dog's tail, slowly, an inch or two. The dog will attempt to follow your hand with its nose, and this should lure him into folding his back legs and sitting. Click when the dog starts to sit. Open your hand and give the treat immediately. The dog may jump up again, and that's okay. Do your best to click as soon as he sits at first and quickly follow the behavoir with a treat. Ideally, the dog will get both the click and the treat while he's sitting. If he does pop right back up the first few times, that's okay, go ahead and treat.

This is usually a pretty easy behavior to lure; however, if the dog doesn't sit at first be patient. If your dog backs up, move more slowly, or do the exercise with your dog's back to a wall. If your dog jumps up, ignore that behavior. Wait for him to settle down. When your dog puts his front feet back on the ground, start luring with the hand movement again. Make sure you're not holding the treat too high, causing your dog to jump up. In clicker training, we start by getting the behavior. Later, when the behavior is reliable, we'll attach a cue to the behavior.

Lure three times with food and three times without food. Then comes the hard part! Be patient and wait for your dog to freely offer this behavior! You can always use a "nose-tease" to remind him you have a treat. When he sits, click and treat.

Sitting Up from Down

Practice getting your dog to sit back up from a down. Even though we still call this "sit," it seems like a new behavior to the dog. He is now sitting up instead of sitting down. If you need to lure it, from a down position, put the treat on his nose and pull the treat up slowly directly over his head. When he sits up to get the treat, click and give him the reward. Don't hold the treat too high or he may jump up.

Down

"Down" means that your dog should lie down. You decide whether you care if he's lying with his legs tucked under him or legs to the side. In my opinion, either one is okay.

Capturing: You can just wait until your dog lies down then click and treat.

A nice way to work with this behavior is while you're watching TV. Just grab your clicker and some treats and relax. Every time you see your dog go over by the fire and curl up, click and toss a treat. He'll get up, get the treat, think about it for a while and probably go lie down by the fire again. Click and treat! Do this a number of times, and before long your dog will offer the behavior. Add the cue and you've just taught your dog to lie down!

Shaping: Click if his head dips towards the ground at first, then if his paws just start to slide out, or if his front elbows start to bend. Wait and give your dog time, each time raising the criteria a little before you click and treat.

Luring: Once your dog is sitting, use your treat hand to lure your dog into a down.

First have a treat in your closed

Hally lies down when given a hand signal by Teah. Sometimes, it's easier to work with small dogs by getting down to their level on the floor or by raising them up and working them on a table or other raised surface (just make sure they don't fall off).

hand, and put your hand to the dog's nose. Then, move your hand down, slowly, between the dog's front paws, and keep your hand very close to the dog. His nose should follow your hand. The dog is likely to lean backwards, and then start to lie down. Click when the front legs start to buckle the first time. Treat. The next time, lure him a little farther down, and begin pulling your hand slowly along the floor in front of him. If the dog lies down, click and treat. Some dogs fold backwards into a down. So when you have the treat between the front paws, you can also experiment with pushing back along the floor towards the dog. As long as he's down when you click, even if he pops right up, go ahead and treat. After working with this a few times, do your best to click and treat while he's lying down.

Lure the dog three times with food and three times without. Then, wait for him to offer the behavior. You can show the dog the food (nose-tease), but don't lure him. You don't need to wait for the complete "down" behavior.

Some dogs (especially ones with really short legs) may not lure as easily into the down position. You may want to either capture or shape this behavior, or you can lure your dog under your legs. Sit on the floor and bend one leg (making a "tent" with your leg) and lure your dog to crawl underneath your leg. This will cause most dogs to lie down. If your dog is scooting backwards, place his hind end towards a wall to work on this exercise. Remember, be patient. Ignore anything that's not a "down." Do not expect perfection immediately!

Lie Down from Stand

Now, teach your dog to lie down from a standing position. If necessary, you can use a food treat to lure him the first few times. Say "down" and move your hand towards the ground. Remember, even though the cue is the same as lying down from a sit, you need to teach your dog to lie down from a stand as a separate behavior.

Stand

"Stand" means your dog should stand up with all four paws on the ground. This behavior comes in handy when you need to examine your dog or give him a bath, etc.

Capturing: Just wait until your dog stands up from a sit or a down and click and treat. Easy!

Shaping: Yes, you can shape a stand as well as any other behavior. This one is so simple though I generally either capture or lure it a few times.

Targeting: Simply teach the dog to "touch" your hand with his nose and use the target (your hand) to cause him to stand.

Luring: Start with your dog in a sitting position.

Use a food lure to move your dog into a stand position. Hold the lure right in front of your dog's nose, and move it forward very slowly. Keep the lure at your dog's nose height until he stands. (Do not move the lure up – keep it parallel to the ground, or you will cause your dog to either jump up or sit as he follows the treat.) It's often helpful to stand in front of your dog and move him towards you while you're moving backwards. Your movement seems to help him get up. As soon as he stands, drop your hand down slightly towards the ground. (Because this causes your dog's head to drop slightly, it helps him to have a more solid stand and not drop his hindquarters immediately.) When you get a stand, click and reward.

Lure three times with food and three times without food. Now give him a "nose-tease" and wait for him to offer the behavior on his own. If you don't get the behavior, go ahead and lure another few times. Now, do the "nose-tease" again and wait for a stand.

Stand from Down

If you've been working on a stand from a sit, also work on a stand from a down position. This is still called "stand," yet seems like a new behavior for your dog.

Puppy Push-ups

In class and in this book, I refer to puppy push-ups. This is what we call a series of behaviors that are used as a training exercise. We don't actually cue this exercise as "puppy push-ups" to our dog. Instead, we (people) just call it that. A basic puppy push-up is a sit, down and stand in a row. A more complex puppy push-up might incorporate any of the following six possible position changes:

- Sit from a stand
- Sit up from a down
- Lie down from a sit
- Lie down from a stand
- Stand up from a sit
- Stand up from a down

Take Hold of Collar

This exercise is simply to teach a puppy or dog not to squirm away when you reach for the collar. Some dogs may be shy or may have already learned to play a little game of "keep away" from their people.

If necessary, slowly shape the behavior by first just beginning to reach for the dog, then finally touching the collar, then eventually taking hold of the collar. Click and treat for each trial where you get closer to touching the collar. Once you can readily take hold of the collar, you can also add it to the "sit" behavior. First, ask your puppy to "sit." After he sits, reach out slowly and take hold of his collar before you click and treat. If he gets up and moves away, do not click and treat. Practice this exercise to make sure your puppy or dog will not shy away when you reach for his collar.

Come

Training your dog to come when called is probably the most important behavior you will teach. This behavior is also called a recall. Training a reliable recall takes thought, attention and some common sense. It also takes patience! Just because your dog will come in the house or your backyard, does not mean she knows a long distance recall around a lot of distractions. Have you ever noticed how when you take your dog to the beach or park, she seems to have "forgotten" what "come" means?

Tips for Teaching Come:

- Never call your dog and then punish her. If she does not come the first time you call, either ignore the behavior and call again in a few minutes, or if she's outside and it's not safe, go and get her and bring her back on a leash. Also, if you have to go after her, do not punish her when you reach her. This will actually teach her to run away from you!
- Never call your dog with a "come," and then do something the dog finds unpleasant (like getting her nails clipped). In this situation, go get your dog.
- Always set your dog up for success. Remember the 80/20 rule. Don't add a cue unless you think your dog will respond at least eight out of 10 times. If you think your dog is distracted and won't come (let's say she's busy rolling in cow manure), don't call her! Instead just go and get her with a leash.
- Do call your dog and give her dinner or anything else fun, like a walk or a car ride.

- Call your dog throughout the day and click and reward when she comes.
- Be consistent with your cue. Have the whole family use the same word such as "come" or "here."
- If you have an older dog that has been ignoring the cue "come" for a long time, start over and use a new cue, such as "here."
- If you are working with your dog outside in an unfenced area, attach a "long line" to the dog for safety purposes (see "Long Line" section of this book).
- Begin adding new criteria to the game. When you call your dog and she comes to you, first take her collar before you click and treat. (Hold the clicker in the other hand from the one you grab the collar with or you'll be clicking right in her ear!) This will help her to learn that you may also want to take her collar when she comes. We want to train her from the beginning that when she comes, we may want to put a leash on or pick her up.
- Once your dog is doing well on "come," you can also request she sit in front of you when she comes.
- If your dog comes, but comes slowly, then do this exercise. Have a training partner hold her back by the collar or hands across the front of her chest. You call her. When she wants to move towards you, have your training partner hold her back just a little bit longer – just a hesitation – and then release her. When she gets to go, chances are she'll come more quickly.

Clients starting training will often come to class and excitedly declare that their dog was off in a field somewhere, and they just clicked and she came running! True, it may work at first or in an emergency, although you want to save the use of the clicker to mark the right behavior – coming to you – so resist the temptation to use it as an attention getting device.

There are a number of games you can play to teach "come." Choose one or more of the following to see what works best for your dog:

Chase Me

Moving away from your dog will cause your dog to want to move toward you. Clapping your hands and shuffling backwards a short distance can work well. Also, moving quickly or running from your dog will help initiate her chase response. In the beginning, you can show your dog a tasty treat or toy and move away quickly. When she follows you and comes to you, click and give her the reward. As she starts to catch on to the game, add the cue by calling her name and say "Come" once. For example, "Skye, come!" and move quickly away. (Resist the temptation to call multiple times, "come, come, come ...") Click and treat for her coming to you! If she runs past you, turn and run in another direction until she catches up with you, then click and treat.

Relay Game

A good way to strengthen this behavior is to have two people kneel down about six feet apart at first. One person holds the dog by the collar and, otherwise, ignores her. The other person encourages the dog to come to them by saying their name and sounding excited. Open your arms and welcome her. Clap your hands against your thighs if necessary. The other person holds her back for a few seconds and then lets her loose. When she comes to you, click and treat. Now you hold her, and the other person encourages her. As soon as she starts to understand the game, you can add the cue "come" when she's on her way to you.

If she's not coming, begin by standing and move back quickly when she looks at you. You can also clap your hands and shuffle quickly backwards – even run the other direction, if necessary. Often the movement will cause your dog to want to chase you.

When you're getting a "come" at this short distance, move out to eight feet and then ten. Progressively increase your distance until you can stand across the room from each other. When this is working, move to a new location (perhaps another room). Then move outside (within a fenced area). You can also play round-robin if you have three or four people participating.

Follow Your Nose

If you're not having much success with the relay game, you might play this game. Begin by standing only a few feet from your dog, and drop a yummy treat right by your feet. When she runs up to get it, click. Move again. Progressively move further and further away. When she's following you around regularly, add the cue "come" right after you drop the treat.

Hide & Seek

This is a wonderful game to use to teach "come," and your dog will love it. It's also great because it requires that your dog listen for the cue even if he can't see you. Obviously your dog will need to know what the cue "come" means, so you need to start with the relay game, chase me or follow your nose.

Have someone hold your dog. Go hide somewhere out of your dog's view. Make it easy at first – around the corner, behind the couch. Now, call your dog clearly and loudly only once. When she finds you, click and treat and praise lavishly! You can make this game progressively more and more difficult. Hide upstairs in the bedroom closet with the door open a few inches, or hide behind the shower curtain, etc. If your dog walks by and seems confused, you could give her a little hint (clear your throat or cough) instead of calling again. If she doesn't find you, hide in an easier place the next time and make the treats better.

Anytime Game

Anytime during the day, not only during official training sessions, call your dog to you. If you get down and open up your arms, this may help entice her, or moving backwards may help trigger her natural chase response. Always click and treat when your dog responds. If your dog does not respond, don't repeat the cue. Let her see you put the clicker and treats away. Repeat the exercise again in a few minutes and see if she will come. Call her whenever you're going to feed her, even if she's already heading for you. Call her to go for a walk or anything else that's fun for her!

Long Distance Recall

Long distance recall is a more complicated behavior than a simple "come" around the house or yard (even though it uses the same cue). The long distance recall requires a lot of practice and involves gradually moving to different locations with higher levels of distractions. You should always work with a long line when teaching a long distance recall (see the "Long Line" section under Training Equipment in this book). You'll need to work in many different settings until your dog is reliable around many distractions.

Once your dog comes reliably in many different settings with a long line on for safety, you'll need to work off leash in a safe, fenced area unfamiliar to your dog (a friend's or family member's fenced yard, a tennis court, a church, school or fenced park). Think of it this way: Actually having a reliable recall around distractions is like a Ph.D. of dog training. We're in elementary school right now, so don't progress immediately to this and expect success. Your dog should always be on a leash or within a fenced area until you're about 95 % sure you've got a reliable recall.

Some Tricks to Use If Your Dog Doesn't Come

The following are not training techniques. Instead, they are tricks you can use in an emergency that will often cause your dog to come to you. Obviously, if you over use these, they will not work.

Catch-Me-If-You-Can!
The "Catch-Me-If-You-Can" game is a technique to use if your dog does not come when called. Do not chase him! All of a sudden, act totally crazy. Begin "yipping" and making all kinds of noise in a high-pitched voice. Swing your arms, jump around, and act generally nuts. Then turn and run fast in the opposite direction away from your dog! Most dogs will follow. When he catches you, praise him and give him a jackpot reward. An alternative approach is to get his attention and, then, either sit down or lie down. A total change in body posture will often surprise your dog and they'll come to investigate.

I Found a Treasure!
This works well for a dog that's playing hard to get. Every time you reach for the collar, he jumps away. Drop down to your hands and knees on the ground. Begin talking in an excited, yet quiet way while looking down at the ground like you found something. (I always say something like, "Wow, look what a wonderful treasure I've found!) Most dogs will come to investigate what their crazy Mommy or Daddy is doing. As they approach, continue talking and calmly reach for their collar – do not lunge for the collar, or they will probably bolt away! When you have him, praise him and give him a jackpot reward.

Emergency Recall

I teach an emergency recall in my classes. The purpose of the emergency recall is that it is used only in a true emergency. Your dog just jumped out of the car and is heading for traffic. You're on a hike, and your dog takes off after a deer. You are walking, and your dog takes after a cow … or cat … o r … you get the idea. I teach a Really Reliable Recall (RRR) popularized by Leslie Nelson at Tails – U – Win Canine Center (see reference section of this book). Take a look at her books and DVD's to learn more. I've had many testimonials from my students on how well this works! My own story below illustrates just how comforting a good emergency recall can be.

Chili and A Dash Of Rooster

The value of a good recall was made vividly apparent to me recently. I had an experience with our little rescue dog, Chili, who came from the streets of Mexico. We were out in the back pasture, and for the first time I saw a rooster in my neighbor's yard. Chili saw the rooster too and locked on with a stare. At the same time I was busy being thankful that I had a fence, Chili spotted a small hole and shot through after the rooster! I panicked and screamed "Chili come" and to my amazement he actually stopped mid-run and returned to me. The funny thing is, I noted the look of surprise on his face while he was headed back to me as if to say, "Why am I going to Mom?" I was thrilled because I realized I had established a reliable recall. The way I did it was to build a strong reinforcement history (a lot of repetitions of come and always good rewards). Secondly, I had worked on Chili's response time on cues until he responded quickly. I could tell he had turned around and was coming to me before he even thought about it (see "Establishing Speed and Accuracy" section of this book). Third, I had worked with distractions that were progressively more difficult until he was successful. This was a situation where all that work paid off!

Let's Walk

The "let's walk" cue means walking on a loose leash without pulling. This is not a formal "heel," instead it is a casual walk where your dog is not pulling on you. A formal heel would mean that your dog would walk directly by your left leg and sit automatically when you stop. Training a "heel" is covered separately. The let's walk training is done with a head collar, no-pull harness or a regular buckle collar, and a standard four-foot or six-foot nylon or leather leash.

Note: Once you begin teaching this cue, you can no longer allow your dog to pull on the leash, because that will compromise your training effort. Also, do not use an expandable leash (or flexi-leash) while training a loose leash walk, as this rewards your dog for pulling by allowing her to go forward when she pulls. You can go back to using one of these later, once your dog understands the cue, "let's walk." If you need to take your dog out without working on the "let's walk" training; then, you can use a head collar or no-pull harness to prevent pulling (see "Training Equipment").

If you have a dog that has already learned to pull, be forewarned that training this behavior can take time and patience. It is not a behavior that necessarily comes easily to dogs. When dogs are out on a walk, they are very interested in investigating their surroundings and walking slowly by our side is not the most appealing idea!

The Stop or Redirect Method

- Decide if you want your dog to walk on your left side or your right side and be consistent. The left side is most commonly chosen.
- Always keep your pace brisk while teaching let's walk. Your dog is more likely to stay with you. Strolling slowly along will give a dog more opportunity to be distracted.
- The main rule is as long as the leash is loose, you can move forward. If the leash tightens, stop and stand still.
- An alternate to stopping is redirecting your dog's behavior. You can either make an about face turn and head in the opposite direction or make a sharp turn. If your dog is on your left, make a sharp right turn. If your dog is on your right, you would need to make a very sharp left turn. This will stop your dog from pulling and automatically put her back into the correct position so that you have an opportunity to click and treat her for being in the right place. I generally randomly alternate between stopping and making sharp right turns as I proceed with this exercise.
- Hold the leash in your hand. Allow only two to three feet of slack in the leash. Think of the leash forming a "J" between you and your dog.
- Wait until the leash is loose before you start moving forward. Once the leash is slack, say, "let's walk" and move forward. Keep walking until the leash tightens up. The second the leash tightens-up, stop or turn. In the beginning, you will probably only be able to take a few steps forward.
- As soon as the leash loosens up, click and let your dog return to you for a treat. Reposition your dog to your side, wait until the leash is loose, and then say, "let's walk." Walk forward again. When you have gone four or five steps with no pulling, click and treat. (It's best to stop to treat so your dog isn't on the run when being rewarded.) Give the cue, "let's walk" and continue stepping forward. If she starts pulling, stop or turn again.
- Start extending the distance going seven or eight steps before clicking and rewarding.
- Keep progressing slowly until your dog can walk about 20 feet. When you arrive at the 20 foot mark, immediately click, and jackpot. Repeat the 20-foot distance several times.
- Change to a new location to practice next time. Use an arbitrary target (a

tree, a sign, etc.). If she pulls, stop. Wait for a loose leash. Click for the loose leash and let her return to you for the treat. Reposition your dog by your side (move her or move yourself), then continue forward, and when the leash is loose, click and treat. Each time you move forward again, use the cue "let's walk."

- Once your dog has become proficient at walking in a straight line, increase the distance slowly.
- Eventually, begin raising the criteria and teaching your dog to walk in more than a straight line. Teach each new variable separately.
  For instance, walk in large circles to the right and left. If you're walking your dog on your left, large right circles help teach your dog not to lag, and large left circles help teach your dog not to cross in front of your left leg, and to pay attention.
  – Add right and left turns.
  – Add right and left about-faces.
  – Add figure-eights.
  – Also vary your speed from slow to fast to normal.

Once your dog has become proficient at walking on a loose leash, you can begin teaching your dog to sit when you stop. However, wait until your dog understands walking on your left on a loose leash before you begin teaching this new variable. Teaching two things at one time will probably confuse your dog.

Now, begin teaching "let's walk" progressively with more distractions – dogs, people, other animals, etc.

If you've been using a head collar, when the behavior is very strong, you can begin weaning your dog from the head collar. Do not do this all in one step (remember generalization?). First, move the leash from the head collar to your dog's regular collar and leave the head collar on. If you're using a Gentle Leader, after several practice sessions, remove the nose loop from your dog's nose and leave the rest of the collar on. Eventually, completely remove the Gentle Leader.

If at any time your dog's behavior deteriorates, "go back to kindergarten." This may include putting the Gentle Leader back on until the behavior is strong enough to slowly remove the Gentle Leader again.

Goal Method

This exercise is another way to teach loose leash walking. You're going to let your dog know that she will get something really yummy if she does not pull on the leash.

- Begin by marking off about a 6 to 8 foot distance. You'll need a start line and an end line. The start and end line can be anything that works for you, such as a line in a sidewalk, a tree, a fence, etc. Place a yummy treat in a small container your dog can see, such as a plastic margarine lid at the end line. (Also, a training partner can hold a treat or you could use a toy.) Begin at the start line. Give your dog a loose leash. If she pulls the leash, immediately back up all the way to the beginning. (Do not turn around and walk the other way.) When she's not pulling, start again. Repeat this exercise until she can make it to the goal line without pulling. When she makes it to the goal point without pulling, click and let her have the treat. It may take several repetitions of this exercise before she realizes that there is something yummy in the margarine lid!

- Once your dog can walk a 10-foot distance successfully a number of times without pulling, you can begin expanding the distance to 20, 30, and 40 feet, etc. Now when you step off from the starting line, say, "let's walk" or "let's go." In the beginning, if she pulls, back up all the way to the beginning. Once you get to about 20 feet, you only need to back up five steps. One of my clients places the treat out by the mailbox where she and her dog walk each morning and has found this exercise very helpful. She actually has the patience to go all the way back to the beginning if her dog pulls.

- Once your dog understands the concept, she may still pull on the leash occasionally. If she does, immediately retreat a few steps and wait for a loose leash before walking again.

Note: Depending on the temperament and hunger level of your dog, some goodies may be too tempting or not tempting enough. For some dogs, if the treat is too good, they simply can't control themselves. For other dogs, if the treat isn't tempting enough, they may not want to bother making it to the goal.

Luring Method

- You can place a tasty treat in your hand on the same side as the dog. Walk three steps with the leash loose. If your dog stays on your side and keeps the leash loose, click and give your dog the treat in your hand. (If you have a very small dog that can't really get all that interested in your hand because it's so far away, you might want to use the targeting method instead.)

- Gradually increase the number of steps you can take without your dog pulling. For example, 5 steps, 8, then 10, 12 and so on. Click and give the dog the treat out of your hand for success. Deliver the treat from the hand closest to the dog. For instance, if you walk your dog on the left, give the treat from the left hand. If your dog pulls forward, just stop and do nothing and reposition your dog (move her or move yourself) and start again.

- Remember anytime you lure, you'll need to fade the lure. After your dog can walk about 15 steps, move the treat back to your treat bag. When you first remove the lure, go back to just a few steps and slowly build back up to 15 steps. Click and treat for success. If your dog starts pulling again, "go back to kindergarten," and build the behavior more slowly.

- Once your dog is staying on your side with a loose leash, begin practicing in different locations. If you've been inside, go to the backyard, the front yard, etc.
- Slowly increase the distraction level.
- Remember, each time you change the location of training or increase distractions; you may need to lower your criteria. That means require fewer steps before the click and reward. Gradually build back up to 15 steps in new locations and distractions.
- Then increase your distance.
- Add turns and vary speed as outlined above.

Catch Me Method

This game is based on getting your dog used to walking by your side and involves more pure shaping instead of luring or restraining with a leash. It's a good way to get your dog to understand the idea of sticking close. This exercise is done off leash, so start in the house or in a fenced area.

- Walk around and click and treat anytime your dog ends up by your left side and is paying some attention to you. You can say her name or make a kissy noise if you want. Don't say a lot though.
- When she comes up by your side, click and treat.
- If she runs past you, turn and walk in the other direction.
- If she loses interest and wanders away, start clicking and treating when she heads back for you.
- Click and treat again when she positions herself by your side.

What do you do if she isn't walking by your side? Nothing. She gets no reinforcement. That's it. Remember, with shaping you can start clicking and treating, as she gets closer to what you want, and then tighten up your criteria as you progress. In the beginning, click and treat for attention and being close to your left side. As time goes on, raise your criteria to be more specific. This is a fun game to play to get her used to being by your side.

Targeting Method

If you use the targeting method, I recommend teaching a more formal "heel" (see "Heel" below). If you prefer, an alternate cue used by many is "let's go."

Heel

"Heel" is a cue that requests that your dog walk by your side (traditionally "heel" means your left side), and close to your leg (not lagging or forging). In general, your dog's shoulder blades are lined up with the seam of your pants. "Heel" traditionally is an off-leash cue and, of course, can also be used on leash. Once the behavior has been taught, your dog should be able to stay by your left leg while you turn or make an about-face, vary your speed, and your dog should sit at your left when you stop.

When working with a young dog that has not learned to pull yet or run ahead of his person, I believe that it's easier to teach a formal "heel" than a casual loose leash walk. A "heel" is very specific and if you take the time to teach your dog what it means, they will know just where they need to be.

When a dog heels, he sticks close to the handler's left leg and does not lag or forge ahead. It's a wonderful off-leash exercise and is highlighted here by Quinn's excellent attention to his person Katie Hawkins.

Shaping Method

• You can get your dog used to walking by your left side by shaping the behavior. It's best to teach this by starting with a big circle. Start counter-clockwise so your dog is on the inside when at heel position. Walk briskly and if you like you can even play some music to keep you going at a good pace. I like to start this work in the living room or kitchen. Keep doors shut or use baby gates, so your dog cannot wander into another room. Have your clicker and some really good treats ready. Any time your dog happens to come up by your left side into the heel position, click and treat. Play this game for a few minutes several times a day. You'll start to notice your dog is showing up at the heel position more often. When your dog wanders away from you, do nothing. When he comes to the heel position click and treat.

- Once he's staying in heel and getting lots of clicks and treats, reverse your circle. Now, the dog is on the outside and has to move faster to keep up with you. Keep up the same game. When he is regularly at your left side, begin changing the movement.
- You can walk straight lines, do right and left angles, eventually move into 270 and 360 degree turns, do figure eights, etc. This method can be fantastic for getting your dog to really understand that lots of good things happen when on your left side!
- Once the behavior is reliable, add the cue "heel."
- Begin working in different locations and bringing in more distractions. Do not go off-leash with your dog outside of a safe, fenced area until your heel is reliable.
- Vary your speed: slow, normal, fast.

Targeting Method

Begin by teaching your dog basic targeting. He must be able to touch and follow a target stick (or your hand) on the cue "touch." Once you have successful application of this behavior, you can move on to teaching your dog to "heel" (see "Touch").

At home you can teach this off-leash in the house or in a fenced area.

- Begin with the dog on your left side. Hold the stick out at nose level by your left leg. Don't worry about a cue yet; just see if he'll follow the stick. Start off by stepping with your left leg. When he successfully follows the stick, even for a few seconds, click and reward. Click while he's heeling correctly by your left leg (or close to correctly in the beginning). Stop to reward and praise him. When he does not "heel," do nothing – no clicks and treats. Give him a little time; then do it again.
- As he begins to heel correctly, increase the time and distance he must heel before clicking and rewarding. (Slowly increase the number of steps from 3 to 5, to 8, to 12, etc.) In the beginning, make sure to click and reward often. As he progresses, raise your criteria to expect a better heel for longer periods of time.
- Once he walks by your side regularly, you can change the cue "touch" to "heel," right before you start walking. When he is successful, click and reward. Stop to reward. Begin again and say "heel."

- When your dog is readily offering this behavior – you walk in a straight line and you can go at least 20 feet – begin performing large left circles (this helps your dog to learn to focus on where you are) and large right circles (this helps a dog that is slightly lagging to work harder to keep up). Then begin doing left turns and right turns. Next, begin doing about-faces and even figure eights. When he's getting this, begin varying your speed: faster, slower, jogging, and walking.
- Finally, start requesting a sit at your left side before you begin "heel." Have him "sit" each time you stop. (Hint: raise the stick slightly so he looks up to help him learn to sit.) If your dog sits crooked or has a hard time sitting on your left side, practice this separately. If necessary, position yourself so that you have a fence or other barrier on your left side to help aid your dog in sitting straight.

As he catches on to heeling and is successful about 90 % of the time, start fading the target. This means, begin moving the stick up further (slowly in increments looking for success) until eventually you're holding the stick in the tip of your hand. Eventually remove the stick altogether, and he should be paying attention to you and walking at your left side.

Once your dog understands "heel" off leash, go ahead and put him on a leash and cue "heel." Remember the generalization principle. If your dog has been taught (inadvertently) to pull while on leash, you may need to review "heel" on leash for several sessions before your dog realizes that "heel" means "heel" whether on or off leash.

When I'm starting with training a young puppy that has little or no leash experience, I prefer to teach "heel" from the beginning and not even work with loose-leash walking techniques. If a puppy hasn't walked on a leash before, you can teach her to heel before she's ever learned to pull on a leash. With older dogs that are already confirmed pullers, many of my clients need help right away, plus we have to change a habit that is already formed. So with these dogs, I may teach a loose-leash walk first and later fine-tune the "heel."

Stay

"Stay" is certainly one of the most important behaviors you'll teach your dog. Stay means that your dog should remain in a location and in a position (sit, down or stand) until released. Stay is not only important in terms of good manners, it is a very important safety behavior. Surprisingly, stay is a natural behavior. All dogs "stay" when stalking prey to catch their meal. Stay is also a great way to teach your dog self-control.

There are three aspects to teaching your dog to "stay," usually referred to as the three "D's". The three aspects are: *duration*, *distance*, and *distractions*. You'll want to teach duration and distance first. Once your dog understands what you're asking, you can begin gradually adding distractions.

Here are a few important points about teaching your dog to "stay":

- When beginning to teach "stay," use either a sit or a down, whichever body posture seems most comfortable and easiest for your dog to maintain. Some dogs that have a hard time sitting still for more than 2 nano-seconds (terriers perhaps!) may be more successful with a "down-stay" in the beginning. "Down-stay" is usually more comfortable for all dogs when you're working on longer durations (3-5 minutes and longer). After your dog starts to understand the concept of stay with one body posture such as sit, you can begin teaching the other positions down and stand.

- Work on one aspect of the behavior at a time. When teaching "stay," work on either the duration of the stay (have him stay for 10 seconds for example) or distance (move 3 steps away from your dog). Do not work on both time and distance simultaneously, as you will confuse your dog. So if you're increasing the time frame, shorten the distance and work close to your dog. If you're increasing the distance, shorten the time frame.

- Vary your duration and distance. To extend the duration of a stay, vary your time around a specific goal. Do not always make it harder. For example, if your chosen goal is 10 seconds, have your dog "stay" 10 seconds, click and treat, then 5 seconds, then 15 seconds, and so on. Slowly begin building the amount of time you have him "stay." Now pick a new goal, say 15 seconds and vary your times around that number. Do the same for distance. Say you pick 5 steps away, vary from 3 steps, 5 steps, 8 steps, etc.

- Build the difficulty of the behavior slowly. If you're not getting success, lower your standards (make it shorter or move closer) until you get success.

- Reset the behavior. If you say "stay" and he moves – either gets up or changes his body position – invite him back into the original posture at the same location and say, "stay" again, then lower your criteria slightly. For instance, if you took 3 steps away and he got up, take 2 steps this time and see if you can set him up for success. Repeat this until he stays. Pause for 5 seconds, click and treat.

- Always release the "stay" so your dog knows it's okay to move out of position. For now, the click ends the behavior. Eventually, when you have faded the use of the clicker, you will need a unique word to release your dog from this behavior. Examples of release words are "go play," "finished," "that'll do," "done," "break" or "release," etc. Another behavior can also act as the release of the stay. For instance, you may ask your dog to "stay" and then call him, "Scruffy, come." However, when teaching the behavior initially, end the behavior and click and treat for the stay – not for another behavior such as come.

Keeping the above items in mind, the following is a step-by-step example of how to teach "sit, stay." This same approach can be used with "sit," "down" or "stand." *Note:* Work only on one of these body postures with "stay" at one time though.

- Begin by asking your dog to "sit" in front of you.
- Start extending the sit by several seconds and slowly build to about five seconds, then click and treat. (This releases the dog.)
- Once your dog can stay for five seconds, you can start using the verbal cue "stay" and then the hand signal (arm extended, palm up in the standard "stop" position) right in front of your dog's face (see "Hand Signals" section of this book).
- Once you've added the "stay" cue, do not click for the sit or down. You are now clicking for the dog holding the sit or down until released. Essentially, this is a new behavior instead of "sit," this is a "sit and stay."
- Ask your dog to "sit" and immediately to "stay." Start extending the time slowly by seconds. Build up to about 10 seconds. Then vary intervals around 10 seconds and build up slowly (by five second intervals) to about a 30-second duration. Always click and treat when your dog does it correctly. If he breaks the stay, reset the behavior and ask him to "stay" again.

To work on building distance from your dog, give him a "sit-stay" cue followed by the hand signal. First, stand right in front of your dog. Take one step back. If he stays, click, and treat. Next, take two steps back. If he is successful, click and treat. Then take three steps back. If he breaks the stay, reset the stay behavior where he was. Do it again – only take two steps this time. Build your distance slowly. Now, begin to vary your distance just like you did with the time (one step, three steps, five steps). Work up to moving about 10 steps away from your dog. Remember not to work on time and distance simultaneously. As you are building distance, drop your expectation for length of time. You may have him stay only five seconds in each new position. As they become successful at distance, you can start building your time back up slowly. If you have a problem getting any distance, instead of moving away take a step to the side, then the other side, then move half way around your dog, etc. This will get him familiar with movement and you'll still be close.

Eventually, you will keep increasing time and distance as your dog becomes proficient at this exercise. Once you've reached one minute, you can move more quickly. (For instance, one minute, one and a half minutes, two minutes, etc.) For long durations, such as five minutes and longer, I suggest you have your dog in a "down" instead of a "sit." For example, if you want your dog to stay out of the way while you're doing something, put him in a "down-stay". You can keep increasing distance until you're out of sight (around a corner or in a different room).

Like all exercises we are learning, remember to help your dog to generalize this behavior. Use new body postures, orientations, and move around to different locations. You will eventually move this outside to your yard, to the front of your house, to the park or the beach, etc.

Also begin adding distractions. Walk up to your dog. Step over him. Have someone else walk by. Bounce a tennis ball, skip around him, clap your hands, get creative. Eventually, you will want to teach your dog to "stay" around other dogs (or cats) as well. (Our cat, Deva, always "helps" me out with this exercise. As soon as I'm working on a "stay," she mysteriously appears and saunters casually by!) Remember, move slowly on this exercise. More time spent in the beginning will get you a reliable stay. Do not increase distractions too quickly.

Work within a fenced area or attach a long line until you have a reliable stay.

It's fun to combine "sit-stay" with hide & seek when your dog understands the "stay" cue. Put your dog in a "sit-stay" or "down-stay"; go hide somewhere (in the shower, closet, etc.); call your dog once. If he isn't finding you, give him clues (cough or clear your throat). When he finds you, click and treat! This game is fun for both of you and also reinforces "come."

Luring Method

If you're not having much luck with stay, you might want to use the luring method. With this method you place a treat on the floor in front of your dog (not too close so he can grab it, not too far so he'll want to get up for it). Show your dog the treat, ask him to "sit, stay." If he gets up and heads for the treat, grab the treat before he gets it and then reset the behavior. Now repeat the exercise. Pretty soon he'll figure out if he moves he doesn't get the treat! This method can be very effective with some dogs. Keep in mind that, as always, if you use a food lure, you'll need to eliminate the lure when he starts to get the idea.

Chili's Cross-Country Adventure

I had an experience with Chili, our rescue dog from the streets of Mexico, that really reminded me how important stay can be in an emergency. Chili is probably a mix of Australian Shepherd, Corgi, Dachshund, and who-knows-whatelse. He has a huge prey drive, and I'm sure has killed live animals in his past literally to survive. Obviously, I've been taking it slow in getting him calm and relaxed around the llamas and most importantly around our new baby goats. This particular day, I had let him out in the back-field to play. I was three fields away, feeding the llamas. All of a sudden, I realized Chili had somehow gotten through the fence (the fence has since that time been completely rebuilt!) and was heading like a crazed maniac towards our two baby goats. I could feel myself starting to panic and, luckily and quickly, yelled out "Down, Stay!" Chili dropped to the ground. I saw him watching the running goats and start to get up, and I firmly repeated, "Down, Stay!" To my amazement he laid there like a little rock. My llama, Snickers, went over to investigate and was sniffing Chili's face. He was not moving a muscle! I quickly ran through the pastures, opened the gate and called him. He immediately came to me! Wow, was I relieved and totally thankful that I had spent time teaching him "stay" and "come"!

Settle

"Settle" is a wonderful exercise used to teach your dog to relax and settle down on cue. It's important for puppies and adult dogs to be able to play hard and then "settle" when requested. "Settle" is another exercise that teaches self-control. It's a good idea to start by teaching this to young puppies. This is one exercise I teach by marking the behavior with a verbal marker "yes!" instead of clicking (besides my hands are full of puppy!) and rewarding with quiet praise and petting. I find the clicker and treats will sometimes get the puppies all excited again! I may use this physical restraint method for very young puppies, however, I prefer the "Park" where a leash and withdrawal of attention is used (see "Park" in the "Self-Control" section).

When a puppy is young, you can physically restrain her by hugging her close to teach her to quit squirming around. Take your puppy on your lap and hook your thumb under her collar. Hold her low enough so that she can't reach up and snap at your face or bump your chin if she decides to have a tantrum. Hug the puppy close against your chest and stomach. You can massage her and speak in a calming voice. When she settles down, give the verbal marker "yes" and praise her quietly. When she quits squirming and you feel her relax, loosen up on your hug. If she goes into a frenzied squirm, hang on! You don't want to release her during a tantrum. Do this a number of times a day to begin teaching your puppy to quiet down.

Once she is beginning to relax, like a rag doll when you hold her, begin adding the cue, "settle," when you're holding right as you feel her begin to relax. As you progress with this exercise, begin to work with the puppy on the floor. At some point, your puppy might be too large to hold in your lap! (Our 4-1/2-month-old Anatolian, Sahara, was 60 pounds!) When you make the transition to having the puppy settle on the floor instead of your lap, you can sit on the floor or on a chair and lean over her, hugging her into a relaxed posture. Be sure to lighten up on your hold, mark the behavior with a "yes," and praise calmly when your puppy relaxes.

Go to Bed

"Go to Bed" is a cue that means go lay down on your bed (or blanket or rug) until released. Some folks prefer the cue "place" or "settle." In other words, calm down and relax. It is a very handy behavior. At first, don't expect your dog to do this exercise for a long period of time. However, as she learns this behavior, she can settle for longer periods. "Go to Bed" is another behavior that teaches self-control. Shaping is a wonderful way to teach this behavior and help you learn how to shape!

"Go to Bed," which means go lie down in your bed and stay there, is a wonderful behavior to use to redirect your dog ("No, you can't beg at the table right now"). It helps with self-control, and it is an easy and fun behavior to shape.

Shaping Method

Begin by placing a towel, a rug or doggie bed on the floor. As you shape this be-havior, throw the treat off the rug or towel each time so that you can "reset" the behavior. (She'll have to move back towards the mat next time.) At first, stand close to the mat. Wait for your dog to get close to it. If she even sniffs it the first time, click and treat. If she puts one paw on it, click and treat. Next time wait for perhaps two paws. Once she steps on it, click and treat. Click and treat about three to five times in a row for her going to the rug and standing on it. Then wait for her to offer the behavior of sitting on the rug. Click and treat. If she repeats, click and treat the "sit" several times. Now, wait for her to offer a "down" on the mat. When she lies down, click and treat. When she repeats this, click and treat each time for about three to five times. Now, begin waiting a few seconds so that she lies down for several seconds. Slowly lengthen the duration of the down. While you are shaping this behavior, move around to different sides of the mat. Do not stand in one place the whole time. Begin moving further from the mat as your dog begins to understand this behavior. You can also move the mat to differ-ent locations. Eventually, she can be trained to go lie down on her bed even if it's in another room. Once she is reliably going to the mat to lie down, attach the cue "go to bed" right before she goes to the mat.

Targeting Method

Place a bed, mat, or towel on the floor. Move a few feet away from the mat. Lead your dog over to the mat by having her follow a target stick. When she reaches the bed, click and treat. Repeat a few times. Now, raise your criteria. Once she reaches the bed, ask her to "down, stay." Have her stay 5 seconds, click and treat. (After you've worked with this for a while, be sure to add a release word prior to the click. This way, once the behavior is learned, and you have faded the clicker, you will also have a word to release your dog from this duration behavior.) Once she is readily going to the bed, begin fading the target stick, and use a hand signal of pointing towards the bed. Change your body posture, move around the mat, and slowly move further away from the mat. Add the cue "go to bed" right before she goes to the bed; gradually build a longer stay on the mat. Eventually, move the bed to other locations. Also, slowly increase your distance until you can go to another room and ask her to "go to bed."

Touch

"Touch" is a wonderful cue that will enable you to teach your dog to focus on a particular location or object. The dog learns to "touch" and then follow the end of a stick. Teaching a dog to touch and follow an object is called "targeting." The overall goal is to be able to move your dog around without needing a leash or a food lure. Targeting is a natural behavior for dogs because they tend to follow their nose anyway. This is also a wonderful behavior for timid dogs. Once they get good at this, they can become very focused on the behavior and forget that they are afraid!

First, teach your dog to recognize the target, and then learn to control the targeting behavior. Once you have "target trained" your dog, there are almost limitless applications. You can use targeting to teach an off-lead "heel," a "go out," "finish," and other directed movements as well as object recognition. One of the best uses of a target stick is to teach a *crossover dog* (a dog that has previously been trained with correction-based training). Targeting will allow your dog to begin offering new behaviors.

Hand Touch

Stand in front of your dog and reach your hand out (palm up). When she reaches up and sniffs your hand, click and treat. Remove your hand, and, then, offer it again. Repeat this number of times until she seems to be readily touching your hand. Start moving your hand to different areas at nose level – to the right a little, to the left, etc.

Once you feel sure that she'll touch your hand, add the cue "touch" right before her nose touches your hand. Now, start moving her. Back away from her and see if she'll follow and touch your hand. Good! Click and treat. Once she's getting really good at this, begin moving your hand up so she'll need to jump up to touch it and move it towards the ground re-

Targeting is an amazing tool to have in your "tool-box" as a trainer. The dog first learns to "Touch" and, then, follow or target your hand as it moves. It's a great tool to help teach other behaviors and can also be used to focus your dog anywhere, anytime.

quiring her to bend down to touch it. The nice thing about teaching a dog to target your hand is that you'll always have your hand with you!

Target Stick

Using a target stick is an easy way to teach targeting. You can also use other objects, a straw, or a plastic lid (like from yogurt or coffee).

Offer the tip of the stick slightly above the dog's nose. Wait for her to touch it. When she does, click and treat. Gradually, start moving the target stick a little farther away and to the left, right, above, and below the dog's nose. When the behavior is happening with regularity, begin giving the cue "touch" right before she touches the end of the stick.

It's easy and fun to teach your dog to first "touch" and then to follow a target stick. Targeting is a great way to teach more complex behaviors such as heel or spin. Target sticks are easier to fade than a food lure, and, because you don't have to bend over, they often make it easier to work with little dogs.

Note: If your dog is not investigating the stick at all, you can start by putting a little peanut butter or soft cheese, or rubbing a hot dog on the end, to get her attention. If your dog is biting the item, try a metal target stick. These are available from many sources online. Most dogs do not like to bite metal.

Remote Target

Once your dog will move after a target, you can start teaching them to touch a target while you move away from the target. Eventually, you will have a dog that you can send away from you to touch an item.

You can start by using something like a small cone. Teach your dog to touch the cone. Once he is readily touching the cone, take a step away while the dog is touching the cone and let him return to you for a treat. Build up one step at a time. Before long, you'll be ten steps away, and he will be running over to touch the target item. Once the behavior is readily offered, you can give this a new cue such as "go-out" or "go-touch."

Remote targeting has many benefits. I have used it to teach a llama to trailer, to teach a dog that was fearful to jump in the back of an SUV or pickup truck, and to teach a dog to go down steps. There are many uses!

Targeting a Mat with Paws

Teaching your dog to target a mat with front paws is a great way to teach other behaviors later as the mat makes it easy to position your dog. Start by free shaping this. Sit in a chair and put a small no-slip mat in front of you. Wait for your dog to pay any attention to the mat. Build behaviors incrementally using the rules of shaping until your dog is consistently placing front paws on a mat. I do not use a verbal cue for this behavior. I use the behavior of placing the front paws on a mat to teach other more complicated behaviors such as "back," "front," and working at a distance.

We can teach dogs to target an object, such as a mat, with their paws. Once Hally was shaped to place her front paws on a mat, Teah then used the mat target to teach other behaviors, including: "front," "back-up," lateral moves (dog moves sideways), and distance behaviors.

Leave-It/Take-It

"Leave-it" teaches your dog to leave something alone. This will also teach your dog not to grab something from your hand or rush to get something on the floor without your permission. Because it's compatible, we are also going to teach "take-it" in the same exercise. "Take-it" means "take something from my hand." Teach all three steps before using this cue in actual real world circumstances. "Leave-it" is spoken in a normal tone of voice – it is not a reprimand. Think of this as a proactive cue, before your dog has that dead bird in her mouth! "Leave-it" is yet another behavior that teaches our dogs self-control.

This exercise has three distinct steps. Make sure your dog is successful at each level before moving on.

"Leave-It" is an important behavior for every dog to know. It means "back away and leave that (fill in the blank) alone." It's also a great technique for helping your dog learn self-control. It's important that you click when the dog moves his head away from your hand.

"Take-It" is easy to teach in conjunction with "Leave-It" and simply means that the dog has permission to take the item. They are not to snatch the item until invited to do so though!

Step 1 – Place a treat in your closed hand. Reward any movement away from your hand.

Show her the treat, then close your hand around it, palm up, and just hold it still at about your dog's nose level. Stay in that position until you see any movement back away from your hand (even just an inch or two). Then click, and open your hand, say "take-it" and allow your dog to take the reward. Repeat this exercise until your dog moves her head away when you present your hand.

Note: Make sure you're putting your hand up to your dog's nose so that she has to back away from your hand. Often, people think they are teaching the dog not to move towards the treat in the hand. Instead, we're specifically teaching the dog to back away from something she wants.

Extend the time she backs-off by pausing before clicking. Have her hold-off from touching your hand for one second, then two seconds, etc. When she moves her head away, click, say "take-it," then reward. Gradually, prolong the click until she stays turned away for 5 seconds or more.

Note: At first, she may check back a few times by touching your hand. Just ignore this behavior and wait until she's backed-off and stayed back a few seconds.

Once your dog is backing-off from your hand readily, add the cue "leave-it," right before you present your closed fist.

Note: In this excercise, click for leaving the object, not for taking it. I also add the word "take-it" from the beginning because I am 99% sure that almost every dog will take the treat. That means that I'm just adding a word to an existing behavior. I do not click for the "take-it" because I'm immediately allowing the dog to take the treat. I consider teaching the "take-it" part of this exercise as a freebie that is easy to get while teaching "leave-it."

Step 2 – Place the treat in an open hand. Even though the treat is readily available, your dog must back away.

Once your dog can back away from the closed fist on cue, it's time to move to the next level. Say "leave-it" and hold the food in your open palm at your dog's nose level. If she starts to take the food, quickly close your fingers around the treat. When your dog moves her head backward, open your hand, click and say, "take-it." Repeat this exercise. Increase and vary the time your hand is open before you click and treat.

Be careful with this part of the exercise. I'll give a dog three attempts at leaving an open hand. If they keep attempting to get the treat, they are not ready for this level. Go back to a closed hand.

Step 3 – Place the treat on floor. Even when something is on the floor, your dog still needs to resist.

Once your dog will respond readily to backing off from an open hand, move on to placing a treat on the floor.

Say "leave-it" and put the food on the floor right in front of your foot. Be ready to cover the food with your shoe if she goes for it. Do not allow her to grab the treat. Click and then pick up the treat and offer it to her with "take-it." This will teach her that all good things come from you and will prevent lunging for food on the floor.

Now say "leave-it" and drop a treat on the floor. Make sure she doesn't get the treat without you giving it to her. You can use body blocking here to keep her away from the food. When you're ready, click and allow her to have the treat. You can either pick it up and say "take-it" or decide when it's okay for her to have a piece of food on the floor. If so, say "get-it." The point is that you have elicited this behavior on cue and under your control, not hers.

Just for fun: Put your dog in a "down" and "stay." Line three goodies up on each leg and say "leave-it." When you click or release her, she can eat the treats off her legs!

Give-It

The goal of "give-it" is to have your dog release an item from his mouth and place it in your hand. I prefer to teach this behavior with a verbal marker (I use "yes") in place of a click. Because you are already holding the toy and food in your hand, using the verbal marker is just easier.

Begin this exercise with something of interest to your dog, but not something too interesting to start. For instance, if you offer him half of a steak or his very favorite toy, he probably won't want to let go. Start with something more neutral, like a toy he likes, although not his favorite toy.

Offer your dog the item and wait until he takes it in his mouth. Wait a few seconds. Place one hand on the toy and simultaneously offer him a luscious treat in your other hand. When you feel his jaws release, and he allows you take it, say "yes" and give him the treat in your other hand. Repeat this a number of times until he's responding well. When the behavior is being offered readily, begin adding the cue "give-it" right before you wave the treat in front of his nose and feel his jaws release.

Now raise the criteria slightly. Place your hand under the toy in his mouth and offer him a treat in the other hand. Wait for him to drop the toy in your hand and then say "yes" and give him the treat you were holding in your other hand. Continue working with this until he is readily placing the toy in your hand. Now, you can choose other items and slowly progress to his favorite toys.

Note: You can also teach "drop," and have him drop an item from his mouth on the floor. However, I prefer to have my dogs place an item in my hand, as this helps avoid the game of who can get the tennis ball first, which usually occurs at some point.

Off

The goal of the "off" cue is to have your dog remove his body or a part of his body from an object or person. For instance, if your dog jumps up on the bed, couch, kitchen counter, or your lap, you can give the "off" cue. My definition for a successful off is four feet on the floor. Once learned, "off" can also become a proactive cue. Let's say you're eating dinner sitting on the couch, as we often do, and your dog is approaching with that "I want to jump up look" on his face. You could say "off" before he jumps up.

To teach "off" I usually start with teaching "up" and "off" a piece of furniture. If you do not allow your dog on any furniture, you can practice with a raised dog bed or a wall or other raised area in your yard or elsewhere. Begin by inviting the dog "up," click and treat, then, toss a treat on the ground, and just as she is jumping off say "off," and click and let her have the treat. If you're working with furniture like your couch, you can simply get up off the couch yourself and your dog will most likely jump off after you. Click and treat. Above all when teaching "off," you need to reward the correct behavior and give no attention to the undesirable behavior. For example, if your dog jumps up on the couch, you could ignore him, and, then, once he gets down, click, treat and praise. If he puts his front paws on the kitchen counter, you could wait for him to put his front feet on the floor and immediately click, treat, and praise. However, I prefer to set up training situations where my dog can get up and off an object at first under my direction and supervision until she gets the idea. Work with "off" throughout the day during any appropriate situation.

Note: This can also be used as a cue for "don't jump up on me." If you have to say something, I would prefer "off" as many folks inadvertently shout "down." To most dogs, that means lie down, and that is confusing for the dog. When your dog jumps on you, wait for them to get off, and once they have four feet on the floor for a few seconds you can click and treat. Once they are getting off readily, you can start saying "off." However, I have found with enthusiastic jumpers that teaching "sit" as a greeting behavior is more effective. Often, we make the mistake of coming home, our dog jumps up on us, we yell "off!" then totally ignore him when his four feet hit the floor. The attention he gets during the jump, even though it's negative attention screaming "off," can actually encourage the jumping behavior in some situations. As mentioned in the section under "Jumping Up" you have to make sure you don't accidentally train a behavior chain where the dog thinks he should jump up and then get "off" for the reward (see "Jumping Up" section of this book).

Kiko's Cuddle

Our dog, Kiko, really wants to come up on the bed in the morning and cuddle with us. We allow him about a 10-minute cuddle first thing in the morning. In training sessions and each morning, I worked on putting "cuddle" on cue (it means come up on the bed and lie down next to us). Then I would say "off," and encourage him to leave (that means I'd turn my back and withdraw attention). He quickly started realizing what I meant. Now, sometimes, he'll come to the bed, and I'll see that cuddly look in his eyes. I extend my hand and say "off" before he jumps on the bed. Then, when I'm ready, I give him the cue "cuddle."

Wait

The goal of the "wait" cue is to have your dog stop all forward motion. It is different than "stay," which means remain in one place until you are released or asked to do something different. For "wait" your dog can stand, sit or lie down, as long as he does not move forward. It's basically a temporary stop. This is also another very good self-control behavior.

"Wait" is a very helpful cue and can be used at the door when you're going out, getting out of the car, before crossing a road, before opening a gate, before going up or down stairs, etc. "Wait" promotes safety, so that you don't have to fight your dog while going out the door, or worry about him jumping out of the car into traffic. "Wait" also subtly establishes that you're the leader in this relationship. In pack behavior, the highest-ranking dogs go first. If a lower-ranking dog attempts to go first, he is immediately corrected.

The easiest way to teach this behavior is when getting in or out of your car, or going out of the house or a gate. (Pick somewhere with a physical barrier.) If you are getting out of the car or somewhere outside where safety is a concern, put a leash on your dog. You don't want him bolting into traffic.

When you get out of the car, open the car door and say "wait" immediately followed by a hand signal in front of his face. You can use a hand signal similar to stay (only spread your fingers). If your dog does not move forward, click and treat. Then invite him out of the car with a release cue or "come." If he does move forward, reposition him with the leash and then go through the exercise again. You can block his escape with your body or by gently shutting the car door part way until he gets the idea.

You can also teach this at your house door. (If your dog has a tendency to rush out the front door, the formal "sit-stay" may be best to teach at this time.) Ask your dog to "wait," give the hand signal, and, then, move towards the door. If he does not move, click and treat. Proceed through the sequence of reaching for the doorknob, opening the door, then stepping through, then turning to face your dog. Click and treat each success. If he breaks the wait, use body-blocking techniques to keep him from moving. Repeat the exercise until you get success (see "Body Blocking").

You can also use this going up and down stairs. It's safer to work on this exercise going up the stairs rather than down the stairs. Position your dog at the bottom of the steps, say "wait," and, then, take one or two steps up. Click and treat if he doesn't move forward; repeat as necessary. You can slowly increase the number of steps you take, clicking and treating for each success. At the top of the steps, you can use your release word "go play!" or call your dog.

Note: Some trainers consider "wait" a temporary pause and do not use a release word. I often use a release word with "wait" just as I do with "stay," especially when getting out of cars.

Release Word

Use a word to let your dog know that the behavior or training session is over, such as "go play," "finished," "done," "that'll do," "break," or "release." ("Okay" is used too often in daily conversation to be useful as a release cue.)

Hand Signals

Sit – Your arm is extended at your side, palm facing forward. Bend your arm at the elbow, and bring your forearm straight up towards your shoulder.

Down – Your arm is extended at your side, palm facing back. Bend your arm at the elbow bringing your forearm half-way up, and, then, make a sweeping motion towards the ground with your palm facing the ground.

Hand signal – *Sit*   Hand signal – *Stand*

Stand – Your arm is extended at your side, palm facing forward. Make a forward motion towards your dog at a 45-degree angle, and, then, bring your arm up in an angle next to your waist.

Hand signal – *Down*   Hand signal – *Stay*

Stay – Hold your arm straight out from your body while making a stop signal with your hand; have your palm and thumbs together facing outward. If your dog is down at your left side (in heel position), simply extend your arm downwards, palm facing backwards.

Wait – Same as the stay signal, only spread your fingers.

Off to the Races –
Playing Games and Performing Tricks

Playing

Playing games and playing with toys is a natural behavior for your dog. Some dogs have not had the benefit of learning to play, so you may need to actually shape this behavior. The important thing about playing games is that you both have fun. Playing is a wonderful way to help build your relationship and bond with your dog. Some dogs can be more motivated by toys than they are by food. I think of my friend Denny's Bull Terrier, Frighty, who loves food, although when you have a ball, the sky's the limit with Frighty!

Create Motivation in Your Dog for a Special Toy: One toy should be a special toy that you can use for special rewards during training exercises, to reinforce other behaviors, or as a retrieve toy. Some dogs do not inherently go nuts over a toy. However, you can motivate your dog to play with a toy. A great technique, developed by a dynamite trainer, Susan Garrett, is outlined in the section "Motivating Your Dog to Play."

Play "Chase Me": Many dogs like to drive us crazy with the chase me game. They grab your old sock and then tear off around the house while you chase them. They bound over furniture and under beds, and it takes all your patience and physical abilities to catch up with them and get your sock back. This is NOT the game I'm talking about! In this game, you control it. You get the dog to chase you! Grab one of his favorite toys and take off with it. Run around the house. If outside, hide behind a tree, run around a tree, go around a corner, etc.

Hide & Seek Is A Wonderful Game: It can be used to reinforce both "stay" and "come." Put your dog in a "sit-stay" or a "down-stay." Go hide somewhere in the house (the shower, a bedroom closet, on top of the washer, etc.) Now, call your dog clearly and wait. If he's having a hard time finding you, you can cough or clear your throat to give him a hint. When he finds you click, treat and give him lots of praise! This game can be played after your dog has a reliable stay. Otherwise, have someone hold the dog while you hide.

Play Tug O' War, But Be Sure To Follow The Rules: There's been a great deal of controversy about playing tug o' war with dogs. Some behaviorists and trainers suggest that this will bring out aggression in your dog. Others claim that your dog is already a predator, and this game is an outlet for that energy. I believe that playing tug o' war is a great game as long as you play by the rules. If you have a dog that is possessive and defends his toys, spend lots of time working up to playing this game by getting success for each step. Don't think of this game as pitting you and your dog "against" each other. Instead, it's the two of you cooperatively playing against the toy. I have only seen two cases of what I would call "play aggression" in clients' dogs. If you have a dog that just goes over the top and becomes aggressive during play, then THIS IS NOT the game for the two of you!

Because tug o' war is allowing your dog to express a natural behavior, dogs generally find tug o' war immensely enjoyable. Therefore, a short tug o' war can become a reward during training. When your dog does something particularly well, you can play for a short time as a reward.

Here are the rules for playing tug o' war:

- You take control of the game. In other words, you start the game and end the game. Having a dog that bugs you hour-upon-hour can become a nuisance! You go get the special tug toy and initiate the game.
- Let the dog know the game is starting. You might ask for some behavior first such as "sit, stay." Then, start the game. It's a good idea to give the game a cue, so the dog knows it's time to play. I say, "Let's tug!" or "Get it!"

Jayne engages her Golden Retriever puppy, Dustin, in a rousing game of tug o' war. Tug is a great game to play with your dog, and most dogs love it! Just play by the rules.

- Before starting tug of war, teach your dog the "give" cue. That way you can get the toy back! I'd suggest you teach "give" first separate from this game (see the section of this book on teaching "give"). Once your dog understands the cue "give," if at any time during the game your dog refuses to relinquish the toy, end the game immediately. Just walk away.
- You can use a release word or a specific word such as "finished" to let your dog know the game is over. It's best to start playing and have the dog release the toy with a "give" a few times during a single play session. Then, you might end the game with "finished" and start it up again in a few moments. That way the

dog doesn't get the idea that "give" or "finished" means the fun is over forever. Stopping the game and restarting it when your dog has calmed down a bit will help your dog learn self-control.

- If the dog takes the object and runs from you, do not chase. You can ignore that behavior and take a little time out. See if he comes back and wants to play or tie the toy to an object such as a dressage whip or long stick, so he can't run away with it.
- Have some special tug of war toys and play this game only with those toys. That way your dog doesn't attempt to play tug of war with anything you happen to be holding!
- Sometimes, let your dog win. Let them grab the toy and run off. This is especially a good idea for dogs that need to build some confidence. Would you want to play a game if you never won?
- Dogs are perfectly capable of knowing where their teeth are. Regardless of whether it is intentional or accidental, if your dog's teeth make contact with your hand at any time during the game, let out a loud "Ouch!" and end the game immediately. However, be fair to your dog and play with a good tug toy that puts some distance between your hand and your dog's mouth. (I had a client once who played with her Rottweiler with a tiny rope and was complaining that the dog was hitting her hand with its teeth! How could he help it?)
- As long as the game is going along well, let your dog get excited. It's natural for them to shake their heads, growl, and pull hard.

Interactive Toys - Consider Getting Your Dog Some Toys That Will Keep Her Busy For Awhile: There are lots of interactive food toys available these days. You put kibble or treats in them, and as your dog knocks them around with their nose or paw, the treats fall out. This can keep some dogs interested for quite some time. You can even give your dog meals in this toy.

Kong toys can be stuffed with goodies and keep your dog busy for quite some time. The stuffed Kong can also be frozen, which will keep your dog busy even longer. Get creative. My favorite recipe (from my friend Katie) is low fat cream cheese and a tablespoon of liverwurst!

It's a good idea to get your dog interested in chasing a toy – especially if they are not that wild about playing at first. Take a fishing pole, long pointer, stick, or dressage horse-whip, and tie a really good tug toy to the end. Move the stick and toy around in a large circle with the toy dragging on the ground – about the same way you would play with a cat. Get your dog playing with it. See the section of this book on "Self-Control" to learn more about this game.

There are many other games. Get creative and create some of your own. The most important thing is that you have fun with your dog! You have to want to play with your dog. If you are not having fun, your dog will figure that out and will be hesitant to join you in a game.

Motivating Your Dog To Play: To paraphrase a great presentation by Susan Garrett at a Puppyworks Dog Training & Instructor's Conference, here's one way to entice your dog to want a toy:

- Start by choosing a toy that you can throw around, but won't roll too much. It could be a stuffed animal or a tug rope for instance.
- Attach a string to the toy.
- Place the toy in a drawer that you can access easily (in the kitchen or living room).
- Several times a day, go through this exercise. Start acting a bit crazy. Jump and dance around and say things like "Where's the toy?" "Do you want this," etc.
- Stop talking for a few seconds and, then, suddenly take the toy from the drawer. Act like you're so excited! Run with it into the next room.
- Now act totally nuts. Swing the toy around. Let your dog know that you are really having fun. Laugh, dance, jump, etc. Now, toss it out to the end of the line and drag it around on the floor, luring your dog! But don't let him get it – yet! Play with the toy for a few moments, and then, run back to the drawer, put it back in, saying something like "uh oh, it's gone."
- Now go about your normal business like nothing ever happened.
- Repeat this crazy performance several times a day for several days. After the second day, allow your dog to put his mouth on the toy, but only for a short time. Pull on the line to steal it away from him. Once you get it away (make this fun, not challenging), play with it a little while by yourself and then put it back in the drawer. Say "uh oh, it's gone."
- Now, gradually increase the amount of time you let him play tug o' war with you with this toy. You will soon have a dog that just loves to see that toy come out of the drawer. Never reprimand your dog or connect the toy with anything negative during this play process.
- Once you've motivated your dog to play with you, always keep this toy as a special toy. Do not leave it out to be played with at will.

Dogs that are afraid or hesitant to play the game can be taught to play the game through shaping and motivation games. Click and treat for each step towards the desired behavior.

The Skye's the Limit

We were attempting to think of ways to keep our Cairn Terrier, Skye, busy. I met Skye when she was 7 years old, and until she passed at 14 years old she ate almost every meal in a Buster Cube! She figured out that if she ran the Buster Cube upstairs and then tossed it down the steps, she could get a treat from almost every step. So from then on, it became her meal game. She would toss the Buster Cube and run down the stairs picking up treats. At the bottom, she would grab the cube run back upstairs and toss it again! It would keep her busy for almost a half-hour! On the other hand, our two Lhasa Apsos, Crystal Moon and Wags, refused to work that hard for food!

Tricks

Training tricks is fun and useful. I hate to admit it, although I remember many years ago saying, "I'm not going to teach my dog tricks. Tricks are demeaning, and my dogs aren't here for entertainment!" My, oh my, I've come a long way. The truth is tricks are great for a number of reasons. First, you'll have fun training tricks, and your dog will have fun too! Trick training loosens up the person! Tricks make every bit as much sense to your dog as a formal "heel" or "stay." They are all tricks to your dog! Once your dog has learned how to learn, she likes to learn. There are a finite number of "obedience" cues; however, you'll never run out of tricks. You can make them up as you go! Tricks are a great way to redirect your dog's energy when you need to. Tricks also help to teach the dog about important handling maneuvers and reinforce other behaviors in a fun way. For instance, when you teach your dog the "Hold the Bone" trick you are actually working on helping her learn self-control and allowing you to handle her muzzle. At the same time, you're reinforcing "leave-it" and "wait."

There are two kinds of tricks: ones your dog does naturally and ones you need to teach. Capture something cute your dog already naturally does, click and treat, and then add the cue. Here are some examples of natural behaviors many dogs already do that can be captured:

- Your dog puts her head down flat in between her front legs when she lies down (Cue: "Are you sleepy?")
- Your dog stands on her hind legs and dances around. (Cue: "Dance")
- Your dog sits up like a little groundhog. (Cue: "Up Pretty")
- Your dog crawls across the floor (Cue: "Crawl")

- Your dog lies down and stretches her back legs way out in back of her. (Cue: "Stretch")
- Your dog comes over and lays her head flat on your leg. (Cue: "Head down")
- Your dog wakes up from a nap and stretches with elbows on the ground and hind end high in the air. (Cue: "Bow")

Other tricks can be taught through using luring in the beginning, targeting, or shaping. We teach tricks just like any other behavior. If you are going to lure, remember to lure at first with food, then lure without food, then when the behavior is offered readily, add the cue and fade the luring movement. Targeting is phenomenal for teaching tricks. Get the behavior started with targeting, add the cue, and fade the target. Start by picking something you think your dog will be good at. For instance, if you have a dog that uses her paws a lot, you might want to start with a paw trick such as "shake" or "wave."

In class we'll go over a number of tricks. For more information, you may wish to refer to several of the books listed in the "Resources" section, including "Clicker Fun" by Deb Jones and "Clicking with your Dog" by Peggy Tillman.

Some Fun Tricks to Teach

Shake: Your dog lifts up her paw on cue and will shake hands with you. This can actually be thought of as having your dog target your hand with her paw. We all taught this when we were kids by grabbing our dog's paw, right? Most of the time they got it. I like to get my dog to lift her paw on her own though. You can shape it a little at a time and also use a food lure to start. Start by having your dog sit, then hold a treat barely out of her reach on her left side. As she shifts her body weight to lean towards the treat, she'll probably lift her right paw. Click her for lifting her paw higher and higher. When she's lifting it regularly, put your hand out and take her paw. Repeat until this is offered readily. Add the cue, "Shake," or "Give me your paw." Another method is to take a treat in your closed fist and hold it right under the dog's chin. Many dogs will immediately paw at your hand. Click and treat! People most frequently shake with their right hand, so I usually teach this with the right paw. If you don't care, you can teach either or you can put them both on cue, "Shake" for right, for instance, and "Give me your paw" for left. Teach one paw at a time.

High-Five: Once you have the shake trained, it's easy to transition the behavior into a high five and just give it a new name. If your dog is offering his paw in response to your hand coming forward into a shake position, simply straighten your

Paw tricks such as "shake" are fun and easy to teach. Many dogs naturally reach out with their paws, so this behavior can often be captured.

It's easy to teach a "high-five" once your dog understands the concept of "shake."

hand into a high-five posture and most dogs will simply touch your hand with their paw.

Wave: Your dog picks up her paw and waves (remember Lassie?). I usually teach this after shake unless the dog naturally lifts her paws a lot. Once you have shake on cue and it's a strong behavior, you can begin teaching wave. Just put your hand out (don't say anything) and your dog will probably lift her paw. When she does, quickly withdraw your hand and click and treat the wave movement. You can shape this to be stronger and stronger. Fade putting your hand out as soon as possible. When it's offered readily, add the cue, "wave" or "bye-bye" and a little waving hand signal. After you have the wave on cue and hand signal, go back and reinforce shake to make sure she's not confused. Teach either shake or wave at one time, don't teach both simultaneously.

Hold Bone: Your dog holds a dog bone on her nose and then when released flips it in the air or drops it on the ground and eats it. Begin holding your dog's muzzle with your hand. Don't restrain her, just keep her nose steady. Place a dog biscuit or object on her nose. (Some dogs' faces – such as pugs – are built so that you may have to place the object on top of their head.) Work with it and find the best place for the object. Now release the object and her nose. Let the treat remain on her nose only a second, then release her. Let her grab the object off the floor. In the beginning, let her have the bone or other object almost immediately. Gradually, increase the amount of time that the object is balanced on her nose. Add a cue such as "Wait" or "Hold" as you place the object on her nose.

As you increase the time, add a release word (in addition to the click). Increase time slowly and make sure you're getting success. *Note:* Puppies can't sit still for very long, so make your times short at first. This is a fabulous trick because it's not just a crowd pleaser, it also helps to teach your dog self-control.

At first, many dogs will drop the treat on the floor and eat it off the floor. That's just fine. Over time, however, many dogs (including my dog Chili!) become confident with the behavior and begin flipping the

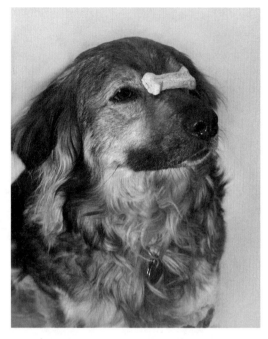

A favorite behavior to teach is the "hold-the-bone-on-your-nose" trick. It's not just entertaining; this trick also reinforces self-control. At first, Chili dropped the bone on the floor when released but, soon, figured out on his own that flipping it in the air would be the quickest way to get it!

treat in the air and munching it out of the air. It's a quicker way for them to get the treat, so dogs often add this variation to the behavior on their own!

Other tips: If your dog does not like his muzzle touched, work with handling the muzzle first (see "Handling"). If you have a hard time with the muzzle, you can also shape the behavior having your dog place her chin in the palm of your hand. Once they learn to steady their muzzle there, you can easily place the bone. Also start with a flat treat. I've worked with bologna or sliced cheese or nice flat, soft small bones to begin with.

Up Pretty: Your dog lifts her upper body straight up from a sit and balances on her haunches. This can be taught with a target stick or treat. Bring the treat/target up just enough over her head so that she'll need to lift her front feet off the ground. Click and treat. As your dog begins to get her balance, raise the treat/target a little higher. Hold it only high enough for her to need to lift up out of the sit. As soon as she's up, click and treat. Make sure the treat/target is centered over her head, so she doesn't lunge forward to get it. Also, make sure you don't hold the treat/target too high or she'll stand all the way up on her back legs (that's "dance"). Build the time she holds it gradually by delaying the click. Some dogs do this behavior naturally. Other dogs need to learn balance. She may even fall over a time or two or she may reach out with her paws to steady herself. For some dogs, especially larger dogs, if you position yourself behind the dog, your legs can act as a safety net if they start to lose their balance backwards. Most dogs will get this fairly quickly. Once the behavior is happening, add the cue, "Up Pretty."

Note: If you have a breed that is prone to back problems or your dog has back problems, you'll want to be very cautious about teaching this trick, if you teach it at all. Also, dogs with long backs such as Dachshunds and Corgis may have problems with this trick.

In the "Up-Pretty" trick, the dog sits back on her haunches and raises her upper body straight up. This is a very natural behavior for some small dogs, such as Crystal Moon, a Lhasa Apso, and is taught by simply clicking and treating when she offers the behavior.

Dance: Your dog balances on her hind legs and usually either turns a circle or backs up. You can start in a sit or stand position. Hold the treat or target stick straight up above your dog's head (and even slightly back) and wait for her to touch it. Don't hold it too far forward, or she may lunge towards it. Don't hold it too high, or she may jump. Hold the treat/target high enough so that she has to lift her front paws up off the ground to reach for it. Click and treat. Gradually move the treat/target higher and higher until she balances on her two back feet. As you progress, click and treat for longer and steadier stands.

Once you have her steadily standing up, you may choose to teach a circle or backing up. To teach a circle, start with an eighth of a circle, then a quarter circle, then half, and so on. Shape the circle a little at a time. Some people prefer to teach the dog to back up instead. Do this by slowly moving the treat/target backwards while she's standing up. Shape the behavior how you want it, then add the cue, "Dance."

Roll Over: Your dog rolls over. Dogs are usually left and right-sided the same way humans are. Begin by figuring out which way is easiest for your dog to roll over. Put your dog in a "down." Bring a treat slowly at nose level back towards her elbow. Does she shift her hips to the side? If not, try the other side. Find out if luring to one side or the other will cause her to shift her hips more easily. Once you have a shift of the hips, you begin slowly bringing the treat over her shoulder in a circular motion approximately even with her elbow. If she rolls and shows tummy up, you're halfway there. For some dogs, you'll need to slowly shape this trick one step at a time. Others can do the whole roll over the first time. Once you've got tummy up, then slowly bring the treat over towards the other side. For many dogs this is the hard part. They may get up and see if they can turn

"Dance" is a trick where the dog stands up on her hind legs. Big dogs, like Meryl, can do this too!

around and get it the other way. Move slowly and steadily and be patient. Once they begin to roll over you can either place the treat near the floor or toss it on the floor very near your dog. Most dogs will roll the rest of the way to get the treat. Click and treat! Repeat until the behavior happens easily, then add your cue, "roll over." *Note:* Dogs with hip or back problems may not be able to perform this behavior.

Bow: Your dog puts her elbows on the ground and rump in the air. Bow can be taught with a target stick or with a treat in your hand as the lure. I like the target stick method best, although your dog needs to be good at targeting. Have your dog stand, place the tip of the stick between your dog's front legs and back slightly under her chest and say "touch." Her nose should follow the stick and she'll

begin bending her front down. She
may come right down on her elbows
the first time, or you may need to
shape this bending movement a little
at a time. When she's offering the
behavior regularly, add the cue,
"bow" or "curtsy." Slowly fade the
target stick. Another fun variation
is to turn your foot into the cue.
After you're getting the behavior
with the target stick, place the stick
on your foot and move your whole
leg and foot forward and ask for
"touch." Gradually, fade the target
stick up your leg higher and higher,
moving your foot forward and turn
it into the signal.

"Bow" is a fun behavior to teach and one that
most dogs perform naturally, when waking up
(stretching) or inviting others to play (play
bow). If you can't capture it naturally, then
teach it with a target stick or food lure.

Now, you can add a verbal cue like, "say hello" and move your foot forward,
and you have a very impressive bow! If the target stick method is not working,
then you can always simply hold a treat in your hand and place it between your
dog's front legs and slightly back under her chest. You need to get the treat back
far enough for your dog to bend the front of her body down on elbows to get the
treat. You can also shape this behavior a little at a time, getting closer and closer
to the bow position as you go. This behavior is also relatively easy to capture as
many dogs "bow" naturally upon awakening (they're stretching) or when initiat-
ing play.

Spin: Spinning is a fun behavior to teach, and some dogs spin naturally. It's also a
good behavior to help build some flexibility in your dog. Generally, dogs will spin
more easily to one side than the other. So start with a clockwise spin, then do a
counter-clockwise movement and see which is easiest for your dog. Whichever
one they do easier, teach that direction first. Begin by using the target stick or a
food lure. If you use the target stick, ask your dog to "touch" and begin moving
the stick in a circle away from your body. Circle your dog consistently to the
right or left.

Soon you can fade the target stick and simply move your hand in a circular
fashion to indicate spin. You can also use a food treat and lure them in a circle spin
in front of you. Fade the food lure as soon as possible. You can use the cue "spin"
and/or the hand signal, moving your hand in a circle in the direction you want the
dog to spin. Just be sure to fade the hand signal to be smaller and smaller as you
go. I generally teach spin in one direction (clockwise) and put the hand signal and

verbal cue such as "spin" on it. Then, I teach the other direction (counter-clock-wise) and put the hand signal (spinning the other way) and a different verbal cue such as "twist" on that behavior.

Crawl: Many dogs crawl naturally, and if your dog does, you can simply capture this behavior by clicking and treating. When the behavior is readily offered, add your cue "crawl." This behavior can also be trained easily with a target stick. Have your dog lie down and slowly move the target stick a few inches at a time away from the dog. Keep the end of the target stick on the floor as you move it. A food lure can always be used as well by moving the treat slowly along the floor away from your dog when he is lying down. Either the food lure or the target stick will need to be faded to finalize this trick.

Some Bumps in the Road – Eliminating Problem Behaviors

Options For Dealing With Problem Behaviors

There are a number of approaches for eliminating an undesirable behavior. Depending on the problem, often management of the environment can be the easiest solution. If that is not feasible, training an incompatible behavior is usually your best bet. Also removing something your dog likes (such as withdrawing your attention) or simply ignoring the behavior can also be used very effectively for a number of issues. For significant problem behaviors like aggression or chasing, you can interrupt and redirect the behavior.

Manage The Environment: This is usually the easiest way to prevent a problem. To manage the environment means controlling the physical environment of the dog so that he cannot perform an undesirable behavior. Even though managing the environment is not training, it does prevent undesirable behaviors. Preventing undesirable behaviors from happening will aid your dog by not further ingraining negative responses to various situations. Dogs are great "actors," and we don't want them to get in too many rehearsals! Dogs are much like people in this way – they form patterns or habits. For instance, if a dog barks like crazy every time he hears the doorbell, soon it will be a habit, and when he hears the doorbell he will bark. However, if you put him in his kennel in another room before someone comes to the door, you may be able to prevent this behavior. Here are a few examples:

- Your dog is chewing up your shoes. Put your shoes away.
- Your dog is running outside of your unfenced yard. Put up a fence or construct a large kennel or dog run.
- "Puppy proofing" your home means managing the environment. For puppies, you may need to really make some changes. Tape down electrical cords, spray chewable items with a safe and yet nasty tasting chew preventative (available from most pet stores), put away anything he might chew (laundry, books, remote controls, etc.). For older dogs, you still need to manage the environment.
- If your dog is getting into the trash, for instance, move the trash can out of reach.
- If your dog is "counter surfing" (getting up on the counter and eating your food), keep the food out of reach.
- Crating Your Dog: Everyone who has a dog will find that purchasing a crate

is a worthwhile investment that will payoff throughout the life of your dog. Crates are a safe place that you can put your dog for a specified amount of time to keep her out of trouble. Crates should not be used as punishment, but they can be used for a short time-out or for longer periods to keep your dog away from something. I usually give my dogs a chew toy or squeaky toy to play with, and I make getting into the crate a happy affair. Most dogs learn to enjoy their crate. I do not agree with crating your dog for an entire day while you go to work (see "Crate Training").

Kiko's Cozy Crate

When I brought Kiko home from the local Humane Society, he went nuts when I put him in a crate – he was barking, anxious, and unhappy. He had been at the humane society for sometime and originally was at animal services, so I suppose he had his fill of time in confinement. I worked with him for some time reconditioning his association with the crate. I did this generally because I believe that all dogs will need a crate sometime in their lives and that it's not only convenient to have a dog that will crate, it's prudent. Several years later when Kiko had to have knee surgery and spend most of a six-month period recovering in his crate, I was so thankful I had trained him to like his crate. A year later, he had to have surgery on the second hind knee! I, again, thanked my lucky stars!

Train A Different Behavior. Train your dog to do something else that will make it impossible for him to continue doing the undesirable behavior. If your dog is jumping up on you and your visitors, train him to sit when someone comes in the front door or when the doorbell rings. If your dog is sitting, it's impossible for him to jump up on people.

- Training your dog to be "quiet" is a good way to stop barking.
- Having your dog "go to bed" will stop him from begging for food at the table.

"Where Does the Dog Go When the People Eat?"

We adopted a 90 pound Lab/Rottweiler named Bear from a friend. He used to sit quite politely about six feet away from the table. He would begin by drooling and before long he'd be blowing big bubbles! Not all our dinner guests appreciated this. So we taught Bear to "go to bed" when we ate dinner and solved the problem!

Training a different and incompatible behavior is my favorite approach to working with many problem behaviors. Play a little game with yourself when you find you are complaining about your dog's behavior. Rather than saying what you don't want, state what you do want. For instance, suppose you catch yourself saying "I don't want my dog eating food off the coffee table." Turn the sentence around "I do want my dog to back off from food on the coffee table." Now, you know what you need to teach: Backing off from food on the coffee table. Teach that, and your problems are solved (see "Leave-it")!

Don't Talk With Your Mouth Full

One of my clients worked out of her home and received phone calls regularly. Every time she picked up the phone, her lab mix would go into a barking fit making her phone conversations intolerable! We trained her dog to run to get her favorite toy when she heard the phone ring (the phone ring became the cue for "get your toy!"). She could not bark well with the toy in her mouth, so it was a great solution to the problem!

Remove Something Pleasant. Removing something pleasant immediately after the undesired behavior occurs can be an effective approach to eliminating some behaviors. Most dogs consider your attention very important. Therefore, removing your attention can be an effective tactic for changing behavior. However, if you have not established a positive relationship – a connection – with your dog, your dog may not care if you're around or not. Unfortunately, I've seen this regularly enough with out-of-control dogs in distracting situations. You can also remove the dog from the situation by putting him in his crate, outside, or in another room, for a time-out. I often use this option if a dog has gone into some kind of frenzy where he's running around and doesn't want to calm down; for instance, when an adolescent dog has what I call the "zoomies" and is tearing around the house around sunset. I've also used this approach if a dog is barking for attention, if a puppy is repeatedly mouthing me, or if a dog is showing aggression towards another dog in the household. Simply walk away and remove yourself or remove the dog for a short time-out.

Never Reinforce Problem Behavior: It's possible to extinguish a behavior by never reinforcing it. However, keep in mind that many canine behaviors such as digging, chewing, and chasing are self-reinforcing. In other words, the dog gets a great deal of enjoyment out of just performing the behavior. Therefore, the behavior itself is reinforcing – like digging for gophers! You cannot simply ignore these behaviors and hope they'll magically disappear. However, some behaviors such as whining in the crate or begging at the table can be extinguished if you never reinforce them.

Let's take whining in a crate as an example: First, be sure that all your dog's basic needs have been met – he's not hungry, thirsty or needing to eliminate. He's in his crate and simply whining to get out. Don't give in. Ignore the behavior. That also means you do not want to be shouting "Quiet, you silly pup!" or going over to comfort him ("Oh, my poor baby ..."). Scolding is still attention and comforting your dog can actually reinforce the whining. So you ignore the whining. When he quiets down for a while, then you can go let him out of the kennel. Be aware that before a behavior is totally extinguished you may observe an "extinction burst." This means the behavior might temporarily get worse (now he's howling or barking as loud as possible) before the behavior actually stops. It's like the animal's final effort to see if this approach will get him what he wants. Patiently wait him out a few times, and, often, the dog will give up the behavior because it's not working for him.

Interrupt and Redirect Behavior: You can use something that will not hurt or harm the dog (either physically or psychologically) to temporarily interrupt a negative behavior so that you can redirect the dog to a desirable behavior. For instance, when the dog is in a huge frenzy chasing your cat around the house, clap your hands sharply and shout "huh-uh." When your dog looks up, you ask him to come or sit. When he accomplishes this behavior, click and treat. Suppose you're walking down the street, and your dog lunges and barks at a passing dog; do an immediate about-face, take him a few steps away, and, then, immediately put your dog to work doing a series of puppy push-ups. The puppy push-ups will help get your dog's mind off the other dog.
Timing is important. Let 8 to 10 seconds pass before rewarding the redirected behavior, or you could inadvertently chain the two behaviors together.

Skye's Story: Scurrying After a Sedan

I adopted Skye from a rescue shelter when she was a year old. She had been seized as evidence in an animal cruelty case and impounded at animal control for almost five months. So she had essentially grown up at the pound. When I brought her home, it was clear that she had no training. She didn't even know "sit." She has a very strong prey drive and was pretty uncontrollable on leash walks. I live in the country, and we often encounter small furry things on our walks, but the most troubling thing was that she tried to chase cars, even on a leash. She was fine in heavy traffic, but when a single car came by she would hit the end of the leash with all her strength, trying to get at it.

The experience that I had prior to taking Teah's class was force-based training; the only thing I could think to do was a leash correction when she went after a car. With this method, the best I could hope for was a cringing dog every time a car came by.

After taking Teah's clicker class, I started asking for a "sit" and clicking her for watching me when the car went by. I will never forget the first time she popped into a sit on her own and turned and gave me this big grin when she saw the car coming. What a difference in attitude. I had a happy dog and still achieved the results I needed.

Katie Hawkins

I'm not going to go into a lengthy discussion of *negative reinforcement* or *punishment* here. There are lots of other books that explain what they are. I'm also not going to claim that I never use either one of them because occasionally I have. In addition, I'm going to avoid a long explanation of what constitutes punishment for a particular dog. I hope it will suffice to say that what I'm talking about here is harsh punishment (shock collars, whacking your dog with a newspaper, screaming nonstop at your dog as loud as you can, slapping, kicking or physically manhandling your dog – you get the idea). In general, harsh punishment and negative reinforcement are not necessary. Although harsh punishment and negative reinforcement can both work in certain situations, one has to take into consideration the consequences of one's actions! First, both negative reinforcement and punishment require that the trainer know how to apply these measures correctly, or she/he will probably do more harm than good. Secondly, these two approaches can negatively influence your relationship with your dog, causing avoidance, fear and aggression. Third, negative reinforcement and punishment both inhibit behaviors and will stifle creativity (just the thing we're looking for when shaping behaviors). In general, it's more effective to reinforce behaviors you want, rather than punishing behaviors you don't want.

Leadership

Being the Pack Leader: "You're Not the Boss of Me"

Wow, what a hot topic these days! It's come and gone as a popular topic during all the years I've been training, and it's popular again now. Let's analyze leadership a little bit. What makes a good leader to you? (Yes, I'm aware you're a person and your dog is a dog.) For me, a leader is someone I trust, someone consistent, someone I can count on, someone who motivates me, someone I look up to and respect. Someone who can be calm and confident when faced with a tough situation. Think of who you would say was the best leader you've ever known. Maybe, you'll pick a parent or other family member, or a boss, or a public figure. I think of Roger Davis. He was my boss when I was 21 years old. He and one of his supervisors hired me to work for them when I was obviously young and didn't have all that much experience. The job was secretary to both the supervisor and manager of the public affairs department of a large utility company. Roger immediately referred to me as his assistant, never as his secretary. He acknowledged when I did a good job. He let me know when what I was doing wasn't quite up to snuff and gave me guidance on how to improve. If he ever asked me to work overtime, I didn't hesitate (while thinking of excuses as to why I couldn't), the immediate answer was "Yes! I'd be happy to." I worked for him for six years. From my perspective, the reason he was such a great leader was because he motivated me, inspired me to want to learn and work hard, and never attempted to manipulate me through guilt, fear, or humiliation. The bottom line is I worked hard for him because I wanted to – not because I had to or because I was afraid of what would happen if I didn't. In the words of Chuck, my husband, who has been both a manager and a leader in his life and who has also had the opportunity to work with several great leaders: "Leaders inspire while coming from a place of love and compassion, while managers control while coming from a place of fear."

With so much talk about being the "pack leader" when you're working with dogs, I can't help but smile when I think about the really fine trainers I've met who work with killer whales and big cats (I'm not referring to an overweight house cat here), or wild animals. I've noticed that they aren't the "pack leader"; they just know how to train.

Now, with a dog it's a bit different. They do come from a pack mentality. And, yes, we've invited them to live in our homes with us. So what would constitute reasonable leadership? I would say that the relationship is more like what you see with a fair parent and small children; you need to decide what your household rules are; you need to be consistent in enforcing them; you need to be calm and confident in the face of difficult situations; you need to find a way to teach your dog to trust you (perhaps you have to trust them also); you need to get your dog to listen to you and to be interested in you; you need to take some time to communicate with your dog about what is expected; you need to let her know when she gets it right and when what she does doesn't work for you; and you need to be patient. Wow! Did you notice all that was about you and not your dog! So a good leader, is just a good leader. We've all met them. This is someone who walks into the room, and all of a sudden everyone is paying attention. An essential trait of leadership is attitude and demeanor – the "energy" so to speak.

Although there is discrepancy among experts as to how close domestic dogs mirror wolf behavior, we know dogs understand pack mentality. From your dog's perspective, somebody needs to be the head honcho. If your dog does not see you (and other humans in the family) as the leader, he'll take over as pack leader by default. Once you've occupied the leadership position, training your dog will be easier, and so will resolving problem behaviors – possibly avoiding many problem behaviors altogether.

In the real world of dogs, "pack leaders" are not bullies. If you watch a true alpha dog, he doesn't have to do much for the other dogs to offer submission. Sometimes, it's no more than a quick glance. I love to watch my little Chinese Crested Powder-puff puppy, Cambria, with my fully adult Anatolian Shepherd, Sahara. Cambria goes to Sahara and literally throws herself on her back with tummy exposed. I've never once seen Sahara throw Cambria on the ground. Submission is offered – not forced. So it's not necessary or effective to scream and yell and show a lot of physical force to convince a dog that you are leadership material. In fact, getting physically tough with an aggressive dog is not a good idea. As you escalate your anger, he may well escalate his. Remember he has teeth, and you'll both lose in the long run. Leadership skills are gained from a psychological understanding of dogs.

Dogs are amazing barometers of how people are feeling. They immediately notice when people are anxious, and that makes them more anxious. Borrowing a wonderful analogy from one of our trainers, Ivy, we can think of a benevolent leader, perhaps, in the same way we might think of a Monk. We probably wouldn't shove him aside to rush out the door in front of him or pull on his robe to get his attention. And yet as a leader, we don't fear him; we simply respect him and recognize his place in society.

It's important to help your dog establish his position in the "pack" (in this case his human family). Any dog will benefit by understanding you're the leader; however, it's particularly important for dogs that are pushy, aggressive, or anxious and fearful. If you're having serious aggression problems, you'll definitely want to consider using all of these suggestions. For dogs that are just a bit pushy or fearful, you may want to pick and choose what works for you. Aggressive dogs may do their best to run the household, and often growl, snarl and snap to get their way. Pushy dogs may insist on having your attention all the time (barking, pawing at you, sitting on you), even when you're not in the mood! Fearful or anxious dogs may run and cower from family members, or they may pace or seem uptight. Remember, fearful dogs can bite, too.

If you're experiencing any serious aggression problems, please contact a professional trainer or animal behaviorist for assistance.

Listed below are basic components of a leadership program:

Self-Control: Teach your dog how to bring his own arousal level down. Many problem issues in dogs are symptoms of a dog that is too aroused (see "Self-Control").

"I Want" Doesn't Get: Be careful of falling into a trap of reinforcing behaviors that you really don't want to reinforce. We have to remember that if a behavior we like originates in another behavior that we don't like, and we keep reinforcing the one we like we are, in fact, also reinforcing the behavior we don't like. So, Kay Laurence taught me a quick little saying, and I often remind myself by saying it "*I want* doesn't get." If your dog is demanding, just make sure they don't get reinforced in any way for that behavior. If the behavior you don't like starts, withdraw all reinforcement, rather than than asking for the behavior you want and paying it.

The Pug Monster

My Pug, Hally, developed a behavior – thanks to me! – I called "pug monster." Each night when it was time to hand out bones, she'd scurry around the kitchen making scary noises and jumping at the other dogs. I made her "go to bed" and settle, and, then, she'd get her bone. Kay Laurence noted (my, it's humbling to have a well-known trainer stay in your house!) that Hally's "calm" behavior – going to bed and settling down – originated out of the "pug monster" behavior, and so "pug monster" wouldn't go away. So I changed the process. Now, when I get out bones, and Hally turns into "pug monster," the bones (for all the dogs) go back in the package, or I leave the room. Hally, now, sits quietly when the bones come out – I don't have to ask for a "sit." After that, I began to notice that when my dogs were demanding, I was responding. Now, they get what they want – all of them – but on my terms, not on theirs. I no longer reinforce a good behavior originating out of an undesirable behavior.

Deference: One way to establish leadership is to simply have your dog work to earn valued resources. Things dogs value include everything from food to getting petted to going for a walk to playing with toys. I've heard this same basic program referred to in many ways over the last few years including: "Deference Protocol," "Learn to Earn," "No Free Lunches," "Working for a Living." Whatever it's called, it basically means your dog needs to do something for you, before you do something for him. This simply means you need to ask your dog to do a behavior, such as sit quietly and pay attention to you for at least a few seconds, before you do anything for him. I actually prefer to "mix it up" and ask for different behaviors all the time, once my dog has more than a "sit" on cue. If you always ask for a "sit" it becomes a bit automatic, and I don't think the dogs are always listening and attentive to you. So ask for different behaviors: Down, shake, watch, roll over, high five, etc. He must now work for feeding, treats, praise, petting and love, grooming, going inside or outside, going through doors or gates, getting in and out of the car, getting up on furniture, or playing.

In short, ask him to do something anytime you give him attention. This program is a subtle and effective way to help your dog learn that he needs to defer to you or look to you for guidance. In a dog pack, members basically agree to defer to the alpha dog. Once a dog knows you're the leader, he'll probably actually be relieved. He's thinking, "Oh, good, I'm not responsible for running things anymore. Whew, now I can relax a little!"

Control the Food: Since food is considered a very valued resource by dogs, you need to control the food. Most dogs can be fed twice a day on a set schedule. Very young puppies and some small toy breeds may require three or more meals per day (check with your vet). You want to teach your dogs that "all good things come from you" including food. When you are first changing the feeding schedule for a dog that has had food available at all times, put the food down for 15 minutes. If your dog doesn't eat, take the food up and wait until the next meal. Believe me, by that evening or the next day, your dog will begin eating when food is offered. (Except for tiny dogs – watch their blood sugar level!)

Sleeping Arrangements: High places or places where people rest are often seen as desirable by dogs. If you're having aggression problems, it's best to keep your dog off the couches, chairs, and bed. If you decide to let your dog on the furniture or to sleep with you, you'll need to teach him to get "up" on the furniture and "off" the furniture on cue. If your dog ever growls or snaps at you from a piece of furniture or your bed, it's safest to remove this privilege. You can have him sleep on a nice soft doggie bed in your bedroom. Alternatively, if necessary, you can always use a crate to confine your dog at night.

Toys and Play: Your house does not need to look like a playground! In fact, it's best if you also control the toys. Why? For many dogs, toys are a very valued resource. Don't worry, he can still have toys; he simply needs to work for them. Pick up the toys and place them in a place where you can control them. Each day, make a point of giving your dog several toys. Just have him do something first! All dogs should always have an acceptable chew toy available. Pick up some of the toys at the end of the day and give out some more toys tomorrow. Rotating different toys may also help to keep him interested. You want to communicate that these are your toys, and you're letting him play with them! Playing retrieve or hide and seek games are great. It's best to stay away from rough wrestling games. Play tug of war by the rules (see "Tug O' War").

Training: Dogs like to learn; learning is intellectually stimulating and, therefore, tires them out. Ever sit through a two-day seminar and feel exhausted when it was over? Ongoing training of some kind is advisable for any dog. You can do 5-10 minutes of basic training, make up tricks, or explore a new avenue, such as agility, musical canine freestyle or tracking, etc. In working with aggressive or fearful dogs especially, it's amazing to see the transformation that takes place once they are actively involved in a training program. Dogs that are fearful often become more confident through training. Dogs that are aggressive seem to more readily remember their place in the family "pack."

I remember working with a family that really brought to mind how important leadership is, and the fact that following some simple psychological and management tools – giving the dog more information about his place in the family and what is acceptable behavior in your home – can greatly improve the dog's behavior.

I arrived at the client's home and was greeted at the door by a lady (I'll call Sarah) and her adult daughter (I'll call Anne), along with their little female, a 3-year-old rat terrier mix (let's call her Mandy). As soon as I knocked, I could hear the barking; when I entered the house Mandy barked ferociously and approached quickly, snapping at my ankles. Sarah picked Mandy up and began reassuring her, "It's OK honey, don't be afraid." I asked her to put Mandy back on the ground and to find a place for us to chat for a few minutes. Mandy continued barking on and off for at least 15 minutes while we talked. She would not move towards me; she hung back under the table by Sarah's feet and continued to bark. We finally had to give Mandy a little "break" or "time-out" in the other room, until we were ready to begin working with her. In taking Mandy's history, I discovered she was adopted at about 2 years old from a local county shelter. It's very possible that she did not receive adequate socialization as a puppy and was now wary of strangers. They both loved Mandy so much, and they thought they were doing the "right" thing by reassuring her when she barked at visitors. I'm sure it was having the opposite effect. First, picking a dog up when they are aggressive or anxious is not a good strategy because in doggie language being on higher ground puts that dog in a more dominant position in her mind. While it might seem appropriate to reassure an anxious child, reassuring an anxious or aggressive dog, (quite frankly depending on the situation and how the dog is responding) may not be the best approach if we don't like their behavior. If every time she freaks at the door, she is getting picked up, stroked and soothed, she will interpret that as a reward for what she is doing. (On the other hand, if a dog is truly afraid of something – it's Halloween and a monster showed up at the door – I might reassure her!)

After discussions with the family, we decided on implementing a program where they would take on the leadership role, provide her with a bit more exercise, begin slow and systematic socialization and desensitization exercises to help her become more comfortable with strangers and begin foundation training. I also suggested a Gentle Leader Head Collar with a light drag-line that could be used when people came to the door.

I'm happy to say when I arrived the next time, Mandy had her Gentle Leader on and only barked a few times as I knocked. When I entered, she hung back and just looked at me. When I asked her to sit, and she responded, I was able to reinforce her. Obviously, that session and subsequent sessions showed great improvement. I believe the leadership component, combined with exercise and training, all contributed to improvement in Mandy's behavior.

Exercise

Every dog needs exercise. There's an old axiom I've heard, "A tired dog is a good dog!" Each dog and breed is different. Some dogs are bred to run 12 hours a day herding cattle while some companion dogs are happy to sit on your lap most of the day. Any dog will benefit from exercise, especially if you're having any behavioral problems. When dogs do not get enough exercise, excess energy often shows up as anxious or destructive behaviors. A tired dog just can't get into as much trouble!

Consider starting your day with a minimum of a half-hour to one hour brisk walk or jog. Keep your dog at your side and don't let him pull. It's best if you're in control of the walk instead of your dog. Some exercise and stimulation first thing in the morning during a dog's active period is a great way to help your dog be calmer and more relaxed during the day.

If you can't exercise your dog in the morning, then evening is another option. Dogs have two high-energy periods during the day – right around sunrise and right around sunset. If they were still wolves, this would be the time they'd go hunting.

If a walk doesn't work for you, then consider a fun game of retrieve or Frisbee. Also, you might consider learning a dog sport such as agility or musical canine freestyle to get your dog (and you!) some exercise.

It's possible to use a dog backpack as a way to increase the effectiveness of exercise time and also help to slow down dogs that pull a lot on leash. I recommend that my clients check with their vet regarding any potential back or neck problems for their particular dog or breed. Also, check with your vet regarding how old your dog should be before carrying weight. You don't want to put the full weight on a dog who's still growing. Start out with about 10% of your dog's body weight and slowly build it up to a maximum of 20% over time as he adjusts to carrying the backpack. Sand is a good option for filling the pack. Distribute the weight evenly between both sides of the pack. If your dog wears a backpack, it's like getting twice as much exercise in a particular amount of time. In other words, your dog will tire more easily, so a half an hour walk with a backpack is more like a one hour walk without one. (If you have ever backpacked yourself, you know exactly what I mean!) T-Touch and other modalities utilize wrapping a dog to help calm them. I have one client who says that just putting the backpack on her extremely active dog, calms him significantly!

I've tried this out on my dog Chili, who as a stray dog in Mexico and a herding mix, was not only incredibly full of energy, he also had no concept of why he should stay close to me on a walk! Chili weighs 35 pounds, and carries 3-1/2 pounds of sand in each side of his backpack for a total of 7 pounds. It used to be that a half an hour walk hardly phased him! Now, his tongue is usually hanging out by the time we get home!

If you are not physically able to exercise your dog, consider hiring an older child or teen in the neighborhood to walk your dog, hiring a professional dog walker or dog sitter, going to a dog park, or dropping your dog off at a doggie day care facility.

Jumping Up

Dogs jumping on their people and visitors is a very common problem. Why do dogs jump anyway? One reason is for attention. Think about how it works in your home. You come home from being gone hours or minutes (it really doesn't matter), and all of a sudden you're greeted by your dog, and she's jumping up! You're not in the mood for that and start flailing your arms and shouting "off, stop it, no!" Your dog finally puts four feet on the ground, and you walk off without saying anything more. Do you see the problem? Your dog receives all kinds of attention for jumping (perhaps negative attention and yet still attention) and no attention whatsoever for not jumping. Another reason I suspect dogs jump is because if you watch a bunch of puppies or particularly adolescent dogs, they will tend to jump up on each other. (Many adult dogs will begin to set them straight that this is not appropriate!)

Jumping Up – Tether Method

You can teach your dog not to jump on you or visitors by using the tether method. This method is helpful if the dog is particularly big and rambunctious or if the person doing the training cannot tolerate the jumping. I also like this method the best because it does not allow the dog to make the mistake in the first place. It does not give them a chance to rehearse jumping up because we can back away before he jumps up. The overall rule for this exercise is no attention until he sits.

This can be done with either a training partner holding the dog on a leash (you can use either the head collar or a buckle collar), or you can tether the dog to something stationary, like a tree, a piece of furniture, or a doorknob. Approach the dog. If he jumps, immediately back away. Approach the dog again and ask him to sit. If he sits, go up to him, and click and treat. If he jumps, immediately back away. Repeat this exercise until you can approach him, and he begins to automatically sit even before you ask.

Once he's doing well with you, ask a neighbor or friend to approach him. It's also a good idea to practice this exercise when meeting people on the street. You can either tether him or hold the leash. Ask him to sit. If he sits, let them approach, you click and they treat and praise. If he jumps, they back up immediately attempting to avoid the jump altogether.

For some dogs, when they do sit and you praise them, don't get them over-excited or they may jump again. Use a calm voice and long, soft strokes on their head and neck. For our dog, Kiko, I like to bend over and whisper in his ear what a good boy he is. Then I go about my business. Don't make a huge deal out of greeting a dog that has problems with jumping.

Jumping Up – Training an Incompatible Behavior

Another effective way to stop your dog from jumping up on you and other people is to train an incompatible behavior. The most common behavior that is taught in place of jumping is "sit." Several other behaviors that can be taught are "down," "go to bed," or "four-on-the-floor" (standing). I suggest you start with sit because your dog is probably pretty proficient at sitting by now. The idea is you (or a guest) come in the door, and you ask your dog to "sit." Do not pay any attention to him until he sits. Then, and only then, does he get his greeting from you or your guest. Sounds simple, right? Well, pretty simple. The problem is that most dogs that jump are so excited in the moment that they may not be listening to you. This takes perseverance on your part. First, make sure you've already taught your dog a reliable response to the "sit" cue. Second, make sure he'll stay in that position for a little while at least.

You have an opportunity to work on this behavior each and every time you come in the door. Don't allow your dog to jump up on you sometimes and not others. The inconsistency on your part will make it impossible to stop this behavior. So if you are working hard to train a "sit" for greeting and another member of the family is pet-

Teaching your dog good door manners is worth the time. It's wonderful when you can answer the door, and your dog sits quietly by your side. Teaching this requires consistency and patience. It will take some time, and you need to manage the situation so that your dog cannot continue to "rehearse" the jumping behavior. Be sure to reinforce calm sitting instead.

ting and paying attention every time your dog jumps on them, chances are you won't be successful at training this behavior. It's best to set this up as an actual training exercise.

Dress appropriately for the session, wearing a jean jacket or long-sleeves to protect against his claws. Drive up in your car, walk in the door and immediately ask your dog to "sit." If he sits, immediately click and treat and praise. (I keep a small container of treats and a clicker by the door when I'm working on this behavior.) If he isn't listening and he jumps up on you, cross your arms and just stand there with no movement looking at the ceiling. Give no attention for this behavior. You can also take a step back to throw him off balance a little. Or, if you prefer, you can use a body block (see section on "Body Blocking"). Some people also prefer to turn their back on the dog. (I find this painful though if it's a large, strong dog.) Not every dog is the same, so experiment and use an option that seems to work with your dog. The bottom line is, whatever you do must be passive and withdraw attention from the dog. When he does quiet down and has his four feet on the floor for about 5-8 seconds, go ahead and ask him to "sit"; when he does, click and treat. Praise him, but do so quietly so as not to get him too excited right now. For some dogs, when they do sit and you praise them, don't get them over-excited or they may jump again. Use a calm voice and long, soft strokes on their head and neck. Then go about your business. It's important to calmy greet a dog that tends to jump.

You're not done yet! The key to training this behavior is repetition. Go out the front door and do this over again. (Or to make it more real for your dog, you can sneak out the back door, get back in your car, drive a little ways and return home.) Come in the door again. Notice he's a little calmer this time, and you can probably get him to sit so that you have an opportunity to click and reward the desired behavior. Now, do this a few more times. Continue this for several days in a row until you're getting a reliable sit when you come in the door.

Now you need to invite some friends or neighbors over and go through this same exercise. When your friend enters, instruct them to pay no attention to your dog until he sits. You ask him to "sit" (hopefully before he jumps up). If he sits, immediately click and let them praise him and offer him a treat. Do this about five times with this person. In addition, do this with a number of people. This is the time to call on your friends and family members to help you out! Invite lots of folks over and work through this with five or ten people a few times in one day!

Note of caution: I've seen many a client (and yes, I've done it too!) actually train a chained behavior when they thought they were teaching the dog to sit when greeting people. A behavior chain is a few behaviors one after the other (like links in a chain) where each behavior in the chain reinforces the last behavior and the final behavior gets rewarded. For example, your dog jumps up on you (behavior one) and while he's up on you, you give him the cue to sit (behavior two), then you click and treat. Your clever dog may interpret this as "OK, you want me to jump up on you, then sit! Got it!" The way to prevent this from happening is to make sure some time passes between when your dog jumps (you ignore), and he puts his feet on the ground and leaves them there (about 5-8 seconds); then, you ask for the sit and click and reward. Also, if you're cueing the dog to "sit," do your best to give the cue before he jumps up on you. For this reason, I often find tethering the dog, therefore not allowing the mistake of jumping in the first place, can be very helpful when teaching this behavior.

Door Rushing

One of the scariest things dog owners can face is having their dog rush out the door and then go running down the street! This used to happen to me many years ago with my German Shepherd mix, Shanti, who decided this was great fun! She would jet out the door or gate before I could stop her and, then, down the street she'd run. I'd be late for work, running after her in the rain, scared she was going to get hit by a car, chase a neighbor's cat, just keep running forever or any number of horrors!

Until your dog is trained to wait at the door and has a reliable recall, you'll want to manage this behavior. That means you make sure there are no options for the dog to run out the front door, garage door or gate! The same goes with a dog jumping out of the car uninvited. I've heard many a horror story from my clients about their dog almost getting hit by a car.

I use one of two approaches to teach dogs not to run out the front door uninvited. One involves teaching a "sit-stay"; the other involves using "body blocking" techniques to teach a "wait" at the door. You can decide which approach you'd rather use.

"Sit-Stay" at the Door/Gate

You can teach your dog to "sit-stay" when you're going out the door. This is especially effective if he's going with you for a ride or a walk. The reinforcement is being able to go out the door. Do this exercise at various times when your dog is going out the door with you. Also, set it up as a regular training session where you're working specifically on this objective.

Be sure that your dog understands and performs a "stay" before expecting your dog to stay around this level of distraction. Ask your dog to "sit–stay." Go outside. If he has been successful, click and invite him outside with you. You can also treat, although the real reward is going outside. You can either have a short play period or go ahead and take him for a walk. After all, he was successful!

For most dogs, this is not that easy. Instead, you need to teach this behavior by breaking it down into small increments and clicking and treating for each successful step. The following is an example of breaking this behavior down incrementally. You may be able to proceed faster, or you may need to go even slower depending on your dog:

- Move towards the door
- Move towards the door and stand there for a moment
- Place your hand on the doorknob
- Turn the doorknob
- Open the door one inch
- Open the door three inches
- Open the door halfway
- Open the door wide while blocking access outside with your body
- Open the door wide and step aside so your dog has access through the door
- Step onto the threshold
- Step out the door
- Do some distracting things outside the door (jumping jacks, bouncing a ball, running around, etc.)

For completion of each successful step, you'll click and treat and move on to the next step. Ask your dog to "sit-stay" as you progress through each of the above steps. If he breaks the stay, reset the stay, and go back to the previous step. Reinforce that step a few times before moving on if necessary. Keep progressing until you can stand on the threshold and, then, finally go outside. Then, bring some distractions into the training. If you're not successful, keep breaking down the behaviors into smaller increments. It could be that your dog does not yet understand "stay." If so, go back to working on stay in a less distracting situation first. Remember to click and reward at each success. The big reinforcement is when he gets it right – then he gets to go for a walk!

Wait at the Door/Gate
Using Body-Blocking Technique

Body blocks can be a very effective way to teach dogs to wait at the door rather than running out uninvited. If you control the space in front of the dog, you are controlling the dog's movement.

You'll need to get your body between your dog and the door and "herd" him backwards away from the door a few feet. Chances are he'll see if he can sneak by you, and you'll need to continue blocking him with your legs until he pauses. Next, move towards the door while you're still facing him and open it partially. Most dogs will move towards the open door, so you'll need to move forward again, blocking the space and, again, herd him away from the door. When he does back off, you need to step to the side of the door and let him decide what to do – wait or make a run for it? Don't continually block the opening. As soon as you see him hesitate, click and go through the door and give him permission to follow (such as a release and "let's go!") and let him go through the door. You can give him a treat, although going out the door is the real reward here. When your dog is no longer rushing the door, you can add the "wait" cue.

It's also a very good idea to teach this in the car. We do not want our dogs jumping out of the car until invited. Go ahead and leave a leash dangling on your dog so you can catch him if necessary. With the car door to help block access to the outside this is easy to teach. Sometimes, I start with teaching it in the car and, then, move on to the front door.

Note: When I begin work on door rushing, I usually start with a long line attached to the dog's collar (see "Training Equipment" section of this book). You can attach the other end to railing or furniture for a large dog and be ready to step on the end for a small dog. Make sure it's loose on your dog though, so he doesn't feel like he's tied up or on a leash. The long line is only there as a safety measure. Once he's readily performing the behavior, remove the long line and practice without it.

Problem Chewing

Dogs chew because it's a natural canine behavior. We don't want to eliminate this behavior altogether; instead, we want to manage and redirect it to what is acceptable to chew on. Dogs chew for a number of reasons. Puppies chew partially because they are teething. Much like a two-year-old child gets into everything, puppies investigate their environment with not just their noses but often with their mouths as well. Adult dogs also chew. I do find that much of the destructive chewing eases off as a dog moves out of its adolescent stage into adulthood. However, they still chew! Dogs chew when they are bored. If they are stuck out in the backyard for 10 hours a day, and you have a nice wooden deck or plastic sprinklers, chances are your dog will chew. Dogs chew because they are anxious. They can't pick up a glass of wine or go to the gym, so they will work out their anxiety partially by chewing. Dogs chew because it's fun for them, and it's a self-reinforcing behavior.

The best way to handle your dog's chewing is to supply her with appropriate chew toys. Some of the best chew toys out there are Kongs and Nylabones. Stuff the Kongs with goodies to get your dog's attention. You can stuff the Kongs with all kinds of creative things (rice and eggs or cottage cheese, cream cheese with a little liverwurst, peanut butter and kibble). You can also freeze it, and it will last longer. This will give your dog something to work on for quite some time. I also like Buster Cubes to keep a dog busy. These are not really chew toys, but they will keep your dog occupied so that he is not busy chewing on your shoe. There are now many kinds of interactive food toys available for dogs. Hollow real bones available from pet food stores or catalogues (they are treated so that they are hard and will not splinter) can be stuffed with cream cheese or other goodies to keep your dog occupied. Just take a stroll down through your local pet food store, and you'll find lots of choices.

In addition to supplying your dog with chew toys, you can also manage the dog's environment. Be sure to "puppy proof" your home. In other words, keep things like shoes, socks, children's toys, and TV remote controls out of reach of your dog. If there are areas of concern, such as your carpet or couch, keep your dog contained in the kitchen or a room where she can do no serious damage. Items like furniture can be sprayed with chew preventative solution available from a pet store such as Bitter Apple. Also, a crate can be used for a short duration to keep your dog quiet and out of trouble. However, I do not suggest crating your dog for 8 hours while you go to work. That's way too long (see "Crate Training" section of this book).

If your dog will not play with a chew toy, you may have to teach it! (Yes, this seems unbelievable, but true.) One way to motivate your dog to play is by tying a string around the toy and dragging it slowly across the floor. You can also shape this behavior, by clicking and treating for each step your dog takes towards playing with a toy. For instance, first click and treat for sniffing, then licking, then putting it in her mouth, etc. (see "Motivating Your Dog to Play" section of this book).

One way to deal with anxiety and boredom is to make sure your dog is getting sufficient exercise. If she is getting enough exercise, this will help alleviate chewing from anxiousness or boredom. Your dog may decide to nap instead!

Keep control of your dog's toys. She should always have at least one chew toy out to play with. However, make sure your dog understands that "all good things" come from you. Let your dog know that these are your toys, and you're letting her play with them. Pick up Kongs and Buster Cubes at the end of the "chew" session. Clean them up and re-stuff them, freeze them, and have them ready for the next day, or clean them and put them away, and, then, the next day make a big deal about getting them ready for your pup. Request that she do a few behaviors (down, roll over, shake) before handing over the goody.

Digging

Some breeds tend to dig more than others (terriers, labs, etc.). Once your dog has begun digging, it's a tough habit to break. Digging is another one of those self-reinforcing and natural canine behaviors. Some dogs dig purely for the fun of it! In the area where I live, dogs dig to hunt gophers – now that's rewarding! Dogs also dig because they are bored or anxious. Sometimes dogs dig to make a cool bed for themselves. If you have a dog that sits in the backyard all day with nothing to do or a dog that is easily aroused, they may turn to digging for release. To help alleviate boredom and anxiety, make sure the dog gets plenty of exercise, has access to at least one room of the house while you're gone, and has interactive food toys available.

Punishment is not very effective with digging. It may stop your dog from digging when you're right there with them. However, since the behavior is so much fun, many dogs will dig anyway and take whatever punishment you want to deal out. It's so much fun it's worth it!

The best way to deal with digging is either to manage the environment or provide an acceptable alternative. Managing the environment means putting up a fence, keeping your dog partitioned somewhere in the yard on cement or wood so he cannot dig, or, keeping him in the house while you're not there to supervise.

When we adopted Bear, our 90-pound Lab/Rottweiler, at 7 years old from our friend, he really liked to dig. He had lived in Arizona with a yard mostly taken up by a pool. He was allowed in the laundry room and not in the house, so he found lots of time during the day to keep busy by digging. When he hit the soft earth of California (compared to the hard earth of Arizona), he was in heaven. And, as an added bonus, our yard was laced with gopher holes and tunnels! It only took Bear about two weeks to turn our backyard into a mini Grand Canyon! We had six dogs at the time. My solution was to put a second fence in our backyard so that Bear would have access to the house and only a cemented portion of the yard while we were gone. I put a doggy door in the fence that allowed all the smaller dogs through, although Bear was too big to go through. All the other dogs still had access to the backyard during the day. Bear was allowed in the backyard when I was there to supervise. That solved our problem!

Providing a place where you will allow and encourage your dog to dig is another great way to handle digging. You can designate a portion of your yard as a "digging pit." If you have a small dog, probably a 3' × 3' area will be large enough. If you have a large dog, it may have to be about 5' × 5'. The trick is to hide yummy treats, bones and toys there. Cover them with a few inches of loose dirt. After your dog catches on, you can bury them a little deeper. Bring your dog to the area and let them start investigating the smells, then start digging. When he does dig and finds a prize, click and praise. As the dog digs more readily, begin inserting the cue "dig" right before he starts digging. Now, you will need to keep this area "stocked" with goodies. The idea is that your dog is going to dig anyway. Why not encourage him to dig where you would like him to? He will probably choose the place where he's found goodies over other places in the yard (you're going to have to make the goodies more exciting than a gopher!). Continue to praise him any time you see him digging in his digging pit. If you see him digging elsewhere, simply interrupt the behavior with a "hey" or a clap of your hands, take him to his digging pit and say, "dig." Click and treat when he digs.

My friend Julie trained her two Cairn Terriers, C.C. and Scout, to dig on cue. Then, she'd take them to the beach a few times a week and let them dig to their hearts content!

Barking

When dealing with a barking problem, it's important to analyze the situation. For instance, is the dog left in the backyard all day with nothing to do? Could he be barking because he's bored, to get attention, or to warn you that someone or something is near your property? Often barking is just a symptom of an over-aroused dog. In many situations, the problem can be solved by management techniques. For instance, if your dog sits on your couch and barks at everyone who walks by, is it possible to shut the blinds? Does this block his visual trigger and minimize the barking? Is the dog running the fence in your backyard because the neighbor's dog is right on the other side? One option is to construct another fence in your yard perhaps three or four feet closer in from the existing fence. Then plant some bushes if necessary to block your dog's vision and close proximity to the neighbor's dog. Is your dog outside all day with nothing to do? If so, ask yourself, "Why can't my dog be left in the house?" If the answer is chewing, housetraining problems, etc., then deal with those problems. Find a way to allow the dog some access to at least some portion of the house.

Once you've determined why you think the dog is barking, if you can't solve the problem with physical barriers or managing the dog or the physical situation, you can look at whether self-control exercises can bring the dog's arousal level down. If your dog doesn't yet know how to control himself, he probably can't stop himself from barking. Barking can be a symptom and will need to be addressed.

Alternately, you may need to begin reinforcing quiet behavior. All dogs, even the most ardent barkers, like our Cairn Terrier, Skye, are still quiet many hours a day. You can also teach your dog to be "quiet" on cue. And believe it or not, you probably want to put the barking on cue as well. You can teach both of these behaviors at once. Since both behaviors are already offered, you can add the cue quickly.

First, you'll need to set up the situation so you can get your dog to bark during the training session. Perhaps a few knocks on the wall will do the trick, or a squeaky toy, or maybe withholding dinner a few minutes. Most dogs get frustrated and start to vocalize in this situation. (Generally, you do not want to choose something like the mailman, as this is probably a situation where you do not want to reinforce barking.)

Now in a training session, see if you can do something to make your dog bark and work with "speak" and "quiet" back and forth. Say "speak," and when your dog goes "woof," click and treat. Immediately say "quiet" and click and treat for a few seconds of quiet. (If you can't get even a second of quiet, wave a treat in front of his nose, which may quiet him down for a second.) Then, begin holding off on the click and prolonging the quiet behavior by a few seconds at a time. The exercise is "bark," dog goes "woof," then "quiet," click and treat for "quiet." I move quickly from giving a piece of kibble for the bark and a piece of chicken (or something much yummier) for the quiet. When you can go though a training session and turn the bark on and off, you're ready to move on.

Now, in a real life situation, such as a doorbell, let your dog alarm bark a few times and then say "quiet." If your dog is quiet, click and treat and praise! If your dog continues to bark, see if you can interrupt the bark and redirect by asking for another behavior such as "sit" (see "Interrupt and Redirect Behavior" under "Eliminating Problem Behaviors" in chapter 8). When your dog is quiet for even a few seconds, click and treat. Begin to teach your dog that once you say "quiet," that if he is quiet, he is rewarded. If he's not quiet, then you need to redirect him or possibly even remove him from the room (time-out). Before long, most dogs get the idea. It's important you teach "quiet" in a training session first so that your dog knows what it means before ever moving on to interrupting the behavior in a real-life situation. It's not fair to yell "quiet" at your dog before he knows what it means!

Barking can be an exasperating problem, and people are often looking for a quick fix. Also, owner-absent barking can literally put the dog's life at risk if the family feels they have to get rid of the dog because the police have been to their house numerous times regarding neighbors' complaints. It would be wise to call a professional trainer or animal behaviorist to help you in a private session.

If you are at the end of your rope, don't be tempted to use a shock collar. Remember that harsh punishment can bring out aggression or fear in your dog. It's far preferable to use a citronella anti-bark collar available from Premier Pet Products. Citronella collars are more effective than shock collars, and at least they are not causing the dog physical pain. A citronella collar uses a microphone. When the dog barks, he gets a quick spray of citronella under his chin. (Most dogs find the smell aversive, since they have a very keen sense of smell.) The collar also hisses when it sprays, which many dogs don't like. The citronella collar is effective with many dogs and can help with owner-absent barking situations. I always suggest that clients do their best to train the "quiet" behavior first, and only use a citronella collar as a last resort. If using a citronella collar, it's important to also reinforce quiet behavior with clicks and treats whenever possible. This will greatly facilitate the training. Also, give your dog breaks from wearing the collar. Your dog should be allowed to bark during a play period or romp in the park.

"I'll Just Be A Minute"

My six-pound toy poodle, Shasta, is well trained with obedience and agility titles and is a certified therapy dog. He has one problem. Well, more than one, but his most annoying behavior is that he does not like to be left in the car. His anxiety starts when I pull into a parking lot and escalates from whining to pulling on my clothes as I attempt to leave the car. His anxious barking draws stares from everyone around the car. What to do? I have tried many different techniques to change this behavior. The technique that has worked is using the clicker and rewarding calm behavior, in very small baby steps. This problem did not resolve itself overnight, and it is something I continually have to work on. But, I have learned that the clicker is a powerful force in overcoming unwanted behaviors.

Donna Hedrick

Working Around the Food Bowl and Bones

Some dogs have food possession issues. Other dogs can eat anywhere, anytime, and don't care what's going on around them. If you think about it, from a dog's point of view, it's doubtful another dog would take your dog's dinner or bone, and, then, give it back. They naturally think you're probably taking it for good. Dogs that are food possessive may guard their food from other dogs or from you. It's a good idea to get your dog used to your being around his food bowl. The easiest way to work with dog-to-dog aggression around food is to feed your dogs in separate locations. Or you can use other management techniques such as crates or X-pens to keep them separate while eating.

Working with the food bowl is something you ideally want to do with a small puppy before he develops any food guarding tendencies. We can, sometimes, inadvertently set dogs up to guard their food. If they are fed in an isolated area (like the backyard or laundry room), they may not be used to having people or dogs around when they eat. Sometimes, we adopt older dogs, so we've got to start wherever the dog is. If you have a dog that is protective of his food, please use extreme caution in working with these exercises. This is not something that should be done by children. An adult should handle these exercises. This is definitely a situation where people get bitten. Look for signs of warning from your dog. He may freeze, growl, snarl, snap, and then, yes, bite! Only go forward with the following exercises if you feel comfortable and proceed gradually. If you think you have serious problems, please contact a professional trainer or an animal behaviorist for assistance.

Food bowl exercises can usually be done fairly safely with young puppies. Get them used to this before they ever get the idea to guard their food bowl. Again, if you have an older dog, use common sense and be cautious. Some ideas include:

- Always ask your dog to "sit" and "stay." Put his food bowl down. Have him wait for your cue to invite him to eat, "okay, eat."
- If you've been feeding your dog all by himself, with no people around, start feeding him in the kitchen or somewhere around people. (Watch the kids though.)
- Hand feed your dog his kibble for several weeks. Let every treat come straight from your hands (as long as he's not aggressive in this situation.)
- Hand feed kibble in his bowl. Start out by having him sit. Put the bowl down in front of him. Put one piece of kibble in the bowl. Say, "okay, eat." As soon as he eats the one piece, click. Now, put another piece of food in his bowl. Follow the same procedure clicking after he eats each piece for about 20 pieces. Now, put a handful of food in his bowl. As soon as he starts eating, click and praise. Follow this exercise for at least three days. Get him

used to your being around when he eats. Also, get him used to the idea that the food is coming from you.

- Another exercise is to feed your dog, then approach slowly, and slip an extra yummy goody (like chicken, beef, etc.) into his bowl. Do this a number of times. This gets him accustomed to the idea that when you (and your hand for that matter) are around, he gets something special in his bowl.

- If he is doing well with the above exercises, ask him to sit in the middle of eating. If necessary, tempt him with something better than his kibble. When he sits, remove his bowl. Place something yummy in it (again something really good), and, then, put it back in front of him and say, "okay, eat." This teaches him that when you take his food bowl away, you'll probably put it back with something better in it instead of taking it away for good.

- You can also hold your dog's food bowl on your lap and let him eat. This will get him used to you being around his bowl. Only do this exercise if you feel comfortable though, as this puts your face much closer to your dog's teeth.

With young puppies, I also regularly play the "trade" game. If they are busy playing with a chew bone (like a Nylabone), I'll go up to them with something edible and yummy, like a bully stick or Greenie, and say "trade-ya." When they give up their bone, I give them the better bone. After a few minutes I also give their original bone back. Just make sure whatever you have is better, or this won't work well!

"Mine"

When we adopted Kiko, our Keeshond-Collie mix, at about 2 years old from the Humane Society, he came to us with serious food guarding issues. When we first got him, if I entered the room in which he was eating, he would begin stiffening, with hackles raised. If I approached, he would begin growling, and if I kept moving towards him, he would start snapping. We worked for some time with his issues. We started with hand feeding and progressed through the steps I've listed above. I'm happy to say that at this point, I can take his full bowl of food away. However, I'm still cautious in that I may ask him to sit and stay before I do it! If he's given a very high value treat (from his perspective) like a Greenie, I put him in his kennel to eat it in peace away from the other dogs. Although I consider him relatively safe, I would not invite someone he doesn't know to pick up his bowl with food in it or a bone even to this day. It is always wise to err on the side of caution when dealing with food guarding problems!

Crate Training

Crate training is well worth your time. I believe every dog should have a crate for his or her entire life. Although one of the major uses of crates is for housetraining (see "Housetraining" section of this book), there are many other uses for a crate. Crates are used in managing your dog. They can be used for a quiet restful period for your dog, a short time-out, to keep them safe in certain situations, to confine them for health reasons (after an operation for example), to let them have a safe den for sleeping, or just because they like them!

The crate should be big enough for your dog to stand up comfortably, turn around, and lie down. For housetraining, you don't want it any bigger than this. For an adult, housetrained dog, you can get a larger crate. If you only want to buy one crate that will be big enough for an adult dog, you'll need to safely block off part of the crate to make it small enough for housetraining. Otherwise, your pup may potty in the corner, and you'll start to diminish the effectiveness of this tool. Some crates that are available come with a removable partition for use when housetraining and, later, can be used for the adult dog.

There are several styles of crates available: plastic airline crates, wire mesh crates and portable nylon crates. Any of them can work.

You'll need to get your dog used to and comfortable in her crate before you use it for any reason. The following are some points for getting her used to the crate:

- Leave the crate out where it's easily accessible (kitchen or living room) and where she can get used to it. After she's used to the crate, it's good to give her access whenever she'd like to go inside.
- Leave the door open, and toss a treat in the crate. When she goes in, click, let her eat the treat, and she may come right back out. That's fine. Do this a number of times. If she won't go all the way in the crate at first, place the treat a few inches inside the crate and slowly move it farther towards the back.
- Once she's going in after the treat regularly, add a cue such as, "in your crate."
- Start delaying the click a second or two or three and give her another treat for staying in the crate a little longer.
- Begin feeding her meals in the crate.

- Give her stuffed Kongs, or another chewy or some wonderful toys in the crate.
- Once she's become comfortable with the crate, begin shutting the door for a few moments while you're close to her in the room.
- Slowly prolong the amount of time she's in the crate.
- If you're sure she doesn't need to go to the bathroom, and that other necessities have been met (is she hungry or thirsty?), ignore whining. If necessary, cover the crate with a blanket or towel to block her view. She may decide to take a nap. Don't let her out of the crate when she's whining. Wait till she's quiet for at least five to 10 seconds, and, then, let her out, if necessary.
- As she becomes more comfortable in the crate with you in the room (maybe 10 or 15 minutes), begin leaving the room for short periods. At first, only a few moments, then, slowly work it up to 5 minutes, 10 minutes, and 15 minutes.
- At this point you can start leaving most dogs in their crate for a half-hour to an hour at a time.

Many young puppies can begin sleeping in their crates very soon. Because they are sleeping, they don't really care that they are in a crate. It's different than leaving them in a crate during the day when they're wide awake. And, then again, for some puppies, you may need to take a few days to get them used to their crate before they will sleep well in it.

Make the crate your dog's safe and quiet spot. Teach children in the household to leave their dog alone when she's in her crate.

When we adopted Kiko from the Humane Society, (he had been at Animal Services first, then adopted for a while, then at the Humane Society), he was very uncomfortable in anything that resembled a cage. With some patience and clicker training, he now sleeps in his crate, and often goes in of his own accord when it's available. Dogs consider their crates a safe "den" and often learn to love it. When I'm packing for a trip and the suitcases come out, I will often find my little Lhasa Apso, Crystal Moon, hiding out in her crate because she's feeling insecure. Crates are a good thing, and dogs like them!

Housetraining

Lucky for us dogs are naturally clean animals. They have an innate preference to keep their dens unsoiled. Housetraining is basically a problem of the dog going in the wrong place at the wrong time. Either you're not supervising him inside, and he needs to relieve himself, or you take him outside and he doesn't need to go at that moment. The trick is to give your dog lots of praise and rewards (and the opportunity) for going potty in the right place and prevent him from eliminating inside the house through proper management. Before long, you'll have a well housetrained dog!

The encouraging thing about housetraining is it can be accomplished relatively quickly for an adult dog, while a young puppy needs some time to gain bladder and bowel control. Depending on your dog's age and breed, you may be able to housetrain within a week or two. For young puppies, housetraining may need to continue until the dog is a little over five months old. On average, housetraining can take two to three months. As far as controlling elimination, small dogs physically mature more quickly, while large dogs mature more slowly. A general rule of thumb is, once your dog has gone about two weeks with no accidents in the house, you can generally consider him housetrained. If you're getting a new puppy, it's a good time to take that week vacation from work! After all, if you had a new human baby, you'd be taking some time off, right? Babies are babies – human or dog.

Here are some of the basic points of housetraining

Pet Doors – If you have a secure backyard, and you can start from the beginning teaching your dog to use a pet door, housetraining will be easier, especially if you have another dog in the house that already understands the pet door. Also, when you're gone for longer periods, you don't have to worry about getting home to let your dog out. Some people who live in apartments, etc. may not have this option. However, if you do have this option, I suggest you consider it now from the beginning. Even with a pet door, you still need to housetrain. However, now, your dog can go out on his own once he understands he needs to do his business outside. Very small dogs or puppies may not be safe outside without supervision.

Feeding Schedule – Put your dog on a set feeding schedule. Twice a day works for most dogs. If your dog is a toy breed or a young puppy (less than five or six months old), she may require food three or more times per day. Check with your vet on that. A set feeding schedule helps with establishing a defecation schedule for your dog. Most dogs need to have a bowel movement anytime from immediately to an hour or so after eating. (Each dog is different, and we'll talk about that below.) Feeding on a schedule will help you to at least narrow down when "the big event" is probable. If you free-feed your dog (leave food out all the time), you will never know when she needs to go. Also, be sure to feed your dog by about 6:00 p.m. in the evening so there's lots of time for a bowel movement before bed. As a side benefit, feeding schedules establish important leadership messages because you're the one who controls the food! You're teaching "all good things come from you!"

Water Schedule – Your puppy or adult dog needs lots of opportunities to drink fresh water. When housetraining a puppy especially (not so much an adult dog), you'll need to keep an eye on the water because he usually needs to urinate almost immediately after drinking. This means that he generally will not get water while he is confined in his crate for housetraining. You may also want to take up the water about an hour before bedtime during the housetraining phase. He can go out for his last potty break and, hopefully, make it through the night, or at least half the night (depending on his age). Make sure that your pup has enough free time outside the crate and that water is available during those times.

Management in the House – Until your dog is reliable in the house, you must manage his whereabouts and keep a close eye on him at all times. You cannot give him the privilege of the full run of the house until he is housetrained. Inside, he is always confined as outlined below (not to punish, just to prevent messes). Also, if he just eliminated, he can enjoy about a half-hour of free time while you're still watching him closely during this free time for any signs of the impending need to eliminate (circling, sniffing the ground, etc.). Remember, if you can stick with the program, this whole housetraining issue will be solved in a short period of time.

- Put him in his crate (he must already be comfortable with the crate – see "Crate Training").
- Tether him to a piece of furniture with a small bed or blanket while you're in the room supervising him. Tie the leash to a piece of furniture and don't give him more than about three feet or so to roam. The leash is attached to a regular buckle collar or harness.
- Tether him to you. Yes, this "umbilical cord" method means he's never out of your sight. Put a belt on and tie his leash to you. Now, you have no choice except to keep an eye on him.

Chart his Potty Schedule – There are some general rules that help you determine when your puppy might need to eliminate:

- After waking up first thing in the morning
- After waking up from a nap
- After drinking water
- After eating a meal or lots of snacks
- After playing or excitement

These rules can help, but what about the other 23 hours in the day? There are more "rules" that I've heard, including "take your dog out every hour on the hour." Others say they can hold their urine about an hour for each month of age

(4 months = 4 hours). The truth is, every dog is different. Some can go for hours, others for only a short period, at first. For instance, our dog Wags could wait an hour or two after eating to defecate. However, Bear had to go out immediately. One good idea, suggested by my friend, Denise Porte, DVM and puppy trainer extraordinaire, is to chart your dog's potty schedule. Then you'll know for sure how long he can be in a crate comfortably. Jot down the following times: feeding, urination, and defecation. Track these events for a couple days, and you'll start to get a feel for your puppy's schedule. This is the most accurate way to determine where your dog is right now. Remember, this will change as he begins to learn to hold it and has better bladder and bowel control. You should re-check your dog's potty schedule at least monthly when he is young or anytime you're having problems with housetraining.

Recognizing the Potty Signal – When your dog is in a crate or confined by a tether to a small area, the idea is he won't want to mess up his den. So that means he's going to signal you (bark, whine or scratch at crate door) when he needs to go out. If you are confining your puppy in a crate at night, you probably already recognize his request for a potty break. So how do you know if he's only whining to get out or if he needs to go potty? (If you let him out every time he whines, he could quickly learn that whining gets him out of the crate.) You can think about how you handle a crying human baby. Figure out if his basic needs have been met (food, water, elimination, play, exercise). Has he relieved himself recently? Could he be hungry or thirsty? If you know he has recently gone potty, eaten and had some water, then maybe he needs some play or exercise. If it's none of the above, then chances are he may just be bored and whining to get out. If that's the case, see if a stuffed Kong or other favorite toy might help ease the boredom.

When he Signals You – When he gives you his potty signal, take him to his designated potty spot. It's helpful to attach a leash or get him to follow you quickly outside or even carry him outside first thing in the morning. Otherwise, he might stop on the way out and mess on the rug. Wait for him to finish relieving himself (don't interrupt him midway), click, treat and make a big fuss over what a wonderful dog he is!

Stay with Your Dog – It's important to stay with your dog while he goes potty. First, how will you know if he went if you aren't there? Second, the most significant part of house training is rewarding the dog for going outside or in a specific area of the yard. You need to be there to click and treat and praise the event. Giving him a bone when he comes in from the yard reinforces coming in, not going potty! If you want to teach him to use a specific part of the yard, you'll need to be there to encourage him to use that spot. You might place a little feces or urine soaked paper towel in your designated potty spot to give him the scent. You may also need to guide him on a leash to the desirable area of the yard and use the leash to keep him from wandering to another area. Don't distract your dog when he's outside to go potty. Be as neutral and boring as possible, and, hopefully, he'll remember why he's out there.

Don't Teach Him Potty Ends the Fun – If you let him potty and always take him right back inside and put him in his crate or leave for the day, he may feel like going potty ends the fun. It's possible that he may start procrastinating while he's outside. At least some of the time, show him that once he potties, then lots of good things happen, including a little extra playtime.

Free Time After Elimination – If he went potty, he can now have about a half-hour of free time in the house. You'll still need to keep an eye on him and watch for signals that he might have to go (sniffing, circling, etc.) After a half-hour, you'll need to either put him back in his crate or tether him again to prevent any accidents. You'll wait again for his signal to go out.

If He Doesn't Go – If you take him out and hang around outside for three to five minutes, and he doesn't go potty, bring him back in and confine him again until he signals. That means no free time in the house until he eliminates. It's "red alert time" (see below). As soon as he signals you with loud whining or barking, he may have realized he did have to go! If you misjudged when he had to go, it might be time to re-chart your potty schedule as outlined above.

Red Alert Time – When he doesn't go potty outside, such as when you thought he had to or when you had just gotten home from work or being gone, and you have no idea when he last eliminated – you need to be on "red alert." This means strict confinement and observation until he signals and goes potty. Suppose you get home from work, and here's this ball of fluff you've missed so much all day. If you take him into the living room to play, you're asking for trouble! Take him immediately outside and see if he needs to go potty. If not – I know this is tough – he needs to be confined (crate, umbilical cord, tether) and observed closely until you get the signal.

Adding the "Potty" Cue – Right before you think he's going to go potty, start saying a designated "potty" cue. Some people like "go potty," "hurry up," or "do your business." It's a good idea to put potty going on cue so that later on you can get your dog to go when requested.

Bedtime – Having your dog sleep in a crate is usually advisable until she's housetrained. If your dog is sleeping with you, you need to make sure she isn't sneaking off the bed and going potty in the middle of the night. That will set up a very negative habit. While you're potty training your dog, it's best to let her sleep in her crate in your bedroom, close to your bed (see "Crate Training" section of this book). I like to face the kennel towards my bed so that she can see me. Dogs like to sleep with their "pack." Very young puppies (less than four months old) will probably need to get up during the night to go potty. They will usually wake up and signal you with scratching, whining, or a special bark. Learn to listen for your dog's specific potty signal as discussed above. It's usually different from the plain old whining that sometimes occurs with puppies. When a puppy needs to potty during the night, she has usually been quiet, and, then, all of a sudden, seems to be doing her best to communicate something to you! (My bladder is full!) Obviously, if your dog were in another room, you wouldn't be able to hear her asking to go out. If ignored, she'll have to potty in her crate, and you don't want that to happen (see below).

Once a dog is a bit older or an adult, most dogs can sleep through the night without having to get up. Just like people, their metabolism slows down, and they can make it through the night (eight hours or so). During the day, they need to go to the bathroom more frequently. As explained previously, for young puppies, you may want to take the water up about an hour before bedtime and feed the evening meal about three to four hours previous to bedtime, so she has time to eliminate before retiring for the night.

Longer Duration Confinement – What do you do when you have to leave the house for longer periods and your dog is not yet housetrained? Don't confine him in a crate all day. If you have a young puppy, he probably can't hold it more than an hour or two, tops. If you have an adult dog, of course, they can go longer. Above all, be fair to your dog. Being stuck in a crate all day while you're at work is just too long. Long periods of close confinement can cause other behavioral problems.

One option is to leave your dog outside in a safe, fenced area while you're gone until he's housetrained. Make sure he has somewhere to get out of the cold and rain or hot sun. This is not an option with very small dogs or young puppies as they are vulnerable to birds of prey and other predators.

Another option is to set up a safe place in the house that limits the damage the dog can do. You can use baby gates or close doors to confine the dog to a kitchen, laundry room, bathroom or garage. "Puppy proof" the area by removing things your dog can chew up or destroy (electrical cords, toilet paper, shoes, etc.) and make sure anything poisonous or dangerous is picked up. Leave him water, toys, a bed or blanket, and perhaps a stuffed Kong and a potty spot (see below). If you have a pet door, you have the best of both worlds: allowing him access to the backyard and giving him limited access to the house while you're gone.

Leave him a potty spot in the confined area. If you don't have a pet door, you need to leave a designated spot for him to eliminate in the room where he'll be staying while you're gone. You can use commercial pee pads (these have an odor that helps encourage elimination), a dog litter box or newspaper. It might be even better to use a piece of turf or imitation turf, as long as you keep it clean, or you might use a small concrete area, such as a patio or porch. Why? Young puppies pick their favorite substrate for going potty (pick what kind of surface they like) when they're young. They then become accustomed to that. You probably want your dog to be comfortable going potty on cement or grass instead of newspaper!

Health Problems – If your dog messes in his sleeping area, he may have a medical problem. Urinary tract infections and other problems can cause a dog to urinate frequently. Unless you know you're to blame for leaving him too long in his crate, it's well worth a trip to your vet.

Diminishing the Usefulness of a Crate – If your dog has to eliminate in his crate (because you've left him too long or he has a health problem), you can ruin the effectiveness of the crate for housetraining. Some dogs which have come from puppy mills, irresponsible breeders, or pet shops where they have had to eliminate in the confined area where they lived have lost touch with the instinct to keep their sleeping area clean. Unfortunately, that means you've lost the crate as a very valuable housetraining tool.

Finding an Accident – If your dog eliminates in the house, and you didn't actually see it occur, just clean it up. Ideally use a product that contains enzymes that will actually remove the odor as well as the stain. Remember, dogs live in the present moment. If you get home from work and there's a mess, there's no point in scolding or punishing your dog. Next time, make sure you have properly confined your dog in either a long-term area, as suggested above, or that you are using a crate, tether or umbilical cord for short periods while you're home. Remember, you need to take responsibility for making sure your dog isn't roaming the house before he's housetrained.

Catching them in the Act – If you catch your dog in the act of eliminating in the house, then simply interrupt the behavior. Usually clapping your hands will cause the little tyke to stop and look up. Now, quickly rush him outside to finish if possible. When he does finish up, click and treat. Go inside and clean up the mess and say no more about it.

Learning to Hold It – One of the points of the confinement (crate, tether, or umbilical cord) is to help your dog learn how to hold it until he's in a proper potty spot. As your puppy gets older, you can leave him in the crate longer.

Learning their "Potty Signal" – Another reason to use confinement (crate, tether, or umbilical cord) is to learn the dog's signal to let you know that she needs to go potty. How else are you going to learn it?

Digestive Upset – It should go without saying – and I'm going to say it anyway – if your dog is sick and is experiencing loose stools or vomiting, don't expect them to get outside or hold it any more than you could!

Housetraining an Adult Dog – Housetraining an adult dog is the same as training a puppy, except the adult dog can usually hold his bladder a lot longer. Keep in mind an adult or older dog that is not housetrained may have established a pattern of going in the house. This habit may be a bit tough to break, so you'll need to be particularly diligent. Make sure to clean your carpets thoroughly (I suggest professionally) and also use an enzymatic odor eliminator as you work through housetraining an older dog.

Retraining Adult Dogs

You probably thought that once your puppy was housetrained that you would never have another problem with soiling in the house. Right? Sorry, that's not always the case. First, examine whether your dog has actually been fully housetrained – or did you just get the behavior you wanted most of the time? Several circumstances can arise during the life of your dog that may result in a housesoiling problem. The first thing to do if you are experiencing problems with an adult dog soiling the house is to have a veterinary examination. Your dog could be having a physical problem that makes it impossible for him to avoid eliminating in the house. Also, it is not unusual for geriatric dogs to have problems, so check with your veterinarian about this.

Secondly, when you move to a new home, remember generalization. In some circumstances, your dog will need to "go back to kindergarten" and be retrained to go outside. Even though he never had a problem in your previous house, a new home presents an entirely new environment for your dog. Also, this same scenario can take place if you're staying with a friend in a different house for a few days. In addition, something like a new carpet can throw your dog off. New smells or a new environment can confuse your dog.

Another situation that can cause adult dogs to urinate in the house is territorial marking. This can occur when new dogs or other animals (sometimes even a human baby) join your household. For example, I used to go to visit my sister and bring my two Lhasa Apsos, Crystal Moon and Wags. They never had a problem with messing in my house. Yet at my sister's home (complete with seven cats) all of a sudden I would discover my little female, Crystal, "marking" on the floor. This may have been a combination of a different house (not generalized) and territorial marking.

Whatever the circumstance, the answer is the same: "Go back to kindergarten," unless your dog is having a physical problem, in which case you need to take care of that. The best way to approach this problem is to re-housetrain your dog, just as if he were a little puppy. The best approach is to use a crate so that you can determine when he will eliminate. Then click, treat, and praise for "going" in the right place outside. Fortunately, he will usually relearn this quickly (within a week or two).

The Geriatric Years

It's tough when people get old, and it's tough when dogs get old. Right now, I'm facing what will probably be the last year or months of my Lhasa Apso, Crystal Moon's life. In a few days, she'll be seventeen years old. She's been an incredibly fun and hearty dog. She's the second dog I clicker trained. I brought her home as a little ball of fur at 9 weeks old in 1990. She's been one of those little dogs that are much bigger than their bodies (If you know Lhasa Apso females you know what I mean!).

It's sad to watch their bodies grow old. At this point, Crystal Moon still has a pretty good appetite, and she has her good days and her bad. She doesn't see or hear so well anymore. She also is getting arthritic. She has some tumors (I suspect malignant) although I don't know and don't need to know for sure. I'm not willing to put her through surgery, at this age, to find out. I just keep an eye on her and make sure she's still having a quality life. So far so good.

When dogs get old, we really need to give them a break. Sometimes, she can't make it outside anymore to go potty. I really don't care, nor do I see

Crystal Moon, our Lhasa Apso, at over 17 years old. Even though her health is not so good these days, she still enjoys doing her "Up-Pretty" trick for a tasty treat.

it as a housetraining problem. She just doesn't feel like going downstairs. So I just clean it up. I don't require her to do too much in the way of training anymore. She gets to take it easy now. I often carry her down or up the stairs just to make it easier on her. I also keep the puppy and younger dogs out of her way. I never leave her alone with my bigger and more assertive dogs. I just don't think it's fair at her age for her to have to put up with those younger attitudes!

All I can do now is be patient, for she is getting slow. My sister, Romlyn, said to me years ago about her two dogs: "They've waited for me all these years; I can wait for them now."

I do my best to watch her eyes and wait for her to tell me she doesn't want to be here anymore. I believe they'll always let us know if we're willing to listen. I just want her to make her transition peacefully and without pain. That is the most important thing. Lucky for me, I believe that Wags (who was her mate for 14 years before he passed) is waiting for her, and me, on the other side.

Note: Crystal Moon passed peacefully on September 4, 2007 at 17 years and 3 months of age.

On the Loss of Our Beloved Dogs

In September 2005 we lost our dearest baby Pug. Saffron was only 8 months old, and one of those "special" dogs for me in which the bond was so strong that we seemed to almost know what the other was thinking. I felt the bond the moment I saw her little face (last one left in the litter – all alone, and parting from her siblings and mother way too early at only 6-1/2 weeks old). Tiny, just two and a quarter pounds. We brought her home, and it was love at first sight for everyone. Even our 125-pound Anatolian and our little crazy mix breed from Mexico, Chili, immediately took over as surrogate mother and father. They loved her so and were so gentle and patient with her. Her training started immediately – as my demo dog and as a therapy dog, and she was doing beautifully. One day I left for about 2 hours to run some errands. My husband, Chuck, called and said, "You have Saffron with you, right?" I exclaimed "No! She has to be there; look in the yard." All I heard was "Oh my God; she's gone." I hung up my cell phone and rushed home. Expecting that somehow she had gotten out of the yard, I was preparing for the big search we'd have on our hands; instead, I found Chuck kneeling over her tiny body in the backyard performing CPR.

We rushed her to the Vet, Chuck continuing the CPR, while I prayed all the way that she would make it. And yet, it wasn't to be. My baby was gone – just like that. Never having lost a puppy before, we were devastated, to say the very least. I've lost many dogs in the past through natural causes, illness or, finally, the decision to euthanize. I could always salve my nerves by knowing that they'd lived a long life and believing that they were uncomfortable and had lost any quality of life, and that it was their time to go. With Saffron, none of these reasons applied. We had a necropsy done because I had to know what happened. She choked and aspirated on some kibble. We don't leave food out, which only means that one of the other dogs must have vomited, and she was eating that when something happened, and she inhaled. I suppose you could call it a freak accident, except I don't believe anyone or anything ever dies by accident.

It was her time to move on; she was done here on earth. She was an angel here for just a short time to light our lives. Even with that thought, the grief was so very intense; I had never experienced anything like it. This grief was even more intense than losing people that I have known.

Saffron's death was very unexpected. Most of my dogs have been old and "ready" to go. Many clients ask me how to tell when it's time to euthanize. I always say just look your dog in the eyes and be willing to listen. They will always let you know. Twice in my life, I was in too much denial to hear them and let two of my dogs live a while beyond when I should have let them go peacefully. For Wags (my Lhasa Apso), it took a dear friend to set me straight and get me to realize that he was ready. I'll never forget the look on the face of my first Akita, Cinnamon Bear, as my husband at the time, Rick, and I had to hoist him onto a blanket to carry him to the car because he could no longer walk. He looked humiliated and seemed to say, "Why did you wait so long?" If you're willing to hear, they will tell you.

Grieving over the loss of our animal friends, for many of us, is losing a member of our family. It's no different than if we had lost a human companion. The grief is just as intense, and the necessity of working through the grief and reaching closure and peace again is every bit as applicable in this situation as with a human death. Yet, many folks feel foolish and silly about grieving for their dogs or other pets in this way. Many people also trivialize the situation because it's not a person. My friend Jerry, in his late 40's, lost his wonderful companion, Casey, a Border Collie cross. It was so difficult for him to go through this. Being single and spending many long hours hiking the back trails and beaches of California, Jerry was lost and alone without Casey. However, to his friends at work and the average person, he found it difficult to explain how he was feeling and didn't

Casey, Jerry Ross' companion and hiking buddy for over 16 years.

think they would understand. Fearing they would judge him as "silly" for grieving so about the death of his dog, Jerry kept it to himself. It took him quite a while to work though this and feel comfortable adopting another dog. I'm very happy to say that he finally did work through it and about a year ago adopted another herding dog cross, Emily. Emily and Jerry now happily practice and compete in Agility.

I believe for those of us who bond with our animal companions deeply, we need to allow ourselves to go through the grieving process, and if possible contact a group that can help us process our feelings. Here in my area, San Luis Obispo, California, there is a local pet-loss group organized by our local Hospice.

Appendix 1

Syllabus & Homework Assignments – Samples

For myself, and for many trainers I've talked with, the hardest part of publishing a dog training book is the fact that training is always evolving. I often attend a seminar, come home and experiment with what I've learned, and incorporate new methods or subtle changes into my classes. Clicker training has changed over the years. Some of the shifts have been very minor and others pretty significant. Clicker training is now used world-wide, and, happily, we now have a whole new global generation of clicker trainers.

In this section, I've included a general class syllabus and homework assignments for my basic Puppy Preschool and Elementary Clicker Classes. We teach many other classes, although these two classes are the basic classes for beginners. I am happy to share this infor-mation with new clicker trainers who are putting together classes. I've created these class formats over an eight-year period. I've experimented with the order to teach behaviors and how much information to present to clients through the years. While the basic format and information has remained the same, as I said above I am constantly looking for new ways to teach clients and dogs more effectively, and I'm sure these classes will continue to evolve. For clicker trainers who would like to use this class format, I grant you the permission to copy homework assignments if you like. For the most recent versions, you can also check my website at www.clicknconnect.com.

Puppy Preschool

Class Description

The Puppy Preschool Class is designed to help socialize puppies and begin training at an early age. Dogs should be approximately 8 weeks to 18 weeks old in this class. Generally, we take about 10-12 puppies per class. We always have one instructor and three assistants in puppy class. My classes focus on clicker training for teaching behaviors such as sit, down, leave-it and come.

The reality is that more puppies are euthanized for temperament issues – that could have been avoided with proper socialization – than die of Parvo every year. While it's critical to keep our puppies safe and out of parks, beaches and open places until their shots are fin-ished, I feel that a well-run, safe puppy kindergarten class is a priority in every puppy and puppy owner's life. We do take every precaution to make sure the puppies are safe. The floor of the indoor training center is sanitized before the puppies enter. A separate potty yard is supplied where only puppies are allowed. All clients are asked to bring on-going shot records (as most puppies are still in the process of receiving shots). And clients are asked to carry puppies from the parking lot into the disinfected building.

The class is broken up into several segments: Socialization with people, socialization with other puppies or adult dogs; introduction to objects; opportunities to do something new which helps build confidence; instruction on basic training; bite inhibition; and, of course, good manners.

The puppies get to meet each of the people in the class (socialization with men, women, and children). We either have people move around or the puppies may be passed around a circle meeting each person in the class. Sometimes shy puppies stay with their families, and people come over to visit with them until, at some point in the class, they may be confident enough to be passed to other people away from their families.

The puppies also get to participate in a short play period with other puppies. The play period is well supervised, and we're always on the look out for a puppy that may be "bullying" others or puppies becoming too aroused. Puppies are divided into several groups (usually 3 to 4 puppies per group) with the smaller, younger and more timid puppies starting together. The more enthusiastic and larger dogs are placed together. Occasionally, just two puppies are put together in an X-Pen or separate area to play. The point is we would like each puppy to have a positive interaction with another puppy and, hopefully, more than one other puppy. Sometimes, by the 6th week of class, all puppies can play together. More often, they are still divided into groups. This depends on the temperament of the puppies attending class. When the puppies return to their people, they get to play tug or otherwise interact with their person. During the class, we also have visits from about three good-natured adult dogs. In this case, dogs are usually kept on leash.

We introduce puppies to items they may encounter in their lives and need to get used to such as hats, glasses, vacuums, and also let them experience doing something new like a tunnel or wobble board.

In the instruction part of the class, we begin teaching basic behaviors such as sit, down, leave-it, come, stay, walk on a leash and touch (hand targeting). We also discuss at length housetraining and crate training. In addition, we talk about how to work with preventing puppy behaviors that most of us don't want, such as jumping up, barking, digging, and chewing. We talk about how important management is at this age. We also discuss how to begin teaching the puppies self-control. Another hot topic is puppy "mouthing" and how to instill good bite inhibition (a light bite if a dog does bite) in our puppies from an early age.

I often tell my clients that if they can make it to only one class because of time or financial considerations, the puppy preschool is the most important. As I continue to work with shelter dogs and private behavior consultations, I think what a different world this would be if each and every puppy owner took their puppy to a positive, safe puppy class. It is a class that is very important for the puppy's socialization and also extremely important for the puppy's person to get off on the right foot in training and raising their puppy.

Puppy Preschool Clicker Class
Syllabus & Homework

6-Week Class
(Class time: 2-hour, people-only orientation, then, 1-¹/₂ hours per week for 5 weeks)

Syllabus

Class 1 – Orientation for People Only (2 hours)
- Basics of Clicker Training
    Why use a clicker?
    Clicker guidelines
    Motivation
    How to get a behavior (shaping, capturing, targeting, luring)
    Adding the cue
    Reinforcement
    Catch them doing something right
- Play the Clicker Training Game
- Housetraining
- Crate Training
- First step in bite inhibition
- Techniques for dealing with chewing and recommended chew toys
- Vaccinations (discuss keeping puppy safe)
- Brief review of puppy developmental stages
- Class information (what to bring to class, lending library, puppy potty area, etc.)
- Demonstrate charging the clicker
- Demonstrate "Attention" using shaping
- Demonstrate teaching the puppies their names
- Demonstrate "Sit" using capturing method

Class 2 – Puppies' 1st Week (1-¹/₂ hours)
- Safe way to meet and greet new dogs
- Everyone circulates and meets the puppies (One family member remains seated with puppy, and all "extra" family members circulate around the room greeting puppies one at a time).
- Review basics of clicker training
- Review "Sit" with hand signal (no lure)
- Discuss using sit for "deference" and to redirect jumping up
- PUPPY PLAY PERIOD
- Review "Attention"
- Review first step in bite inhibition (yip/growl when mouthing hurts)
- INTRODUCE PUPPY TO NEW THINGS – (wheelchair, walker)
- Teach "Settle" in lap

- Teach "Come" understanding the basics of teaching "come" (relay game)
- Teach "Release" word (Begin using release word such as "go play" or "free puppy")

Class 3 (1-1/2 hours)
- Pass the puppies (People sit on floor, puppies move around the circle by themselves or with class assistant or handler if necessary. People can ask puppies to "sit" or "settle.")
- Teach "Take hold of collar" – work with getting puppies comfortable with having collar grabbed
- Teach "Settle" (on leash)
- Review of "come" add the "Hide & Seek" game this week
- PLAY PERIOD (release puppy with release word)
- Second step in bite inhibition (yip/growl for any pressure)
- INTRODUCE PUPPY TO NEW EXPERIENCE (tunnel)
- Teach "Down" capturing or with lure and hand signal
- INTRODUCE PUPPY TO ADULT DOG
- Teach "Leave-It/Take-It" (Step 1 – closed hand)
- Discuss how to be a benevolent leader
- Introduce concept of Self-Control
- Demonstrate "Tug and Calm" game

Class 4 (1 hr. 15 minutes)
- Review "Settle while excited"
- Pass the puppies (People stand, and can ask puppies for "settle," "sit," or "down.")
- Review "Down" with hand signal (no lure)
- Review "Leave-It" (add Step 2 – open hand)
- PLAY PERIOD
- Teach "Off" – four paws on the floor
- Demonstrate Handling (sensitive areas such as feet, tail, mouth, ears, bathing, nail clipping)
- INTRODUCE PUPPIES TO NEW THINGS (vacuum)
- Teach "Touch" hand (teach the basics of targeting)
- INTRODUCE PUPPIES TO NEW EXPERIENCE (Wobble Board)
- Teach "Stay"
- Discuss Techniques for dealing with Digging

Class 5 (1-1/2 hours)
- Pass the puppies (People sit and can practice handling puppies)
- Discuss head collars & no-pull harnesses
- Introduce target stick ("touch" stick)
- PLAY PERIOD
- Teach "Heel" (shaping or target stick)
- Teach "Loose Leash Walking"

- INTRODUCE PUPPY TO NEW THINGS (umbrella, Dremel tool for nails)
- Introduce exercises around the food bowl (avoid food protection)
- Self-Control – Excercises: Parking, Calming Ovals, Getting from point A to point B (for pups 16 weeks and older)
- Review "Leave-It" add (Step 3) and discuss as the third step in bite inhibition to decrease frequency of mouthing.
- Discuss techniques for dealing with Barking

Class 6 – Graduation (1-1/2 hours)
- Pass the puppies (People stand and can wear hats, sunglasses, use canes, etc.)
- Review any behaviors class would like reviewed
- Review anti-biting exercises and discuss how to check for lifelong bite inhibition
- PLAY PERIOD
- Discuss vaccinations
- Discuss pros and cons of dog parks
- INTRODUCE PUPPIES TO ADULT DOG
- Discuss psychological/health benefits of spaying/neutering
- Discuss the importance of continued training
- Introduce emergency recall (taught more in-depth in Elementary and Clicker High)
- Games & prizes (tail wag/recall race/sit-stay (5 sec.)/down-stay (10 sec.)/leave-it)
- Graduation ceremony, certificates, prizes, photos, refreshments
- Sign up for next class

Puppy Preschool Clicker Class
Session One Homework

Charging the Clicker – Introduce your puppy to the clicker during the first training session. Simply start with the clicker in your pocket. Click and give your puppy a treat. Do this a number of times. Next, move the clicker behind your back, click and treat. Repeat several times. Finally, move the clicker out into plain view and click and treat a few more times. The puppy will only need to be introduced to the clicker once. From now on, you can use the click as a marker and reward for a specific behavior such as "sit."

Clicker Training Game – Play the clicker training game at least twice. Be the "dog" once and be the "trainer" once.

Timing Game – If you want to practice your timing, have someone throw a tennis ball for you and click each time it hits the ground. Another option is to watch a video and select a behavior (like someone speaking or lifting an arm). Hit the pause button each time you see this behavior.

Attention – Begin teaching your puppy to look at you (and give eye contact). Work with shaping this behavior. If you like when the behavior is being offered, you can put this behavior on cue with a word such as "watch" or you can leave it as a *default behavior* where the puppy will choose to look at you if it's not sure what else to do.

Dog's Name – If your puppy does not know his name yet, say your puppy's name, and when he turns to look at you, click and treat. Repeat this 20-50 times for the puppy to learn name recognition. (I teach the puppy's name separate from attention. For attention, I use the word "watch.")

Sit – Begin teaching your puppy to sit this week. Work with capturing this behavior. Click and treat every time you see your puppy sit! Before long, sits will be offered readily and just add the verbal cue "sit" prior to the behavior. We will also want to teach the hand signal.

Reading

Concepts:
Chapter 1 (p. 17-20)
Chapter 4:
    Training Concepts and Tips (p. 37)
    Guidelines for Beginning Clicker Training (p. 39)
    Motivation (p. 41)
    Reinforcers (p. 42)
    Getting the Behavior (p. 44)
    Adding the Cue (p. 49)
Chapter 5
    Developmental Stages (p. 64)
    Socializing Pups and Introducing Dogs to New Things (p. 70)
Chapter 10
    Crate Training (p. 153)
    Housetraining (p. 154)

Behaviors:
Charging the clicker (p. 39)
Dog's Name (p. 79)
Attention (p. 80)
Sit (p. 81)

Motivation Exercise:
After reading the section on "Motivation" in this book, select five things your puppy will work for enthusiastically. Now, gather these items and have them available for training sessions. (Example: real chicken, hot dogs, salmon treats, stuffed Kong, squeaky toy.)

Puppy Preschool Clicker Class
Session Two Homework

Socialization and Introduction to New Things:
Introduce your puppy to 5-10 new people this week.
Introduce your puppy to something new (example: broom, rake, etc.)

New Behaviors:
Settle – Begin teaching your puppy to "settle" in your lap this week as demonstrated in class. This means to calm down and lie quietly in your lap. It's important to be able to get your puppy to settle down when asked.

Come – Begin teaching "come" this week by using the relay game we went over in class. Remember moving quickly away from your puppy will help stimulate a come response. Be sure to keep your puppy safely indoors, in a yard, or on a leash until he or she understands how to come when called.

Redirecting Jumping Up – Work with the exercises we reviewed in class to begin teaching your puppy to sit to greet people instead of jumping.

Bite Inhibition – This week work on lessening the pressure of your puppy's mouthing. Begin yelping loudly or growling if your puppy mouths you hard enough to hurt. Read over the section on "Bite Inhibition" in this book.

Begin using your release word this week.

Review And Expand Behaviors:

Attention – If you would like to add a cue to this behavior, add "watch" this week. Review the section on "Attention" behavior in this book.

Sit – This week work with your puppy on "sit," using the hand signal and a verbal cue. If you captured this behavior, you have no lure to fade. If you started with luring, get rid of the food in your hand as soon as possible! Continue to click and treat as a reward.

Reading

Concepts:
Chapter 5
    Bite Inhibition (p. 65)
Chapter 4
        Generalization (p. 53)
        Distraction Training (p. 54)
Chapter 8
    Options for Dealing with Problem Behaviors (p. 127)

Chapter 9
    Jumping Up (p. 139)

Behaviors:
Settle (p. 102)
Come (p. 86)

Puppy Preschool Clicker Class
Session Three Homework

Socialization and Introduction to New Things
Introduce your puppy to 5-10 new people.
Introduce your puppy to something new that rolls (bicycle, skateboard, roller blades)
Introduce your puppy to a good-natured adult dog (check with friend, neighbor, family member)

New Behaviors:
Take Hold of Collar – Begin teaching your puppy to be comfortable having you take hold of her collar. Begin by reaching for your puppy's collar. If the puppy backs up, use less movement (reach partially towards the collar) until you can reach all the way and touch the collar. (Remember building a behavior through small increments is fine. Go ahead and take baby steps!) Eventually, you can ask your puppy to "sit" and, then, reach out and take hold of the collar before you click or treat. This exercise is designed to prevent the puppy from backing away when you reach for his collar.

Down – Begin teaching your puppy to lie down this week. This is another easy behavior to capture (like sit), or you can use a lure. Once she is getting the behavior, use your hand as the lure and get rid of the food in your hand. Small puppies and puppies with short legs can be guided under your leg as demonstrated in class to begin getting this behavior if necessary. For some "low rider dogs" like Dachshunds, luring is not all that effective because their nose is already on the ground!

Leave-It/Take-It – Begin teaching "leave-it/take-it" this week. Remember, there are three steps in teaching this behavior (closed hand, open hand, treat on floor). Make sure your puppy is successful at each step before you move on to the next step. Review this section in your book.

"Tug-and-Calm" Game
Begin teaching your puppy self-control. Read Chapter 4 of this book and play the "tug-and-calm" game as demonstrated in class.

Review And Expand Behaviors:
Settle – Begin getting your puppy to "settle" on the floor and on a leash this week.

Come – Continue working with "come" this week. Continue to move further apart on the relay game. You can add "hide & seek" this week.

Bite Inhibition – Work on lessening the pressure of your puppy's mouthing even more. We want them to think that people are so tender that they can hardly take any pressure at all. This week yelp or growl for any pressure whatsoever. Review the section on Bite Inhibition in Chapter 5 of this book.

Reading

Concepts:
Chapter 8
      Leadership (p. 132)
      Exercise (p. 137)
Chapter 3
      Teaching Your Dog Self-Control (p. 27)
      "Tug-and-Calm" Game (p. 31)

Behaviors:
Take Hold of Collar (p. 86)
Down (p. 83)
Leave-It/Take-It (p. 107)

Puppy Preschool Clicker Class
Session Four Homework

Socialization and Introduction to New Things:
Introduce your puppy to 5-10 new people.
Let your puppy do something new this week (stairs?)
Introduce your puppy to something that makes noise (vacuum, weed eater, leaf blower).

New Behaviors:
Touch – Begin teaching your puppy how to target this week by teaching the "touch" behavior. Wait until you have the behavior of your puppy touching his nose to your palm before you add the word "Touch." Review the "Touch" section in this book.

Stay – Review the "stay" exercises in this book. Begin teaching your puppy to "stay" this week. You can start with either a "sit-stay" or a "down-stay." Remember, young puppies have a hard time focusing for long so progress slowly on this behavior and set your puppy up for success.

Off – You can begin teaching your puppy the meaning of "off" this week. Get "off" the furniture (or whatever) when asked.

Handling – Begin handling exercises demonstrated in class (work with your puppy's ears, eyes, mouth, paws, tail, etc.) and continue for the rest of your dog's life!

Review And Expand Behaviors:
Settle – Begin by getting your puppy to "settle" while excited this week.
Down – This week, teach your puppy to lie down using the hand signal and a verbal cue. If you have lured this behavior, eliminate the treat as a lure and just use your hand. The hand-luring movement will transition into your hand signal. Continue to click and treat as a reward when your dog lies down.
Leave-It/Take-It – Continue progressing to step 2 of "leave-it" this week. Are you ready to place an open hand under your puppy's nose?

Reading

Concepts:
Chapter 5
   Handling (p. 66)
Chapter 9
   Digging (p. 146)

Behaviors:
Touch (p. 105-107)
Stay (p. 98)
Off (p. 110)

**Puppy Preschool Clicker Class
Session Five Homework**

Socialization and Introduction to New Things:
Introduce your puppy to 5-10 new people.
Introduce your puppy to things people carry or wear. (Example: hat, bags, sunglasses, umbrellas, uniforms, or Halloween costumes.)

New Behaviors:
Heel – Review the "Heel" section of this book. Begin teaching your puppy to "heel" with the target stick and the shaping method. Start in your living room, and then progress to the backyard or a safe, fenced area. Work this behavior off leash to begin with and, then, later add the leash. Since you have a very young puppy, now is a perfect time to teach "heel." If you teach "heel" from the beginning, there will be little need for teaching a loose leash walk. Your puppy will never learn to pull on the leash.

Let's Walk – If you have an older puppy, and you are already walking him on a leash, then practice with the techniques for teaching walking on a loose leash. If you decide to use a head collar or no-pull harness, you can, also, use that during the leash training exercises. Work in an area with a fairly low level of distractions (like right in front of your house on the sidewalk). Review the "Let's Walk" section of this book. Begin working with the stop and redirect and/or the goal method demonstrated in class.

Work Around the Food Bowl – Do some work and handling around the food bowl as discussed in class. Remember – adults only at first!

Introduce Self-Control Exercises: Calming Ovals, Parking, Getting From Point A to Point B.

Review And Expand Behaviors:
Touch-Target Stick – Make sure you've added the cue "touch" for the behavior touching your hand. Now, introduce your puppy to a target stick. Once the puppy is following the target readily and the behavior is on cue, you can begin using the target stick to teach "heel."

Stay – Continue working with "stay" this week. Have your puppy stay a little longer and move a little further from your puppy. Remember to progress slowly on this behavior for puppies.

Come – Continue working with your puppy on "come." This week move out to the backyard and make the distances even longer.

Leave-It – Teach Step 3 ("leave-it" even if it's on the floor)

Bite Inhibition – Begin using "leave-it" to decrease the frequency of mouthing.

Reading

Concepts:
Chapter 2
    Head Collars (p. 22)
    No-Pull Harnesses (p. 24)
Chapter 9
    Working Around the Food Bowl and Bones (p. 150)
    Barking (p. 147)

Behaviors:
Heel (p. 96)
Let's Walk (p. 91)
Calming Ovals (p. 28)
Parking (p. 30)
Getting From Point A to Point B (p. 30)

Puppy Preschool Clicker Class
Session Six Homework

Congratulations on completing Puppy Preschool Clicker Training! Your puppy has now been introduced to lots of different people (men, women and children) and lots of puppies. This is a very important part of socializing your puppy during her developmental stage when she will most readily accept new things. Your work is not over! Keep introducing your puppy to lots of people. Talk with friends, neighbors, and family members and also find some adult dogs (that have all their shots and a good temperament) and let your puppy continue to meet adult dogs as well as other puppies. If your puppy particularly liked another puppy in the class, consider setting up a "puppy play date" for your puppy. Also, continue introducing your puppy to new things and new experiences as well. You are off to a wonderful start with your new puppy having experienced Puppy Preschool.

However, training is not over! Your puppy has now learned to learn and is "clicker-wise." In addition, your puppy is developing a longer attention span. Your puppy is now moving out of the puppy stage into adolescence (yep, that's like a teenager!). Now is the time to continue training by bringing your puppy to a Puppy Enrichment or beginning dog training class: Elementary Clicker Training. In Puppy Enrichment Class, we will focus on teaching your puppy self-control and building confidence and a great relationship with you. In Elementary Clicker Class, we will continue working on the basic behaviors such as sit, down, stay, come, walk on a leash and leave-it. Now, the challenge is teaching your puppy to focus on you and learn to perform the right behaviors while distractions are present. Plus, your puppy will be able to be exposed to dogs of all ages in a beginning class. Don't stop now. Begin fine tuning your behaviors while further enhancing your relationship with your puppy.

New Behavior: Emergency Recall – Read "Really Reliable Recall" handout from Leslie Nelson, TAILS-U-WIN CANINE CENTER© (This behavior is covered in-depth in Elementary and Clicker High classes.) Also, refer to "Resources" for more information on available books by Leslie Nelson.

Elementary Clicker Training Class

Class Description

The Elementary Clicker Training Class is a 6-week class designed to teach people how to train their dogs to do basic behaviors including: sit, down, stand, heel, walk on a leash, come, stay, leave-it, and off. In addition, we discuss how to deal with issues such as jumping up on people, rushing out doors, digging, barking and chewing.

The focus of this class is for the dogs to learn to pay attention to their people as opposed to all the other dogs and distractions in the class. This is a great beginning level training class for dogs older than 18 weeks. Ideally, clients start with a Puppy Preschool then take a Puppy Enrichment before moving into Elementary Clicker Training. I find that the dogs and people, who have taken a previous clicker class, benefit even more from this class. However, if that is not possible, this is a good beginning-level training class.

The Elementary Clicker Class is also the basic class required before clients move on to more advanced training classes such as Clicker High, Musical Canine Freestyle, Rally-O or Agility.

Elementary Clicker Training Class
Syllabus & Homework

Syllabus

6-Week Class
(Class time: 1-1/2 hour people-only orientation + 1 hour per week for 5 weeks)

Class 1 – People-Only Orientation (1-1/2 hrs.)
- Introductions (brief introductions from clients & staff)
- Class information (location of restrooms, lending library, potty cleanup, etc.)
- Basics of Clicker Training
  Why use a clicker?
  Clicker Guidelines
  Motivation
  How to get a behavior (shaping, capturing, targeting, luring)
  Adding the cue
  Reinforcement (continuous versus variable)
  Catch them doing something right
- People Games
  Play the Training Game

Practice click timing (toss tennis ball, etc.)
Practice mechanical skills of clicking and treating (bean game)
- Discuss Leadership
- Discuss Exercise
- Discuss Self-Control
- Generalization & Distraction Training
- Brief introduction helpful equipment – head collars/no-pull harnesses – recommend checking out DVD/video
- What to bring to class (buckle collar, 6' leash, treats, dog, chewy)
- Demonstrate "Charging the Clicker"
- Demonstrate "Attention" (shape and capture)
- Demonstrate "Sit" (capture)
- Demonstrate Calming Ovals

Class 2 – Dogs' 1st Week (1 hour)
- Click and treat as many times as possible in one minute
- Review "Attention" (If you want to put on cue, are you ready?)
- Review "Sit" (Add verbal cue or hand signal?)
- Teach: Self-Control Exercises:
    "Calming Ovals"
    "Park"
    "Getting From Point A to Point B"
- Discuss Head Collars & No-pull harnesses briefly & fit for interested clients
    Discuss how to fit them, how to put them on and take them off
    General rules of using a head collar for "maintenance" walk to prevent pulling
    Suggest clients check-out Gentle Leader DVD/video
- Review basics (don't move hands, watch timing, reinforce often)
- Teach "Down"
- Teach "Leave-It/Take-It" (Step 1 – closed hand)
- Introduce Hand Signals
- Demonstrate Redirecting Jumping behavior by tethering and teaching "sit" for greeting people
- Discuss teaching an incompatible behavior (what to do, instead of what not to do)
- Teach trick: "Shake"

Class 3 (1 hour)
- Review "Down"
- Teach "Stand"
- Teach "Come"
- Discuss the concepts to teaching a reliable recall
    Relay Game
    Hide and Seek
    Tactics for getting dog back before they know their recall
- Teach "Off"

- Teach "Touch" (hand)
- Discuss management as a tool for problem behaviors
- Discuss how to minimize Digging/Chewing/Barking
- Demonstrate Self-Control Game "Tug and Calm"

Class 4 (1 hour)
- Teach "Take Hold of Collar"
- Discuss "Long Distance Recall"
    Use of long-line
    Working towards off-leash recall
- Review "Leave-It/Take-It" Step 2 (open hand)
- Introduce "Puppy Push-ups" (all 6 position changes)
    Sit – from stand and from down
    Down – from sit and from stand
    Stand – from sit and from down
- Review "Touch" – progress to step 2 using a target stick
- Demonstrate how to shape "Go to Bed"
- Teach "Stay"
    Discuss strengthening behavior with additional duration, distance, distractions
    over time
- Discuss withdrawing attention (time out) as a way to deal with problem behaviors
- Teach trick: "Bow" or "Spin"

Class 5 (1 hour)
- Review "Leave-It/Take-It" – add Step 3 – treat on floor
- Teach "Let's Walk"
    Stop-Redirect, Goal Method, Luring, Catch Me
- Teach "Heel"
    Targeting method
    Shaping a "Heel"
    Discuss "Heel" covered more in-depth in Clicker High
- Discuss body blocking techniques
- Demonstrate "Wait" – momentarily pause and do not move forward
- Demonstrate how to prevent "Door Rushing" – teaching stay/wait at the door
- Demonstrate handling (mouth, ears, paws, tail, etc.)
- Discuss how to use an interrupt and redirect
- Discuss why harsh punishment is not advisable

Class 6 – Graduation (1 hour)
- Introduce Emergency Recall – distribute handout from Leslie Nelson, TAILS-U-
  WIN CANINE CENTER© (Discussed more in-depth training in Clicker High and
  "Come" mini-seminars.)
- Introduce a Shaping Exercise – (example: ring bell or sneeze and take tissue)
- Discuss exercises around the food bowl to work with or prevent food possession

- Fading the clicker and treats
- Mastering a few important cues (come, stay, attention, sit, walk on leash)
- Taking the training on the road (generalization & distractions)
- Socialization & Desensitization
- Additional training opportunities
     Next Level Class: Clicker High, Musical Freestyle, Agility, Rally-O, or Mini-Seminars
     Other Activities: See Appendix 3 in Book (CGC, Therapy Dog, Tracking, Herding, etc.)
- Games & prizes
- Graduation Ceremony; certificates, photos, prizes, refreshments
- Sign-up for next class

Elementary Clicker Training Class
Session One Homework

Before beginning training, please review "General Training Tips" and "Guidelines for Beginning Clicker Training" in this book and apply these principles during training this week. Charge the clicker only the first time you introduce your dog to the clicker. It does not need to be done again.

New Behaviors:
Attention – Shape eye contact and your dog checking in with you. Read over the "Attention" section in this book and work on shaping this behavior. It's easy and fun. When your dog is offering the behavior readily, if you choose you may add a cue such as "Watch" or you can allow this to be a default behavior.

Sit – Work with capturing the sit behavior. Simply click and treat each time you see your dog sitting. Soon this behavior will be readily offered! If your dog already sits on cue, practice asking for the behavior and then clicking and treating.
For this week, click and treat EVERY time your dog performs the behavior.

The Training Game – Play the Training Game at least twice. Be the "dog" once and be the "trainer" once. You will learn a lot playing this game!

Timing Game – If you want to practice your timing, have someone throw a tennis ball for you and click each time it hits the ground. Another option is to watch a video and select a behavior (like someone speaking or lifting an arm). Hit the pause button each time you see this behavior.

Mechanical Skills – Practice clicking and treating as we did in class. Take a handful of kibble and see how many clicks and treats (placed in a bowl) you can master in one minute.

Calming Ovals – Begin walking your dog in the oval pattern as demonstrated in class.

Reading

Concepts:
Chapter 1 (p. 17-20)
Chapter 2 (p. 21)
Chapter 3
    Teaching Your Dog Self-Control (p. 27)
Chapter 4
    Training Concepts and Tips (p. 37)
    Guidelines for Beginning Clicker Training (p. 39)
    The Training Game (p. 41)
    Motivation (p. 41)
    Reinforcers (p. 42)
    Getting the Behavior (p. 44)
    Adding the Cue (p. 49)
    Varying the Reinforcement Schedule and Rewards (p. 51)
    Generalization (p. 53)
    Distraction Training (p. 54)
Chapter 8
    Leadership (p. 132)
    Exercise (p. 137)

Behaviors:
"Charging the Clicker" (p. 39)
Calming Ovals (p. 28)
Attention (p. 80)
Sit (p. 81)

Motivation Exercise:
After reading the section on "Motivation" in your handbook, make a list in priority order of five things your dog will work for enthusiastically. Now, gather these items and have them available for training sessions. (Example: real chicken, roast beef, stuffed Kong, ball, tug toy.)

Elementary Clicker Training Class
Session Two Homework

Continue your daily training sessions.

New Behaviors:
Self-Control Exercises – Practice "Calming Ovals" and "Parking" this week to help teach your dog self-control. Also practice walking "Getting From Point A to Point B" when necessary.

Head Collar/No-Pull Harness – If you are using a head collar, or no-pull harness spend time getting your dog used to the new equipment this week, including walking when wearing the device. If you walk your dog this week, use your head collar or harness, keeping your dog fairly close to you. Do not allow pulling and do not use an extendable leash for teaching walking. Pick a side to walk your dog on, either left or right. The left side is the most commonly used side. Be consistent, whichever side you choose. Just get your dog used to the new equipment and practice walking as demonstrated in class. We will progress further with this behavior in two weeks.

Down – Teach your dog to lie down on cue this week. Read over the "Down" section in this book. You can work with capturing this behavior, shaping it or luring it. If you lure, fade the food as quickly as possible.

Leave-it/Take-It – Review this section of your handbook. Begin teaching "leave-it" and "take-it." Progress to the next level only after your dog is successful at the current level. For instance, start with a closed fist (step 1) and make sure that's working before progressing to an open hand (step 2). If your dog is having problems, drop back to the prior step and reinforce that behavior before moving on.

Problem Behavior – Jumping Up – Review this section of this book, and use one of the methods outlined to begin teaching your dog to sit to greet people. I prefer the tether method as you can avoid the jumping up behavior altogether and, therefore, bypass possibly reinforcing a chained behavior of jump up and, then, sit.

Trick – "Shake"

Review Behaviors:
Attention – If you want to add a cue to this behavior, you can add "watch" this week. Otherwise, this can be trained as a default behavior. Have your dog look at you progressively longer. You can also begin moving a little and see if your dog can keep attention on you while you move slightly (back and forth to start).

Sit – Continue reviewing sit. If you are getting the sit behavior readily, you can add the cue (hand signal or verbal) if you're ready, and begin helping your dog generalize by changing location/body posture, etc.

Reading

Concepts:
Chapter 2
    Head Collars (p. 22)
    No-Pull Harness (p. 24)
Chapter 8
    Train a Different Behavior (p. 128)
Chapter 9
    Jumping Up (p. 139)

Behaviors:
Down (p. 83)
Leave-It/Take-It (p. 107)
Shake (p. 120)

Review:
"Parking Your Dog" (p. 30)
"Getting From Point A to Point B" (p. 30)

Exercise:
My dog's distracted by ...
Write down everything that distracts your dog, from a leaf falling to a car to something you can't get her away from. Instead of saying "my dog won't do this when ...," let's work on making the distractions a part of our training. Prioritize distractions with 1 being least distracting and a 10 being very distracting. Now, you can introduce distractions in a systematic way. Don't go from a 1 to a 10. You need to move systematically from least distracting to most distracting. Do not put your dog in a situation where the distraction is greater than her level of training. Remember, we want to set our dogs up for success. If you've moved too quickly, don't blame your dog! For now, the rule will be the higher the distraction the better the treat!

Elementary Clicker Training Class
Session Three Homework

New Behaviors:
Come – Use one or more of the exercises outlined in the section on "Come" to begin teaching your dog to come on cue. Do call your dog to dinner, click and treat. If you call your dog during the week, be ready to click and treat (even if it's not an official training session). If your dog does not come to you, do not call again. Wait and if possible set up a new training situation where you're more likely to have success, and then call her. Do not call your dog for anything unpleasant. I suggest you do not let your dog out in an unfenced area until you have a reliable response to "come."

Stand – Work with teaching your dog to stand. You can simply capture this behavior or lure it.

Off – Teach your dog how to get up and "off" a piece of furniture or raised wall or other area this week.

Touch – Review the instructions for "touch" in this book. Start working on targeting this week by teaching your dog to touch your hand. This is a really fun behavior, and there are lots of fun things to teach your dog with it as we go on.

Quiet – Begin teaching your dog what "quiet" means this week. Review the section on "Barking" in this book.

Tug and Calm – Play the game as demonstrated in class.

Review:
Review "Down." Are you ready for a verbal cue or hand signal?

Continue your 5-10 minute training sessions at least twice daily. Continue strengthening and working on all the behaviors we've already learned: attention, sit, down, stand, and take collar.

Be sure to have your dog work in different locations in the house and perhaps, even the backyard on behaviors you've worked on for several weeks. Also, begin changing your orientation to your dog. For instance, have your dog sit or lie down on your left side instead of in front of you. Change your body posture also. If you've been standing, sit down and ask your dog to sit or lie down.

If you haven't added the cue yet to any behaviors from the last two weeks, decide if it's time. Review the section on "Adding the Cue" in this book.

Remember to incorporate training into your life. Have your dog do a behavior (such as sit, down, stand – vary them!) before serving his meal, before going outdoors, etc. Consider hiding some treats around the house and surprising your dog at unexpected times when he does something right.

Reading

Concepts:
Chapter 8
    Options For Dealing With Problem Behaviors (p. 127)
Chapter 9
    Chewing (p. 144)
    Digging (p. 146)
    Barking (p. 147)

Behaviors:
Come (p. 86)
Stand (p. 84)
Touch (p. 105)
Off (p. 110)
Quiet – Barking (p. 147)
"Tug-and-Calm" Game (p. 31)

Elementary Clicker Training Class
Session Four Homework

New Behaviors:

Take Hold of Collar – Work with your dog on "take hold of collar" this week.

Long-Distance Recall – You can continue increasing the distance between two people on the relay "come" exercise we learned. This week you should be able to put your dog within a fenced area, attach the long line, and call your dog from increasing distances. Once you've worked in a fenced area, in subsequent weeks, you can move eventually to the front yard, park, beach, etc. If your dog does not respond, you can ignore her for a short time before performing the exercise again. Set yourself up for success, so you may need to move closer this time and, perhaps, have a better treat. Remember do not call your dog to punish her. I do not recommend letting your dog off leash outside a fenced area until you have a reliable recall.

Stay – Review the instructions on "stay" in this book. Work with stay this week. Your goal is to work up to a 30 second stay while standing up to 10 feet away. Remember work on time and distance and distractions separately and progress slowly. Start with your dog either in a down or a sit (whichever your dog likes best). Once you have a stay in that position, begin working the other position. For instance, if you started with "down, stay," progress to "sit-stay" as soon as you have a reliable "down-stay."

Go to Bed – Shape this behavior as demonstrated in class. Review this section in this book. This is a great exercise to teach self-control, so don't skip it.

Puppy Push-ups – You can begin practicing "sit," "down," and "stand" in a series of behaviors which we call "Puppy Push-ups." Remember, your dog can sit from a stand or a down; they can lie down from either a sit or a stand, and stand up from a sit or a down.

Tug-and-Calm Game – Play the self-control game "Tug and Calm" and begin teaching your dog how to bring down his own arousal level.

Trick-"Bow" or "Spin"

Review and Expand:

Touch-Target Stick – Make sure your dog can do a hand "touch" and that you've added the cue. Now, introduce a target stick. Have him touch, and then follow the target stick.

Leave-it/Take-it – Progress to Step 2 of "Leave-It/Take-It" using an open hand.

Continue progressing with the behaviors we have worked on so far: attention, sit, down, stand, touch, leave-it/take-it and come. Review the individual instructions on each of these and progress accordingly. Is your dog performing these behaviors consistently? Have you added the cue? Generalize behaviors by moving around the house, changing your orientation to your dog and using different postures (for example, you sit instead of stand) when you give the cue. Remember to use your release word such as "go play!" when the training session is over. Also, be sure to do your training before you feed the morning or evening meal. If your dog is hungry, he or she will pay closer attention to you. Also, start working with problem behaviors as appropriate when they occur and set them up in a training session.

Reading

Concepts:
Chapter 2
   Long Lines (p. 25)
Chapter 4
   Shaping Guidelines (p. 46)
   Varying the Reinforcement Schedule and Rewards (p. 51)
Chapter 8
   Remove something pleasant (negative punishment) (p. 129)

Behaviors:
Take Hold of Collar (p. 86)
Puppy Push-ups (p. 85)
Long Distance Recall (p. 89)
Go to Bed (p. 103)
Stay (p. 98)
Leave-It/Take-It – Step 2 (p. 107)
Bow (p. 124)
Spin (p. 125)

**Elementary Clicker Training Class
Session Five Homework**

New Behaviors:
Let's Walk – Read over "Let's Walk" in your book. Choose a method you want to use: Stop/Redirect, Goal Method, Luring, or Catch Me. You can use all of these methods and inter-mix them in a training session. Begin walking your dog on leash. Remember, you want to teach your dog to walk on a loose leash, so the leash must have some slack in it. Begin working on walking 10 feet or so, then increase the distance to 20 feet. Use your head collar or no-pull harness if you have one. Click and treat often for a loose leash.

Heel – You can also choose to teach your dog to heel. One method is to use the target stick in which case you must teach "touch" first. You can also use the shaping method. I usually teach this behavior off lead in a safe, fenced area (or even the house at first). Once you add the leash, remember generalization, and work with your dog a little while with a leash until he understands heel is both for off-leash and on-leash work.

Door Rushing – Read over the section on "Door Rushing" in this book. Decide whether you will work on a "sit-stay" or a "wait" cue at the door. Work with your dog to make sure she either sits and stays or waits (does not move forward) at the door until she is invited out. When working with problem behaviors, remember you need to be consistent. You cannot let your dog barrel out the door one minute and expect her to stay quietly the next. Work on this every time you leave. Also, set up specific training sessions several times this week to work on waiting or staying at the door.

Wait – Work with "wait" when getting in and out of the car, or going out a gate, door, etc.

Handling – This week start working with your dog's paws and tail, and begin to slowly desensitize your dog to nail clipping or filing, grooming, or bathing.

Review & Expand:
"Leave-It/Take-It" – Progress to Step 3 this week, placing the food item on the floor in front of your shoe.

Continue practicing and progressing on all behaviors learned to date. Review the applicable section in this book on each behavior to determine how to progress. Make sure you are not luring too often. If your dog is still requiring a lure, work towards fading the lure. Offer it less and less often. Offer hand signals to help your dog; they are a natural outgrowth of the luring movement. If your dog will not perform without food, "turn the tables." Lure with food, then praise, but do not click and treat. Now, lure without food; if you get the behavior, click and treat. This will change the whole game and may get your dog performing without a lure.

Reading

Concepts:
Chapter 5
    Handling (p. 66)
    Body Blocking (p. 69)
Chapter 8
    Interrupt and redirect behaviors (p. 130)

Behaviors:
Let's Walk (p. 91)
Heel (p. 96)
Wait (p. 112)
Door Rushing (p. 142)
Leave-It/Take-It Step 3 (p. 107)

Elementary Clicker Training Class
Session Six Homework

Congratulations on completing the six-week dog training course! Now, you know quite a bit about training. The good news is this is only the beginning of a wonderful relationship between you and your dog.

You and your dog have been introduced to many new behaviors during this training course. Some of you may not be interested in working on all of the behaviors we've covered. At a minimum, pick a few of the most important behaviors (such as sit, come, stay and walk) and master these few behaviors. You will find your life is much easier with your dog once he will respond to these basic cues.

Now that your dog has learned to learn, it will become easier to teach new behaviors or tricks. It's fun to continue training your dog by reviewing exercises they already know to keep them proficient and also training new tricks and behaviors just for the fun of it. Understanding how to communicate and how to train your dog using positive reinforcement and a clicker, the possibilities are limitless!

Take it on the Road

Now that your dog is performing the behaviors in familiar areas, the next step is to "take it on the road" by working your dog in new situations and in different locations with greater distractions. Begin with the lowest level of distractions and "set up" training sessions, progressing to more intense distractions. Do not jump from a 1st degree distraction to a 10, or you will be setting your dog up for failure. Move slowly through greater and greater distractions while working your dog. Remember, you may have to "go back to kindergarten" and lower your criteria and make it easier in the beginning. Don't worry though, as your dog will catch on much quicker now. The basic rule is, the greater the distraction, the better the treat! Work up to your front yard, the park, the beach, etc. Once you have reliable response to the cue, you can begin to eventually fade the clicker and short-term reward. I always continue to reinforce my dog although the rewards are now delayed, and it's certainly not always food – we can choose also from "life rewards," praise and toys and games. I always dust off my clicker to teach a new trick or behavior, or if I'm taking my dog into a tough situation with lots of distractions (like the vet).

New Behavior:
Practice the *Emergency Recall* we went over in class. This behavior is practiced in-depth in the Clicker High Class.

Additional Training – There are so many wonderful things to do with your dog these days. Consider contacting trainers or dog groups in your area and select something entertaining to do with your dog. See "Activities to do with Your Dog" in Appendix 3.

Reading

Concepts:
Chapter 4
    Fading the Clicker and treats (p. 60)
Chapter 5
    Socializing Puppies and Introducing Older Dogs to New Situations (p. 70)
Chaper 9
    Working around the food bowl (p. 150)
Resources
    Review the "Resources" section in Appendix 4, and see if there is a book or video of interest (p. 202).

Behaviors:
Emergency Recall (see handout) from Leslie Nelson, TAILS-U-WIN CANINE CENTER©
Refer to "Resources" for more information from Leslie Nelson.

Private In-Home Training Sessions

Private in-home training sessions are tailored to meet the client's needs. Most clients require from one to six sessions depending on what they need help with. Some clients do not have the time or inclination to travel for group classes. Other clients find that their dog, if reactive, does better to start in private sessions. Some clients only have one or two issues to work on such as barking, digging or housetraining. Private classes to teach the basics including: attention, sit, down, stay, come, walk on a leash or heel, and leave-it, generally require at least three private sessions. If the client is experiencing behavioral problems with the dog such as jumping up on people, door rushing, digging, barking or chewing in addition to the need for basic behavior training, these issues may require an additional session. If the client is experiencing either significant fear issues or aggression, three sessions may be just a start. It's very possible that additional sessions would be required depending on the issue.

Appendix 2

Glossary of Training Cues
and Training Terms

Glossary of Training Cues

Attention	The dog looks you straight in the eyes and focuses on you instead of the environment. Some people use a cue such as "Watch" while others prefer this be taught as a default behavior.
Come	Your dog comes to you immediately.
Down	Your dog lies down either with four legs underneath or on his side.
Go to Bed	The dog goes to a mat, blanket or doggie bed, lies down and stays until released. The mat, blanket or doggie bed can be moved to different locations.
Give-It	Your dog releases an item from his mouth and places it in your hand.
Heel	Your dog walks next to your left leg and sits when you stop. Ideally, this will become an off-leash as well as an on-leash behavior.
Leave-It	Your dog is to leave whatever he's doing and back off. Do not sniff or investigate any further. Turn away.
Let's Walk	The dog is to walk on a loose leash without pulling.
Off	This means your dog should remove any part of himself from objects or people. This is used to let your dog know you want him off the furniture, counter, or off your lap.
Settle	Your puppy immediately calms down and lies down quietly.
Sit	The dog places his hindquarters on the ground.
Stand	Stand with four feet on the floor.
Stay	Your dog is to remain in one place and in the same position until released or asked to do something different. (Can be used with sit, down or stand.)
Take Hold of Collar	This exercise is designed to prevent the puppy from backing away when you reach for his or her collar.

Take-It	Your dog takes what is in your hand, such as a food treat or a toy.
Touch	Your dog touches your hand or the end of a stick with his nose. This is a way to teach targeting behavior where your dog will touch or follow your hand or a stick. This can be used to teach your dog to focus on a particular location or object and can be a great aid in teaching behaviors such as an off-lead heel or various tricks.
Release	Use a word to let your dog know that the behavior or training session is over such as "go play," "finished," "done," "that'll do," "break" or "release."
Wait	Your dog stops forward motion. (He can change position – sit, down, or stand – just not move forward.)

Glossary of Training Terms

Classical Conditioning (also called *Respondent* or *Pavlovian Conditioning*) Classical Conditioning specifies that the animal responds to his environment without conscious actions. His action does not affect the consequences. The dog hears the doorbell ring. The ringing bell tells him someone has arrived and the door will open. He is conditioned to expect visitors when he hears the doorbell ring (see Operant Conditioning also).

Conditioned (Secondary) Reinforcer – Something that is connected with a primary reinforcer and which takes on pleasant properties due to this connection. For us, money is the ultimate conditioned reinforcer, because it can be used to buy many primary reinforcers. For dogs, the clicker can be a secondary reinforcer, which means an award is available. Or, when you take your dog for a walk and you bring out the leash and he gets very excited. The leash has become a conditioned reinforcer, which means a walk is coming.

Continuous Reinforcement – Giving a reward for each and every correct behavior.

Default Behavior – A behavior offered by your dog in lieu of a cued behavior or when they are not sure what else to do.

Jackpot – An extra large and unexpected bonus. Used to communicate to the dog that the response was excellent.

Luring – Use of a Primary Reinforcer to cause the animal to perform a behavior. Example: Luring a dog into sit with a treat in your hand held above his head and slowly moved backward.

Negative Reinforcement – A negative reinforcement is an ongoing, unpleasant event that your dog will attempt to avoid. The negative reinforcement is applied until the dog performs the desired behavior, then, it is removed. A negative reinforcement is intended to increase behavior. An example is the "ear pinch," used by some trainers to get a dog to pick-up the dumbbell. His ear is pinched until he picks it up, and, then, the ear is released.

Nose-Tease – Briefly offering a treat and then removing it. Communicates that a payoff is available if the dog figures out what behavior to offer. For example, place a treat in your hand, hold it up to your dog's nose and then hide the treat behind your back.

Positive Reinforcement – A positive reinforcer is something that your dog will work to obtain and that is meant to increase the behavior it follows. Food and toys are two examples of powerful positive reinforcers.

Primary Reinforcer – Anything the animal will work for. For example, food, play, freedom, and praise.

Punishment – Punishment is used to decrease the behavior it follows. There are two kinds of punishment. Positive punishment is the application of something unpleasant after the undesired behavior. An example is spritzing a dog with a spray of water from a water pistol. Negative punishment is the removal of something pleasant after the undesired behavior. An example is removing your hand if a puppy is play-biting on it.

Reinforcer – Anything that brings about an increase or repetition of a behavior.

Secondary (Conditioned) Reinforcer – Something that is connected with a primary reinforcer and which takes on pleasant properties due to this connection. For us, money is the ultimate conditioned reinforcer because it can be used to buy many primary reinforcers. For dogs, the clicker can be a secondary reinforcer, which means an award is available. Or, when you take your dog for a walk and you bring out the leash and they get very excited. The leash has become a conditioned reinforcer, which means a walk is coming.

Shaping – The process of reinforcing approximations of a desired behavior and raising the criteria required to earn a reinforcement until the desired behavior is achieved.

Stimulus – Anything that can be sensed by the dog. Examples are sounds (click), light, etc.

Variable Reinforcement Schedule – A variable number of responses is required to earn reinforcement. For humans, an example is a slot machine. For dogs, an example is asking for a "two-fer" (two behaviors before you reward) or a "three-fer" (three behaviors before reward.)

Appendix 3

Other Activities To Do With Your Dog

Thirty years ago when I first got into training my German Shepherd mix, Shanti, pretty much all that was available to do with your dog was conformation shows or formal obedience through the American Kennel Club (AKC), which only allowed purebred dogs. There were not many options for fun activities to do with your dog.

My, how things have changed! Now, there are so many wonderful sports and activities that you can do with your dog; the sky's the limit! For one thing, there are opportunities with mixed breeds through the American Mixed Breed Owner Registry (AMBOR) which was founded in 1983. In 1994, they reached an agreement with the United Kennel Club (UKC) allowing mixed breeds into UKC events. Now, owners of mixed breeds have many more opportunities to participate in events such as agility or obedience.

Below, I'll highlight just a sampling of some of the fun things you can do with your dog. It's best to search the internet for more up-to-date information.

When Teah and Hally discovered Musical Canine Freestyle, they both loved it immediately. When you find an activity where you have fun with your dog, pursue it! Your relationship will naturally improve as a result of the training, and, simultaneously, your strong relationship will make training easier and more fun.

Musical Canine Freestyle – Musical Canine Freestyle is a choreographed musical program performed by handlers and their dogs. In simple terms, it's dancing with dogs to music! It's a fun sport for dogs and their people, and the audiences love it! We incorporate basic obedience behaviors, rally-o and tricks along with other dimensions such as music, timing, costuming, routine development and showmanship to put together programs. These programs can be performed in the privacy of your own home, to compete for titles or just to please a crowd. Musical Canine Freestyle beautifully demonstrates the joys and fun of bonding with your dog! Organizations you can contact for more information include: World Canine Freestyle Organization (WCFO), Musical Dog Sports Association (MDSA), Canine Freestyle Federation (CFF).

Agility – The sport of dog agility involves a handler guiding their dog around an obstacle course which is judged on the basis of speed and accuracy. Each unique course is made up of standard obstacles including jumps of various types, tunnels, weave poles, a pause table, and the contact obstacles of an A-frame for climbing, a dog walk for traversing, and a teeter-totter for balance. Training involves teaching the dog individual obstacles, learning handling maneuvers to move around the course, and how to get your dog to respond to those handling cues. In competition, handlers walk the course without the dog and memorize the 14-20 obstacle pattern while planning a handling strategy. After the walk through, each dog and handler team, in turn, runs the course while being timed and judged. Everyone who runs the course correctly within the allotted time earns a qualifying score. Dogs compete against other dogs of similar size, and jumps are set according to their height. Serious competitors like to train dogs with a lot of enthusiasm for work, but all dogs can have fun at this sport as the number of venues, levels of competitions, and variety of games provide plenty of opportunities for everyone.

Agility has become a very popular dog sport, for fun or for competition. The activity can help build a dog's confidence and establish teamwork and communication between handlers and their dogs. Dogs of all shapes and sizes can have fun with Agility.

www.usdaa.com
www.akc.org
www.cleanrun.com
www.nadac.com

Tracking/Trailing – This is the foundation work of canine search and rescue and involves training dogs to use their highly developed sense of smell to find lost humans or animals, detect drugs, bombs or other animals. Tracking dogs are used in police K-9 tracking, search & rescue trailing, sport tracking, and for recreation. Dogs are also now being used in research projects to detect and sniff out cancer in patients! Tracking titles can be earned through the American Kennel Club (AKC).

Rally Obedience (Rally-O) – Rally-O is a fun, challenging sport that showcases the teamwork between dogs and their people and is a more relaxed competition than traditional obedience. It is often used as a bridge towards traditional obedience where the team learns to be comfortable in the ring doing prescribed exercises. Rally is like a board game where the team walks to each station in a heel position and completes the exercise requested. Humans are allowed to talk and/or use hand signals to show their dog what is expected at each station. Dogs seem to enjoy this game because they can be constantly cheered on and praised for their efforts. All the exercises learned in Rally-O are useful to make you and your dog better partners in everyday living. Some people just like to work with their dogs in learning these exercises towards a stronger bond, and some want to go on to compete for Rally- O titles. Rally-O is a sport that is open to anyone who wants to achieve a higher level of training with their dog and have a lot of fun while doing it.

AKC's Canine Good Citizen (CGC) Program – The CGC is a certification program designed to reward dogs who can pass a CGC test showing that they have good manners in public and at home. The CGC Program stresses responsible pet ownership for people and good manners for dogs. Dogs that pass the 10-step CGC test may receive a certificate from the American Kennel Club. The CGC is often a first step towards pursuing more formal training in obedience or other dog sports or working towards a therapy dog certification. Obtaining your CGC is a nice goal for family pet owners. Contact www.AKC.org for CGC evaluators in your area.

Service Dogs – Service dogs assist children and adults with disabilities. Guide dogs help the blind or visually impaired; hearing alert dogs assist the hearing impaired by alerting to important sounds; mobility assistance dogs help handlers who need help balancing or are in a wheelchair and need assistance with many other items (picking things up; hitting the elevator button, turning lights on); seizure/alert response dogs respond to a person's seizures and either alert to a seizure or go get help; psychiatric service dogs assist people with disabilities such as agoraphobia (fear of going out in public) and help to keep the handler calm or may help an autistic person to stay focused or distract the owner from repetitive movements.

Herding – Over time a number of breeds have been developed to help with the stock management practices. Many herding breeds can be instinct-tested for herding ability, for a small fee. From there, they may pursue a long and rewarding journey learning "stock dog training." Some breeds were bred for herding cattle, like the Corgi's, and Australian Cattle Dogs. Some were bred for sheep herding such as the Border Collie. Each breed can be trained for trial on stock in the different venue such as American Herding Breed Association (AHBA), Australian Shepherd Club of America, Inc. (ASCA) and AKC, as well as for actual ranch work. It is important to find a trainer who can work with your particular breed of dog and work with its individual herding ability.

Therapy Dogs – Therapy dogs and their handlers work together to bring joy and comfort to patients in hospitals, nursing homes, and retirement homes. They also visit child day care centers, and go to libraries to help children learn to read. A very rewarding experience for both you and your dog, and the people you visit. Check out Therapy Dog International (TDI) or Delta Society online.

Frisbee – On the surface, playing Frisbee with your dog may seem like just a bit of fun, but it actually holds many other benefits as well. A bored dog may tend to create their own interesting diversions to entertain themselves. At times, their idea of fun may be something that you consider to be destructive behavior. Playing Frisbee with your dog may help to curb some of your dog's destructive behavior by giving your pup an outlet for all of his pent-up energy. There are competitive events related to this sport. For more information contact the International Disc Dog Handler's Association (IDDHA).

Search and Rescue Dogs – Search and Rescue Dogs are specifically trained dogs that are used in searching for victims trapped in rubble created by earthquakes or explosions, Alzheimer's patients who have wandered away, children who have become lost, victims of boating accidents, evidence in criminal cases, and even assisting in locating lost pets.

Schutzhund – Schutzhund is a German word meaning "protection dog." The purpose of Schutzhund is to demonstrate the dog's intelligence and utility. It also measures the dog's mental stability, endurance, structural efficiencies, ability to scent, willingness to work, courage, and trainability. Schutzhund work concentrates on three elements: obedience, tracking, and protection work similar to what police dogs do. Look up the United Schutzhund Clubs of America, and AKC "Working Dog Sport" online.

Flyball – Flyball is a relay race with four dogs per team. Dogs spring over a series of jumps, run to a box, and step on a pedal which flips a tennis ball from inside. The dogs catch or retrieve the ball and return over the jumps to the start/finish line. Then, the next eager dog is released until all four dogs have successfully completed the run. The team with the fastest time wins the race. It is a fast and exciting sport, not only for the handlers and their dogs, but for the spectators as well. Any dog may compete and earn titles awarded by the North American Flyball Association. There are competitions held all over the world.

Carting – From competition carting where dog and handler go through a series of maneuvers, to pulling festive carts in parades, giving cart rides to kids, and helping with yard work by loading clippings and leaves into the cart. Cart pulling is an activity that can be enjoyed by the entire family.

Weight Pulling – Just as we have tractor pulls, and horse pulls, we also have weight pulling competitions for dogs. Weight pulling is a sport in which your dog, wearing a specially designed harness, pulls a load for a set distance within a specified amount of time.

Dog Pulling – Skis, Bicycles, Rollerblades, Scooters, – Dogs pull for recreation and exercise. Skijoring involves one to three dogs hitched directly to a person on cross-country skis. Hitch your dog to your bike, and you have bikjoring, hitch your dog to your rollerblades, and you have bladejoring. Have them pull a scooter and you're doing dog scootering! With a proper harness and training cues such as left, right (gee and haw), stop and go, the possibilities are endless.

Sled Dogs/Mushing – Sled dogs are a group of dogs that are used to pull sleds or toboggans over snow or ice. Mushing can also be done with wheeled rigs when there is no snow. The Iditarod Sled Dog Race, held every first Saturday in March in Alaska since 1973, has popularized the sport. You might look up the Alaska Dog Musher's Association for more information on races.

Earthdog trials – Many terriers are bred to go to ground and flush out the quarry from its den or earth. Most terriers are not bred to kill the quarry. Dachshunds are also bred to go to ground. Earthdog tests are designed to enable dogs bred for this work to be assessed on their natural ability to do the task when presented with an underground hunting situation. A mock den is laid in the ground – the dog must pick up the pre-laid scent, arrive at the quarry, and work the quarry for a given time. The hunting encounter is controlled and neither dog nor quarry, a rat, are in any real danger.

Hunt and Field Trials – Hunting situations are simulated and dogs are judged against a standard. The simulations can involve difficult hunting situations and often at long distances requiring excellent marking, trainability, and drive from the dog. Refer to AKC for more information on titling events in this sport.

Dock Diving – The idea of dock diving sprang from dock workers waging bets on how far their dogs could jump into the water. A dog who loves water, and a favorite ball or toy, is all you need to compete. The handler throws the ball or toy into the water and lets his dog loose to jump. The length of the jump is measured to determine the "winner."

Hiking/Backpacking with your dog is an excellent way to get away from the routines and commitments of daily life. Most dogs love to get out and enjoy the sights and scents on the trail. Packing is a wonderful way to enjoy the world through the eyes, nose, and ears of a dog.

Walking or Running – Put on your athletic shoes, hook up your leash and enjoy the health benefits to both you and your dog by going for a run or a vigorous walk. Equipment such as hands-free leashes, and reflective clothing for you and reflective collars and leashes for your dog, are available to make evening exercising safe and fun.

Dog Camps – Dog camps allow you to spend vacation time with your dog and other dog enthusiasts. While some camps are geared towards specific dog sports, others offer a variety of activities and sports to explore with your canine companion.

Obedience Trials – Obedience trials test a dog's ability to perform specific exercises, and recognizes the dog's ability to perform those exercises in public, and among other dogs. AKC offers competitions for registered, purebred dogs only. UKC offers competitions that can include purebred and some that can include mixed breeds through an agreement with AMBOR.

Conformation Shows – Conformation shows are intended to evaluate breeding stock. Along with the thrill of competition, there is the opportunity to see some beautiful dogs. Conformation events, for registered, unaltered, purebred dogs only, are held at All-Breed Shows, Specialty Shows (restricted to a specific breed), or Group Shows (restricted to a specific grouping of dogs, such as working breeds, sporting breeds, etc.). See AKC or UKC for more information.

Lure Coursing – Sighthound breeds including Greyhounds, Whippets, Borzoi and Ridgebacks are eligible to participate in lure coursing trials. In lure coursing, dogs run three at a time and follow an artificial lure around a pre-determined course pattern. Coursing dogs are scored on speed, enthusiasm, agility, endurance and their ability to follow the lure. Lure coursing is truly an exciting sport and is almost as much fun for the handlers as it is for the hounds. For more information on lure coursing check out the AKC website and the American Sighthound Field Association (ASFA).

Appendix 4

Resources

Books

When I started writing this book and resource guide for my students in 2000, there were only a few books published on the subject of clicker training. Now, there are many great books about clicker training, positive dog training, and dog behavioral issues. And more great books and DVDs are becoming available all the time! Listed below are some of my favorite, current authors of dog training material, and some of the books I've personally read. Please note that this is in no way a complete list of books I could recommend. Instead, this is a list of the books I most commonly recommend to my clients. There are, of course, many more books that can be helpful once the handler understands the basics of training. It's best to search the internet for up-to-date information on what's available.

Books by Kay Laurence (www.learningaboutdogs.com)

Kay is one of my favorite trainers. She combines incredible knowledge and insight about dogs, with a profound understanding of how and why clicker training is so effective, topped off by a wonderful ability to communicate with the human species! I recommend anything by Kay Laurence! Listed below are a few of my favorites that I have available for my students:

Clicker Foundation Training – She explains the basics of how and why clicker training works and gets you started with targeting and shaping skills.
Clicker Novice Training – This book builds on the behaviors you started in the previous book and gives you more insight into shaping to acquire precision behaviors and how to develop reliability.
Clicker Intermediate Training – This book takes you even further into the magic and precision of clicker training, including how to wean off the clicker and short-term rewards.
Clicker Dances with Dogs – If you want to do Musical Canine Freestyle, whether for public demonstrations, competition or just for fun, Kay's innovative methods will enhance your dog's learning and your routines.
Clicker World Obedience Training – Learn from one of the world's best trainers how effective clicker training can be in teaching obedience behaviors.
Learning Games – Play is a natural form of learning. In this book, Kay outlines over 50 games and variations that you can use to help resolve conflict, strengthen bonds, and provide physical workouts for your dog.

Books by Patricia McConnell (www.patriciamcconnell.com)

If you want to learn more about people and dogs, read McConnell's books!

Beginning Family Dog Training, Patricia B. McConnell, Ph.D., Dog's Best Friend, Ltd, Black Earth, WI, 1996. A great little book about the basics of dog training using positive reinforcement. Easy to understand, full of helpful information and fun to read.

The Cautious Canine: How to Help Dogs Conquer Their Fears, Patricia B. McConnell, Ph.D., Dog's Best Friend, Ltd., Black Earth, WI, 2002. The best little booklet I've seen to help clients to deal with a fearful dog. This practical guide outlines specific steps for helping a dog if the behavior is motivated by fear.

The Other End of the Leash, Patricia B. McConnell, Ph.D., The Ballantine Publishing Group, New York, NY, 2002. This is a wonderful book that gives you more understanding of how dogs and people communicate. It's also full of real-life stories and practical solutions to common problems.

For the Love of A Dog: Understanding Emotion in You and Your Best Friend, Patricia B. McConnell, Ph.D., Ballantine Books, an imprint of the Random House Publishing Group, a division of Random House, Inc., New York, NY, 2006. You'll learn more about emotions in both people and dogs. Like *The Other End of the Leash,* this book is a combination of scientific fact, stories, and practical advice that will help you deepen your relationship with your dog. For people who love their dogs, this is a must read!

Other books by Patricia McConnell (some with other authors):
I'll Be Home Soon! How to Prevent and Treat Separation Anxiety
How to Be Leader of the Pack, and Have Your Dog Love You for It!
Puppy Primer (with Brenda Scidmore)
Feeling Outnumbered? How to Manage and Enjoy Your Multi-Dog Household (with Karen B. London)
Way to Go! How to House-Train a Dog of Any Age (with Karen B. London)
Feisty Fido: Help for the Leash-Aggressive Dog (with Karen B. London)

Books by Suzanne Clothier (www.flydogpress.com)

Suzanne Clothier also has many booklets available on a variety of topics from puppy temperament testing to self-control. Review her website for more information.

Bones Would Rain From the Sky: Deepening our Relationships with Dogs, by Suzanne Clothier, Warner Books, 2002. Suzanne offers information on her childhood and relationship with dogs. This book is sure to help you understand more about your canine friend and enhance your relationship.

Books by Ian Dunbar (James and Kenneth Publishers (800-784-5531)

Ian Dunbar is often considered "the father of puppy training." His books are clear and concise and will get you off to the right start with puppy training.

After You Get Your Puppy, Dr. Ian Dunbar, James & Kenneth Publishers, Berkeley, CA, 2001. Lots of great information for the puppy owner, including developmental deadlines and the importance of socialization.

Before You Get Your Puppy, Dr. Ian Dunbar, James & Kenneth Publishers, Berkeley, CA, 2001. Important information everyone should know before they get their dog, including developmental deadlines and housetraining.

Doctor Dunbar's Good Little Dog Book, Dr. Ian Dunbar, James & Kenneth Publishers, Berkeley, CA, 1992. This is an all-around good book on dog training. It's very short and concise and includes some nice photographs to aid understanding. Although Dunbar does not use a clicker, his training methods are quite compatible. Just add the clicker before the reward to do clicker training.

Behavior Booklets, Center for Applied Animal Behavior – Dr. Ian Dunbar and Gwen Bohnenkamp, James & Kenneth Publishers, Berkeley, CA, 1985. This is a series of nine behavior booklets including: *Preventing Aggression, House-Training, House-Training Supplement, Barking, Chewing, Digging, Shyness/Fearfulness – Towards People, Fighting and Socialization*. Even though these are not books about clicker training, they are positive training techniques and very good. You can figure out where to add the click.

Books specifically related to clicker training

Click to Calm: Healing the Aggressive Dog, Emma Parsons, Sunshine Books, Waltham, MA, 2004. This book includes many creative and effective ways to manage aggressive behavior through clicker training.

Click to Win! Clicker Training for the Show Ring by Karen Pryor, Sunshine Books, 2002. This book includes collected articles from the AKC Gazette for conformation handling in the show ring.

Click for Joy! Questions and Answers from Clicker Trainers and their Dogs, Melissa C. Alexander, Sunshine Books, Inc., Waltham, MA, 2003. This book lists questions and answers pertaining to clicker training. It's a helpful reference for experienced trainers or people just learning about clicker training.

Click Here for a Well-Trained Dog, Deborah Jones, Ph.D., Howln Moon Press, Eliot, ME, 2002. A good basic book on clicker training. Lots of information.

Clicker Fun, Dog Tricks and Games Using Positive Reinforcement, Deborah Jones, Ph.D., Howln Moon Press, Eliot, ME, 1998. An easy-to-read little book full of many different tricks and games to entertain you and your dog and make training more fun!

Clicking with Your Dog, Peggy Tillman, Sunshine Books, Waltham, MA, 2000. This is a wonderful book on clicker training. It gives step-by-step instructions with illustrations for a whole bunch of behaviors. This is worth having in your resource library.

The Clicker Training Manual, Volume I, Gail T. Fisher, All Dogs Gym, Manchester, NH, 1997, revised 2003. A manual full of great articles and lots of information for the beginning dog trainer. This is Gail's training manual at All Dogs Gym in New Hampshire.

Clicker Training for Obedience, by Morgan Spector, Sunshine Books, Waltham, MA, 1999. Morgan has put together a very detailed "how to" book. He writes it with emphasis on people who want to take their dogs to a level of professional obedience – dog shows.

Don't Shoot The Dog! – The New Art of Teaching and Training, Revised Edition, Karen Pryor, Bantam Books, New York, NY, 1999. This book is a classic in the field of clicker training and a must read for clicker trainers wanting to know more.

Quick Clicks, 40 Fast and Fun Behaviors to Train with a Clicker, Mandy Book and Cheryl S. Smith, Legacy by Mail, Carsborg, WA, 2001. A quick guide to training lots of behaviors with a clicker.

More Books on Clicker and Other Positive Training Methods

The following books relate to how dogs learn, how to train behaviors and work with behavioral issues using clicker training and other positive methods of training.

The Bark Stops Here by Terry Ryan, Legacy by Mail, Carsborg, WA 2000. This book offers some great information on why dogs bark and some effective behavior modification techniques to deal with the issue.

Control Unleashed, Leslie McDevitt, Clean Run Productions, LLC, South Hadley, MA, 2007. Learn how to turn stress into confidence and distraction into focus using positive training methods. The versatile "Control Unleashed" program is designed to help "dogs with issues" learn how to relax, focus, and work off-leash reliably in either stimulating or stressful situations.

The Culture Clash, Jean Donaldson, James & Kenneth Publishers, Berkeley, CA, 1996. An incredible book with lots of information. Donaldson makes a powerful case for thinking in terms of behavior modification rather than the older and more anthropomorphic dominance models of dog training.

Dogs Behaving Badly, An A-to-Z Guide to Understanding & Curing Behavioral Problems in Dogs, Dr. Nicholas Dodman, Bantam Books, New York, NY, 1999. This is a great A to Z manual on dealing with dog problems written by Dr. Dodman, head of the Animal Behavior Clinic at the Tufts University School of Veterinary Medicine. It's written in a witty style and includes many real-life stories about dogs.

The Dog Whisperer: A Compassionate, Nonviolent Approach to dog Training, Paul Owens, Adams Media Corporation, Holbrook, MA, 1999. This is a good and positive book on training. It contains some information on nutrition, breathing techniques (for the human), and other beneficial material that you don't find in most books.

Excel-erated Learning: How Dogs Learn and How Best to Teach Them, Pamela J. Reid, Ph.D. James and Kenneth Publishers, Berkeley, CA, 1996. This book gets into greater detail on how dogs learn and how dog training works. This is another book for the student who wants to delve deeper into understanding dog behavior and training.

How Dogs Learn, Mary R. Burch, Ph.D. and Jon S. Bailey, Ph.D., Howell Book House, New York, NY, 1999. This book explains the basic principles of behavior and how they can be used to teach your dog new skills, diagnose problems, and eliminate unwanted behaviors. This is a good book for the student who wants to understand more than the basics.

Positive Perspectives, Pat Miller, Dogwise Publishing, Wenatchee, WA, 2004. A complete dog training, puppy raising, problem solving, and basic health guide. Written as a series of columns in *Whole Dog Journal*, *Positive Perspectives* gives you information on day-to-day living with dogs in small, easily understood "bites." For puppy owners as well as adult-dog owners.

The Power of Positive Dog Training, Pat Miller, Hungry Minds, Inc. New York, NY, 2001. This is a wonderful book on training with positive methods, including clicker training. Pat Miller writes wonderful articles for *The Whole Dog Journal*, and her training advice is compassionate and pragmatic.

Purely Positive Training, Companion to Competition, Sheila Booth, Podium Publications, Ridgefield, CT, 1998. This is a great book about using only positive reinforcement in working with your dog. It includes how to raise your puppy positively and how to build a positive relationship with your dog.

Taking Care of Puppy Business, A Gentle Approach for Positive Results, Gail Pivar and Leslie Nelson, Tails-U-Win!, Canine Center, Manchester, CT. 1998. A very short and concise little booklet on how to raise puppies with a gentle approach.

When Pigs Fly – Training Success with Impossible Dogs, Jane Killion, Dogwise Publishing, Wenatchee, WA, 2007. Some breeds of dogs and mixes have a reputation as "impossible" to train. Hounds, terriers, and other breeds are often called pig-headed and even "untrainable." Learn these "Pigs Fly" methods and take advantage of the natural strengths of these independent and intelligent dogs. Help your dog become a wonderful companion or a formidable canine athlete. Clicker and reward-based training that is fun to use.

Web Sites/Phone Numbers

Clicker Trainers and other Positive Training information

Kay Laurence, Learning About Dogs: www.learningaboutdogs.com
Karen Pryor Clicker Training: www.clickertraining.com
Steve and Jen White: www.i2ik9.com
Gary Wilkes: www.clickandtreat.com
Suzanne Clothier: www.flyingdogpress.com
Patricia McConnell: www.dogsbestfriendtraining.com
Corally Burmaster: www.clickertrain.com
Leslie Nelson, Tails-U-Win Canine Center: www.tailsuwin.com.
Dawn Jecs, Choose to Heel: www.choosetoheel.com
Ian Dunbar's Publisher: James & Kenneth Publishers 800-784-5531
Canine Training Systems (includes Deb Jones' videos): www.caninetraining.com
Terry Ryan's Website (includes sound DVDs): www.legacycanine.com
Linda Tellington-Jones T-Touch: www.lindatellington-jones.com

To Find Clicker Trainers:
The Association of Pet Dog Trainers (APDT) www.apdt.com; 800-PETDOGS
List of Clicker Trainers: http://www.clickerteachers.net

Dog Training Books:
Direct Book Service www.dogwise.com; 800-776-2665
Sit Stay.com www.sitstay.com
J&J Dog Supplies www.jandjdog.com; 800-642-2050
Many trainers have books available on their own websites.

Bulk clickers (purchase in quantities for training classes or retail outlets):
LC Advertising, Inc. www.clickercompany.com; 480-706-1884

Miscellaneous dog supplies such as dog gates, crates and treats:
Doctors Foster & Smith www.DrsFosterSmith.com; 800-826-7206
Pet Edge www.petedge.com; 800-738-3343

Head Collars (available in bulk for trainers or pet stores):
Gentle Leaders – Premier www.gentleleader.com; 800-933-5595
Snoot Loops – Animal Behavior Consultants, Inc. www.animalbehavior.com; 800-339-9505
Comfort Trainer – Mariam Fields; 540-659-8858

Citronella Collars:
Premier www.gentleleader.com; 800-933-5595

DVDs / Videos

Click and Go, Deborah Jones, Ph.D. Presents the basic principles of clicker training.
Techniques presented include shaping, luring, and targeting.
Click and Treat Training Kit, Gary Wilkes. A comprehensive introduction to clicker
training dogs.
Clicker Magic, Karen Pryor. Footage from seminars showing a variety of behaviors and
different species.
On Target, Gary Wilkes. An introduction and how-to for using targeting in dog training.
(This is good information, although the tape quality is not so good.)
The Clicker Training Center Presents Puppy Kindergarten, Corally Burmaster. A good
introduction to clicker training with emphasis on how to start with young puppies.
Take a Bow Wow – Easy Tricks Any Dog Can Do. Virginia Broitman & Sherri Lippman.
A great collection of functional dog tricks.
Bow Wow, Take 2. Virginia Broitman & Sherri Lippman. A collection of fun and func-
tional dog tricks.

The How of Bow Wow: Building, Proofing and Polishing Behaviors. Virginia Broitman & Sherri Lippman. A great video on fine tuning behaviors.

On Talking Terms with Dogs: Calming Signals. Turid Rugaas. Learn about dog body language and how you can better communicate with your dog.

Really Reliable Recall Booklet/DVD. Leslie Nelson, Tails-U-Win Canine Center. How to teach a reliable emergency recall. I recommend this to everyone.

Training Companion Dog tapes (set of 4), Dr. Ian Dunbar. James & Kenneth Publishers; 800-784-5531. More detail using Dunbar's training techniques. Good, positive training techniques, even though it's not clicker training. You can figure out where to add the click. The set of four includes: Vol. 1 Socialisation/Early Training; Vol. 2. Behavior Problems; Vol. 3 Walking on Leash/Jumping up; Vol. 4 Recalls/Stays.

Training Dogs with Dunbar, Dr. Ian Dunbar. James & Kenneth Publishers; 800-784-5531. An excellent overview of Dunbar's positive training techniques. Although this is not clicker training, it's good. You know where to add the click.

TTOUCH of M.A.G.I.C. for Dogs & Puppies. The basics of the T-Touch techniques demonstrated on dogs and in different situations.

Periodicals and Magazines

Teaching Dogs
Learning About Dogs
   www.teachingdogs.com
   www.learningaboutdogs.com
The Whole Dog Journal
   P.O. Box 420235
   Palm Coast, FL 32142
   Phone: 800-829-9165
   E-mail: wholedogjl@palmcoastd.com

Appendix 5

Index